Nick Mayhew-Smith is a writer and researcher specializing in sacred landscapes and the natural world. He began his career as a journalist working at the *Financial Times* and moved on to found the publishing agency Wardour Ltd, before embarking on a series of media projects looking at Britain's spiritual and natural heritage.

His previous books include *Britain's Holiest Places* (2011), which became a BBC television series in 2013, and *Bare Beaches* (2004), a guide to skinny-dipping in the wilderness. This latest book builds on such eye-catching journeys, but is most closely based on his PhD at the University of Roehampton, looking at the nature rituals of the early Celtic Christians, which was completed in 2018.

He lives in south-west London with his wife Anna, an icon painter, and daughter Alexandra. He works as a writer, researcher and lecturer on all manner of theological topics and is a lay minister in the Church of England.

THE NAKED HERMIT

A journey to the heart of Celtic Britain

Nick Mayhew-Smith

First published in Great Britain in 2019

Society for Promoting Christian Knowledge
36 Causton Street
London SW1P 4ST
www.spck.org.uk

British Library Cataloguing-in-Publication Data
A catalogue record for this book is available from the British Library

ISBN 978–0–281–08154–7
eBook ISBN 978–0–281–07735–9

1 3 5 7 9 10 8 6 4 2

Typeset by Falcon Oast Graphic Art Ltd
Printed in Great Britain by TJ International

eBook by Falcon Oast Graphic Art Ltd

Produced on paper from sustainable forests

This book is dedicated to the memory
in perpetuity of Bill Taylor (1961–2016).
A friend and brother from the mountains

Contents

Acknowledgements

I wrote this book with my body as much as with my mind. It was a deeply personal and solitary journey, yet more collaboration has gone into it than is strictly appropriate for a would-be hermit. Not one word would have been possible without the support, encouragement, guidance and at times sobering bewilderment of so many friends, family, colleagues and fellow travellers. Closest to me as always have been my wife Anna and daughter Alexandra, offering a robust blend of orthodoxy and innocence when it comes to discussing plans and accompanying me on some of the gentler outings. My family have always been good to me on my travels, my parents Richard and Christine and my brothers Peter and Alex and their families.

Professionally, this book has been built on some labour-intensive university research, guided with unfailing decency and intellect by two inspirational teachers, Professor Tina Beattie and Dr Charlotte Behr at the University of Roehampton. It would also not have been possible without the funding and support of the TECHNE consortium, which distributes PhD funding from the Arts and Humanities Research Council, ably managed by Carol Hughes and Jane Gawthrope. Fellow students, colleagues and university teaching staff who have helped me include Britton Brooks, Mandie Iveson, Neal Cahoon, Kaveh Abbasian, Lia Shimada, Sue Miller and John Eade, and with particular respect to a cohort of students I was privileged to teach, including John Dawson, Amina Khan, Gavin Singh, Jess Oughton, Naima Khanom and Aine Campbell.

Friends and fellow travellers on the journey include many who have watched my explorations unfold over decades, including school friends Martin MacConnol, Peter Dzendrowskyj and John Frater, and university friends Warren Pearson, Donal Lawler, Hamish Macdonell and Oliver Mason. We all turned 50 in the year I wrote this book, a well weathered company by now. My other long-standing friends, Jane Porter, Kath Coleman and Louise Wilson, have helped me to test the water with some of the ideas that make this book, cheered on by Rosamund Bartlett and Dan Driscoll.

Some church and creative collaborations have provided direct inspiration, from theological, physical and emotional perspectives, including my fellow Reader Marion Gray, Mary Colwell, Fran Hollinrake from

St Magnus Cathedral, and John Bimson from Forest Church. Suzanne Piper, Myra Nichols, Geoffrey Parkin, Robert Green, Bob Horrocks and Keith Williams are friends who have helped in various ways to keep body and soul connected in my thoughts. Vanda Inman, custodian of the holy well of St Clether, and the painter Ramsay Gibb have inspired me with their heroic dedication to their own journeys into sacred landscapes, Ramsay's paintings offering a thought-provoking perspective on the marks that love leaves on the land. For this book specifically, I owe many thanks and much respect to the editorial, production and marketing teams at SPCK. And creatively, I must thank four inspiring accomplices who helped to turn my previous book on holy places into a television series, presented by Ifor ap Glyn and brought to life by Nia Dryhurst, Rhys Edwards and Emyr Jones.

From a slightly more sober perspective, numerous priests, ministers and church leaders and their partners have helped me on my way: Moyna McGlynn, John and Scilla Ansell, Alison and Peter Judge, Sarah Dawson, Belemo Alagoa, Duncan Swan, Chris Palmer, David Pennells, Jackie Cockfield, Joseph Skinner, John Musther, and Stuart and Alison Wallace from Wimbledon Quakers. Several local bishops have offered generous and imaginative support over the years, particularly Bishop Christopher Chessun of Southwark diocese, Bishop Richard Cheetham of the Kingston area, and Bishop Michael Ipgrave of Lichfield diocese. Any mistakes, potentially heretical statements and embarrassing incidents contained in this book are however mine alone, and jealously guarded as such.

Timeline

Third or fourth century

Alban becomes the first recorded British martyr, killed for sheltering a priest during one of several empire-wide Roman persecutions of Christianity. His shrine at St Albans, which can still be visited today, attracts pilgrims from at least as early as the fifth century.

397

Martin of Tours dies, an innovative and popular leader who combined the power of a bishop with the poverty of a monk. Several of his Gaulish contemporaries write about the pioneering monastic communities of the Eastern deserts, notably Sulpicius Severus (d. *c.* 425) and John Cassian (d. *c.* 435), generating texts that were hugely influential on Celtic Christianity.

c. 400

The British Bishop Ninian becomes one of the first missionaries to carry Christianity outside the boundaries of the Roman Empire when he crosses Hadrian's Wall to convert the Picts in south-west Scotland, founding a church dedicated to St Martin at Whithorn.

410

Withdrawal of imperial army and administration from Britain, ushering in the poorly documented, sub-Roman era in which the church and other institutions were left to fend for themselves, enabling independent Celtic traditions to develop.

420s

First Saxon invaders arrive, taking advantage of the post-Roman power vacuum.

429

Germanus, Bishop of Auxerre, travels to Britain to support both the church, which was beset by the Pelagian heresy, and the native Britons, who were under attack from their Saxon and Pictish enemies. His *Life*, written in *c.* 480, is the most substantial surviving narrative text about fifth-century Britain.

c. 430s

Patrick, a native Briton, joins an influx of missionaries organizing the conversion of Ireland to Christianity, initially under the supervision of Rome, although ties gradually loosen over the next two centuries as independent Celtic traditions evolve.

452

The Council of Arles in southern Gaul forbids veneration of trees, springs, stones and fountains; nothing similar is recorded in British Christianity until as late as the eleventh century.

c. 480–550

The British monk Gildas writes *On the Ruin and Conquest of Britain*, lamenting the collapse of church and society in the face of invasion and internal failure, a rare surviving documentary record from the period when Celtic Christianity was emerging.

563

Columba, the Irish prince and missionary, establishes his monastery on Iona under the protection of the kingdom of Dál Riata, an Irish colony that extended along Scotland's west coast. He conducts missionary expeditions into the land of the Picts, devoting considerable attention to the landscape, according to the *Life* written by his eventual successor on Iona, Adomnán.

597

Augustine of Canterbury arrives from Rome on a mission to convert the Anglo-Saxon Pagan kingdoms and to regularize Celtic Christian practices, particularly the dating of Easter and the method of baptism. Coincidentally, this is the same year the great Celtic leader Columba dies on Iona.

c. 610–820

The *Life* of the Welsh Bishop Samson of Dol (d. *c.* 565) is written in a monastery in Brittany. Although difficult to date accurately, it is the only early *Life* of a Celtic missionary from western Britain, recording Samson's travels from Llantwit Fawr in south Wales to Ireland, Cornwall and eventually Brittany. Nearly all other Welsh saints' *Lives* were written from the twelfth century onwards.

635

The Anglo-Saxon King of Northumbria invites Aidan from Iona to establish a monastic community on Lindisfarne. The conversion of the English subsequently takes place as a pincer movement, with Celtic missions from the north and west and Roman missions from the south.

664

The Synod of Whitby is convened to settle the long-running dispute about the Celtic versus the Roman method of dating Easter, alongside other unspecified 'ecclesiastical matters'. The synod comes down firmly in favour of the Roman method, and the Celtic influence on British Christianity begins to wane.

665

Cuthbert becomes Prior (and later Bishop) of Lindisfarne, mixing ecclesiastical duties with time as a hermit on Inner Farne island. He also conducts missionary expeditions to the Picts, where Columba laboured before him.

687

Cuthbert dies and is soon recognized as a saint, his acclaim no doubt helped by his work converting the churches under his authority from Celtic to Roman practice.

697–c. 735

A flurry of saints' *Lives* appears, written by monks from Iona, Lindisfarne, Whitby, Ripon, Monkwearmouth-Jarrow and East Anglia, including three about Cuthbert and one each about Columba, Pope Gregory the Great, Wilfrid, and Guthlac of the Fens. In 731 Bede completes his *Ecclesiastical History*. All these texts appeared as the conversion of tribal Britain to Christianity, sometimes known as the Age of the Saints, was coming to an end.

716

The monks of Iona agree to accept the Roman method of dating Easter, many years after their counterparts in Ireland and Northumbria had abandoned the Celtic method in a series of seventh-century synods.

768

Celtic Christians in Wales agree to accept the Roman method of dating Easter.

793

A deadly raid on Lindisfarne marks the start of the 300-year Viking Age. The British and Irish transition to Christianity had produced remarkably few martyrs, something that rapidly changed with the incoming raiders.

909

The last supporters of the Celtic method of dating Easter, in Cornwall, finally accept the Roman system, marking an end to this particular Celtic Christian practice.

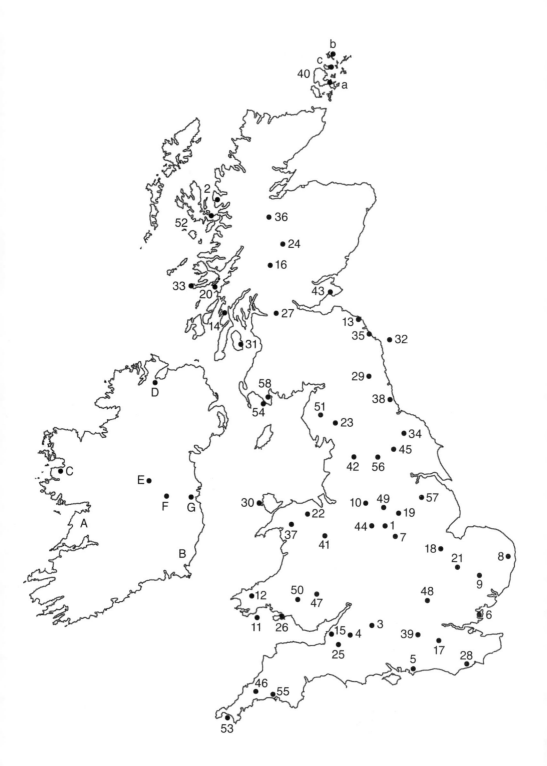

This map shows the main British and Irish locations described in this book

Key

Britain

1. Anchor Church, Ingleby, Derbyshire
2. Applecross, Highlands
3. Avebury, Wiltshire
4. Bath, Somerset
5. Bosham, West Sussex
6. Bradwell-on-Sea, Essex
7. Breedon on the Hill, Leicestershire
8. Burgh Castle, Norfolk
9. Bury St Edmunds, Suffolk
10. Buxton, Derbyshire
11. Caldey Island, Pembrokeshire
12. Carningli, Pembrokeshire
13. Coldingham, Scottish Borders
14. Columba's Cave, Ellary, Argyll
15. Congresbury, Somerset
16. Crianlarich, Stirling
17. Crowhurst, Surrey
18. Crowland, Lincolnshire
19. Dale Abbey, Derbyshire
20. Eileach an Naoimh, Inner Hebrides
21. Ely, Cambridgeshire
22. Ffynnon Fair, Nant-y-Patrick, Denbighshire
23. Firbank Fell, Cumbria
24. Fortingall, Perthshire
25. Glastonbury, Somerset
26. Goat's Hole Cave, Gower peninsula
27. Govan Old Church, Glasgow
28. Hastings, East Sussex
29. Hexham, Northumberland
30. Holyhead, Anglesey
31. Holy Island, Arran
32. Inner Farne island, Northumberland
33. Iona, Inner Hebrides
34. Lastingham, North Yorkshire
35. Lindisfarne (Holy Island)
36. Loch Ness, Highlands
37. Maentwrog, Gwynedd
38. Monkwearmouth-Jarrow monastery, Tyne and Wear
39. Newark Priory, Surrey
40. Orkney Islands
    a Kirkwall, Mainland
    b Papa Westray
    c Egilsay
41. Oswestry, Shropshire
42. Pendle Hill, Lancashire
43. Pittenweem, Fife
44. Repton, Derbyshire
45. Ripon, North Yorkshire
46. Roche, Cornwall
47. Skirrid/Ysgyryd Fawr, Monmouthshire
48. St Albans, Hertfordshire
49. Stanton in Peak hermit's cave, Derbyshire
50. St Cynog's Church, Powys
51. St Herbert's Isle, Derwentwater, Cumbria
52. St Maelrubha's rock, Isle of Skye, Inner Hebrides
53. St Michael's Mount, Cornwall
54. St Ninian's Cave, Galloway
55. St Samson's Cave, Golant, Cornwall
56. St Wilfrid's rock, Burnsall, North Yorkshire
57. Stow, Lincolnshire
58. Whithorn, Galloway

Ireland

A. County Clare (district)
B. County Wexford (district)
C. Croagh Patrick, Co. Mayo
D. Derry, NI
E. Durrow, Co. Offaly
F. Kildare, Co. Kildare
G. Tallaght, South Dublin

Note: precise locations and visitor descriptions for nearly all the British sites are in the author's previous book, Britain's Holiest Places.

Introduction

————•·•————

I arise today by the power of heaven,
The light of the sun, the brightness of the moon,
The splendour of fire, the flash of lightning,
The swiftness of wind, the depth of sea,
The stability of earth, the firmness of rocks.
St Patrick (attributed), *The Deer's Cry* (fifth century)[1]

This is a story as old as humanity itself. A naked man in a primal wilderness, alone with the animals, contemplating the vastness of creation, taking shelter beneath the limbs of a sacred tree, tending a garden paradise, at peace with the natural world. To tell this story I have followed ancient patterns of belief from the edge of recorded history, conversing with birds, bleeding myself dry through dripping sweat and scourging thorns, stripping at dawn to stand in the crashing sea, praying on a mountain where angels gather, bathing in the ruins of a holy well disused for half a millennium, and experiencing solitude as if I were the only human being on earth. My voyage took me to a place where all this is possible, a journey that was ten years in the planning as I navigated a course to the sacred landscapes of sixth-century Britain. And then as Celtic mists rose from the green swathes of virgin landscape, when my night's vigil was done, the angels greeted and demons vanquished, I would climb in my car and head off for a spot of lunch.

This is in many ways the original story of humanity told and retold through the lens of human progress. From the simplicity of first creation to the most modern of inventions, there are points of contact that remain: we still relate to our land, to the waters, to our bodies themselves. What I discovered in the ancient ways and wisdom of our ancestors has turned out to be far more relevant and revelatory than I had imagined possible. My deep adventures into the patterns of Celtic nature rituals have also turned out to be more connected to mainstream religious tradition than I had ever imagined. Consigned to the fringes of Christian history and all too often hijacked to suit a contemporary agenda, the roots of all this colourful Celtic nature spirituality can be found in the earliest Christian texts, in their original context in other words, but it takes some patient digging to unearth them. There has always been a vague sense that this enigmatic period of Christian/Pagan history was somehow bound up with the natural world, and I felt it would be productive to take a very hard look at this specific dimension to see what could be learned. Quite a lot, is the short answer.

I stretched myself to the limits to produce this account of what happens when the Christian faith enters with wholehearted and full-bodied enthusiasm into creation. Intellectually what follows in these pages is based on three years of systematic study into nature rituals for a thesis, a test of patience, solitude and sleep deprivation that prepared me surprisingly well for the physical journey ahead, when I went to see what happens when you follow the early saints into the wilderness. Even my most vivid dreams and dramatic discoveries while sitting in a library could not prepare me for the adventures that followed. But then, I hadn't expected to find so much in the library either before I began, a set of insights at the most profound level into the degradations we inflict on ourselves as we damage the land beneath our feet, the air we breathe, the water we drink and bathe in.

This is a story about sin and loss, but also of hope and restoration, of innocence and experience both mental and physical. It is a story for those of any religion, or none at all, because it is the story of humanity and our troubled relationship with the natural world.

On my journey I discovered what creatures inhabited the wild places of the early British imagination, what fears haunted the missionaries and their would-be converts. I went to experience the life of these pioneers, the raw spirituality of a time when most of the land was uncultivated, unsettled and replete with stories, myths and legends, a time when there were spirits and powers behind the animation of the natural world. I discovered that there is much to learn from living at the edge, in the marginal places of our land: caves, mountains, tiny islands, rivers and lonely stretches of shore. There is, I discovered in the life of a Celtic hermit, cold and hardship but also joy and comfort, solitude but also solace, discomfort along with a feeling of remarkable connection to the natural world. There is also, disgracefully, a little bit of swearing.

I did my best to enter into this world as far as I could, for all the difficulties it presented, and have indeed returned with some stories to tell. What emerged from the mist and the mud turns out to be an entirely authentic and coherent expression of belief, yet one that has been forgotten by the mainstream churches. There are indeed bodies in this story, conversations with animals, sacred trees, mountains in the mist, Celtic shores, hermits' islands, holy springs and the odd cave where demons lurk. My studies and my adventures alike were not always easy or comfortable, but I did find every step of the journey fascinating, every corner I turned offering an unexpected vista of a landscape wreathed in legend and etched by ritual use.

The sky was once quite literally the limit when it came to the possibilities of Christian devotion, and it would appear that this free-ranging spirituality was both authentic and once entirely supported by the church. What I experienced in the outdoors was on a continuum with the more recognizable patterns of liturgy that were practised then as now inside a church building. Rituals of baptism, reconciliation, fasting, hospitality, foot washing and even the Eucharist itself were so potently conceived they could not help but bleed out into the land surrounding a church or a monastery, and even the land surrounding a solitary man or woman as they walked through the wilderness. Today this spiritual overlay has been more or less rolled up, the numinous and the transcendent trimmed to fit inside the four walls of a church building and often locked inside for most of the week. We know very little about the forms and orders of early Celtic liturgy in Britain, but read any of the stories that survive and it is overwhelmingly obvious that the church leaders worked and worshipped in the great outdoors with enthusiasm and purpose. The leading Irish missionary St Columba, who founded his monastery on Iona in 563, was one of many wonder-workers who strode the land, dispelling storms and conversing with beasts, calming the elements and protecting the trees, in between finding time to talk to the people themselves. In one of the rare glimpses we have of formal church activities, Columba's earliest *Life* suggests in passing that he celebrated most of the regular Sunday church service outdoors: 'he entered the church as usual on the Lord's day after the Gospel had been read' in order to celebrate the sacrament of the Mass.[2] Even the most formal church service of the week began in the fresh air, since the Gospel reading takes place perhaps halfway through this liturgy, which makes it less of a surprise that ritual became so entwined with trees and birds. I write about a service I conducted in a churchyard while finishing this book, in the chapter on sacred trees, and what happened was entirely unexpected, in a good way.

Natural sacred places

The journey behind this book began a decade ago with a project to visit every major holy site in British Christian tradition, a task that took me five years to complete and encompassed 700 locations, of which about 500 made it into my book *Britain's Holiest Places*. I expect I have visited more holy places in Britain than anyone else alive, which is in itself little more than a demonstration of what pig-headed determination and a very high boredom threshold can achieve. Mostly it was wonderful to see the variety of places that have been marked out as special by ancient tradition, some very familiar but some surprising and profoundly moving in their simplicity or eccentricity. And so that journey was published, followed by a mini-reprise for a BBC television series, which looked at six locations in each of six episodes, 36 of the more telegenic and interesting places, which went down well with critics and viewers alike. There was nothing more I could do, nowhere left to go on a journey that had been something of an obsession, and I was glad to shake the dust off my sandals and start looking for a proper job.

And so it would have been, except for one tiny question that kept nagging me: what on earth did people do at all the natural holy sites I had unexpectedly encountered? I know what to do at a church or cathedral. We all know what people did there in the past; these places have been made holy by use and reuse, and they still more or less retain their original function. But I really did not know what devotional acts could make holy so many enchanting landmarks and features that this island has in great abundance. To put it bluntly: what did Christians do at a sacred tree? What was supposed to happen at the top of a holy mountain, in the cold waters of a sacred spring or pool? All I could do was guess that there was something important embedded in these places. It turns out there was, and I needed to take a long hard look at the evidence to get there. Whether or not their spiritual agency could then be reactivated, in the same way a church building still serves its original purpose each Sunday morning, directs the narrative thread of this book.

The ancient texts talk of a dazzling and exotic array of saintly interactions with nature: planting sacred trees, talking to animals, exorcizing lakes and rivers, retreating to islands, fighting demons in caves and on mountain tops, preaching to birds, and the odd spot of prayer standing naked in ice-cold water. All good fun in its day, one might think, but hardly the stuff of Christian tradition, and not something that any modern church would actively encourage, revive or even claim as its heritage. Several of these places see active use by Neo-Pagan traditions in Britain today, and they often attract a commendable degree of local affection and activity (I'm thinking here of an After Eight mint placed reverentially beside a holy well in Monmouthshire). But what is their place in mainstream Christian tradition, if any? What exactly can you do today beneath a sacred tree, in a holy pool, on a mist-wreathed mountain or shivering at the entrance to a cave crawling with spiritual power? These questions mounted the more I thought about them, until the nagging doubt could be ignored no more. I decided I had to go back to basics and study them properly, systematically, under the watchful gaze of academic scrutiny. So I signed up at Roehampton University to undertake a three-year research project, with a scholarship from the Arts and Humanities Research Council, no less. If you are a UK taxpayer, therefore, you have already contributed to this book, for which my thanks twice over. But I intend to pay it back as best I can here, to encourage that healthy relationship between people and place that forms the basis of any true religion and indeed any reasonably cohesive and thriving society. In a sense too none of this is actually my work, I am merely attempting to recover the wisdom of certain ancient ways of approaching the environment before we had bulldozers, pesticides and wetsuits at our disposal.

Doing a PhD in any of the humanities is a pretty effective way to prove the old adage true, that you can take a joke too far. Being immersed in such concentrated research does stop being amusing or entertaining after a while, but you do get a chance to really dig into a subject. And the more I dug the more I found. In the following chapters of this book I will tell the urgent story that all of this study consistently demonstrated: a way in which humans can usefully and spiritually connect with the natural world. Trees, animals, water courses, the wilderness, islands, caves, mountains and many other landmarks and features can be approached afresh in the light of an older, more reverential attitude in ways that feel remarkably relevant to modern anxieties about over-exploitation and degradation. More remarkable still is that all these interactions are based on one simple and entirely biblical premise, grounded so deeply in Judaeo-Christian tradition you have to go back to the very first book of the Bible to find the source.

In a nutshell the story of this book is this: when humans first sinned, the immediate effect was to damage the relationship between humans and the natural world. A spiritually minded person will help to put that right. And yes, this was expressed explicitly in the early British texts. It was, I believe, the backbone of Celtic Christianity as it was understood in the sixth and seventh centuries. It is not a modern spin on a vague but richly suggestive set of tales. The source material is tricky to deal with but not impossible when you get to grips with what survives, who wrote it, where they borrowed ideas from and what was done with their finished works. The earliest missionaries constructed a compelling narrative, a story that allowed Christianity to grow in our damp northerly climate, a story that can still be followed today.

Green theology before environmentalism

It is a common assumption that Celtic Christianity was highly sympathetic to the natural world, but I have never heard anyone explain why that might be in a way that sounds authentically sixth century. Digging deep into its motivations and storytelling to research this book has produced what I think is the fundamental reason for this extraordinary impulse to approach the entirety of the natural world in a loving embrace. It does not come from the same place as our ecologically motivated, environmental points of view today, because they had different anxieties and aspirations to deal with. As I will explain in Chapter 2, I think the fragments of evidence show that it was related to the missionary focus of the early church during a long period of transition from Paganism, a time when the Christians sought to write a new narrative over the forces that shape and move all of creation. But as I hope this entire book demonstrates, the logic behind it can serve as a basis for approaching the natural world from a completely different perspective from the one that has seen us over-exploit and degrade it. If you are looking for a theological justification for environmentalism, in other words, Celtic Christianity offers it, a robust and interesting set of principles to consider and to adapt to modern circumstances. It is a theology that reaches so far back into the human story and the human condition it would, if followed through to its full conclusions, do away with the need for any environmental activism serving as a back-stop to limit the damage we cause. It is a starting point rather than a rescue operation.

Any assertions on this topic do require a level of proof, and my book offers both a recovery of the historical context and then quite a lot of wading into the wilderness to test my theories in the field. There is certainly a vague but popular sense that Celtic Christianity had a sympathetic attitude towards the natural world. Beyond this any further generalization is likely to be met with scepticism and outright opposition from some quarters; it is a rich culture that invites speculation but is also wide open to debate. So I have zoned in very specifically on the one topic of the relationship between humans and nature in an attempt to work out exactly what was going on. And I will be the first to admit that it does look at first sight rather like some sort of primitive environmentalism when you hear tales of wild animals flocking to hermits, of trees venerated for their connection to a saint, even rules against collecting the eggs of seabirds. But I am uncomfortable with the idea that there was any sort of ecological awareness comparable to today, when mass pollution and destruction of the environment are as unarguable as the piles of plastic rubbish I found washed up on every shore.

I wanted to know what else might motivate a religious impulse that, at its greatest stretch, appeared to seep out of the walls of the church to suffuse all of creation with a sense of the numinous. Was there really a spirituality that allowed people to worship freely and enthusiastically by ritually engaging with the natural world, that saw the entirety of the cosmos as a canvas on which divine purpose has been painted, in every hue and every colour? And if so why? The very notion that there was ever such a cosmological vision in any Christian church, and that it might be recovered and motivate us towards greater sympathy with nature today, might sound close to deluded, so ambitious is its scope. I would be the first to admit that writing a PhD thesis is an institutionalized form of psychosis, a belief that the more narrow and fixated your mind becomes the more important your work. But I think it has now come to that, to take seriously the wisdom of ancient beliefs and practices to see what we can learn from an age before mass destruction of the environment was within our capability. There was certainly a sense of going back to the drawing board as I stood on a remote, litter-strewn beach in the garb of Adam and wondered if we might benefit by starting from scratch in our approach to creation.

I use the words Celtic Christianity freely in this book because this is the popular way to describe an early form of spirituality in Britain and Ireland, with a few caveats about the term given below. There is no end to the theories that have been floated as to what was going on in this early expression of faith, all of which are useful because the picture is so large it benefits from as many different perspectives as possible. Many other writers have noted that the Celtic period serves as an invitingly blank piece of paper on which anyone can project their personal desires for a primal form of religion – before going on to do exactly that themselves. A love of the natural world is one of the first things that is ascribed to this regional expression of Christianity, the spirituality of a people who 'lived closer to nature' than we do, although it would be interesting to know exactly what that phrase is supposed to mean.[3] The air we breathe and the human body itself can be considered dimensions of 'nature'. There are just such implications for the body in Celtic Christian culture, an enormously charged and deeply visceral place to talk about spirituality. An incarnated religion such as Christianity, which is based on the notion that God took on a complete human body, can be the starting point for a broad-minded discussion of our physical footprint on creation.

Indeed, some of the story of this book is about finding comfortable compromise for the human body in Christian ritual. I think it might have been one of the sticking points between Celtic Christian culture and the Roman church when they debated the correct method of baptism. Bodies are so often the focus of disagreement and argument in religious differences: how we cover or uncover them, how we modify them and feed them all sit at the visceral end of theological debate. And of course they are the vehicle for an embodied form of faith that moves towards the natural world in a physical way. All forms of ritual are just such a combination of bodily action motivated by intellectual concept, ideas that are expressed through some sort of active performance.

It is the limitless horizon, the all-encompassing scope of Celtic Christian theology, that is most important of all when it comes to thinking about the environment. Religion is so often an expression of local, national or regional concerns, but a truly fundamental orientation towards the environment will have to be capable of transcending all of those boundaries. I think Celtic Christianity did do that and remains able to do that. As will be seen, there is clear evidence that its sensitive spiritual appreciation of nature was not confined to the edges of Britain and to Ireland but for a time greatly inspired the Anglo-Saxon people too, those who live in what is now England. In the specific area of nature rituals and devotions, it is clear that the Anglo-Saxons not only admired and copied their brothers and sisters in Irish, Welsh, Scottish, Pictish and other British tribes but actually gave it impeccable theological status and hard-wired it into their own tales of the landscape.

An intense love of nature or something remarkably similar to it has also cropped up sporadically in other parts of the world. It is up to the reader to decide, but my own view is that this is very much an understanding of Christianity and other religions whose full realization lies in the future. You could consider it a prophetic voice from the margins, but I think it might also be a happy quirk of history that Celtic spirituality records the flowering of the faith in a non-urbanized, non-imperial environment for the first time, when Christians needed to adapt their message to deal with a wholly unexpected and unfamiliar terrain. I think they did so superbly, in ways that echo down the centuries.

What is Celtic Christianity?

The notion that Celtic Christianity was a remarkably prophetic form of environmentalism is only one of several theories advanced to explain its motivations and messages. Others have suggested that it was simply Paganism disguised behind a Christian veneer, a deliberate rejection of the institutionalized norms of the Roman church, or an ethnic expression of belief that somehow adheres to anyone in Britain and Ireland who is not English.[4] If you set off looking for evidence for these theories you would find something that matches, because the material is so suggestive and our understanding of the context so patchy. But often these are no more substantial than beguiling patterns in the mists that obscure our view of early medieval Britain. Some indeed are modern concepts that have little meaning in their original context, such as the environmentalism discussed above and perhaps the notion of a strict ethnic divide between the English and everyone else.

The reality of Celtic Christianity is more prosaic than some of the romantic versions would have it, the concerns more practical and focused on getting through a fairly difficult life in a society that was still largely tribal, Britain lacking the major urban centres that were typical in other European regions under more direct Roman imperial control. In terms of Christianity and the church, Celtic spiritual culture is certainly a lot more mainstream and its theology more accessible than the myths would have it. Caitlin Corning and Thomas O'Loughlin are among two of the most coherent and careful writers in determining what was and was not special about this regional expression of Christianity in terms of its culture, church organization and theology. There was certainly never a conscious attempt to build a parallel church to the one based in Rome, nor was there any deliberate attempt to violate Roman conventions as a rebuke to 'organized' religion. In reality there were only three Celtic practices that were ever considered problematic by the wider church, and only two of these were common to the entire Celtic region: calculating the date of Easter and the shape of the tonsure for monks. A third divergence was over the practice of baptism in Britain (but not, so far as evidence indicates, in Ireland), due to some unspecified deviation in the ritual.[5] I think I have worked out what that deviation was, presented in my chapter on devotional bathing rituals. But other than these three matters, the missionary bishops from Rome and even the popes themselves were entirely happy to let Celtic Christian regions enjoy their own expressions of faith. Many of the nature-loving practices and devotions echoed on for centuries across Christendom before the church moved to sweep everything up into the four walls of its buildings and lock the doors.

The term Celtic is sometimes used to describe people on the islands of Britain and Ireland who are not of English (or Anglo-Saxon) origin, but ethnic division does not work on any level as a way to understand and articulate such profound and far-reaching faith as Celtic spirituality offers. Ian Bradley's fine book *Celtic Christianity: Making Myths and Chasing Dreams* is an exercise in demolishing much of the wish-fulfilment of Celtic studies. Yet Bradley twice highlights the ethnic origins of modern scholars and the preponderance of southern English accents at Celtic conferences and claims that 'outsiders' have been most interested in the Celtic Christian revival, despite the fact that many chapters of his own book quote a clear majority of writers he would presumably consider ethnically 'Celtic'.[6] Why any of this even matters is unclear, although to be fair to Bradley he has re-evaluated this and other positions with a degree of self-criticism and fairness to the evidence that is admirable to a fault. 'Celtic' in this book simply refers to the expressions of Christian faith that developed in Britain when it was somewhat isolated from the continental church. This situation gradually changed after the pope sent a mission to regularize British Christianity in 597. The arrival of his missionaries highlighted the fact that a number of distinctive practices had evolved in British ritual and belief, many of which lingered happily for generations. It would be helpful if there were another word for this peculiar expression of Christianity that had no modern ethnic connotations, but 'Celtic' is the one that is commonly used, and is done so here with a health warning attached.

Ethnic delineations are a strange way to interpret an expression of Christianity that deliberately sought out universal narratives to explain the human condition. They don't even match the evidence in any case when it comes to Britain's tribes. The notion that 'Celtic' always means 'non-English' is a particularly persistent stain left by political, cultural and national issues that have nothing to do with spiritual boundaries, and does not in any case align with the hard evidence of how far Celtic centres of Christian mission spread. Irish missionaries went deep into Gaul and Italy, so seriously did they take their calling to touch every corner of creation with their message, a topic for another day and perhaps another book. In south-east England, Bede records a Celtic monastery at Selsey in West Sussex, and another at Bradwell-on-Sea in Essex. If you draw a straight line between these two you divide the island of Great Britain into 2,500 square miles that might have been untouched by Celtic Christianity

(Kent, more or less), and nearly 81,000 square miles that were entirely touched by it.[7] In the Celtic heartlands to the north, there were English Christians living on Iona long before Augustine of Canterbury arrived from Rome to convert the Anglo-Saxons in 597. One of them worked the ovens in that island monastery, a man whose name has been recorded for posterity: Genereus the baker.[8] The notion that Celtic Christianity is foreign to English history is indefensible, and could in any case be refuted by a single word: Lindisfarne.

Ethnic identity made – and continues to make – no difference whatsoever when it comes to enjoying the unique mix of beliefs and practices that make up Celtic spirituality. It appears to have been most vibrant at a time of mass conversion, because it was designed to manage the transition from Pagan narratives about the landscape to Christian revelation, as will be explored throughout this book. The vastness of the entire cosmos is embraced by a Celtic belief system, ultimately offering a new relationship with all of creation. Closing this down again to focus on the exceptional nature of one national or regional culture is contradictory in the extreme. It emerged at a time of transition, a time when Christianity had to be articulated in new ways to people who lived beyond the boundaries of Greek and Roman empire. Philosophical ideas about mercy, forgiveness, the afterlife and sin itself simply did not resonate with the folk of Britain. It is an easy point to overlook, but this island might have been the first place where Christian mission moved outside the Graeco-Roman sphere of intellectual influence and culture. The Bible itself records ways in which missionaries such as St Paul had to adapt their preaching to their audience, to talk of the gods of the marketplace in Athens, to hold them up respectfully and confidently against Christian revelation. The same thing had to happen in Britain. It is possible that St Ninian was the first to carry the gospel across the boundary of the Roman Empire when he passed through Hadrian's Wall on his way to convert the Picts of southern Scotland around the year 400. His missionary church at Whithorn is surrounded by evidence of early Christian devotion. In the cold twilight at the remote St Ninian's Cave to the west of here, the reality of this undertaking and its achievements hit me brutally hard, in a way I describe in the final chapter. Something happened to me there that shocked my understanding of creation and God to the core, leaving me reeling in the soft gold light of a midsummer sunset.

I once gave a talk about my work at university and ended up fielding questions about Brexit and ideas of nationalism generally, a reaction I suppose to modern, nativist discourse about tribal identity but not even remotely my area of expertise or interest. I know all too well that many people subordinate their religion to patriotic sentiments of national, regional, political and cultural difference and exceptionalism, but I have seen enough of the world to know that this does not foster a positive or universal spirituality, and it has never been Christian. Satan's last throw of the dice when he tried to tempt Jesus was to urge him to use spiritual power and authority to accumulate political glory, to establish the greatest state in human history. In case any Christian needs reminding, Jesus rejected the idea outright, yet it remains the last and the most dangerous temptation of all to anyone who claims a faith. God sits above all of us and cannot be defined by humanly made boundaries, languages and traditions that each country jealously protects. The notion that matters as small, artificial and changeable as cultural, national and ethnic divisions should be used to hedge and qualify God, to compartmentalize his creation, seems to be a tempting prospect in all manner of religions, but it is more or less the opposite of what this book represents. Rather, this is a local expression of a universal set of ideals, which can and have been articulated in other places and cultures just as well.

Indeed, the most notable exception I found in these universal expressions of faith relates to the frustrating absence of women saints, a bias that I am certain reflects a blindness in the historical records. To illustrate how far this extends, I can point out that there is not a single reference to veneration of the Virgin Mary in any of the four early records of the life of St Cuthbert, yet his very own wooden coffin, made just 12 years after his death, has the earliest depiction of the Virgin and Child anywhere in the Western world outside Rome. All too often there is a bewildering gap between the textual records and the physical evidence, one that my own adventures seek in their own small way to bridge. Just enough early written evidence makes it through to indicate that women also rolled up their sleeves and got stuck into the physical landscapes of Britain, even though precise references are few and elusive. In one such passing mention, Bede writes that the founder of Ely's monastery and later cathedral, St Etheldreda, decided to refrain from taking hot baths except before the major church festivals, hinting that she too joined her male counterparts in a fortifying cold-water plunge of spiritual significance.[9] Over in Ireland there is no ambiguity about the wonderworking St Brigit's nightly regime, bathing herself in a pool even when it was surrounded by snow and ice. According to one *Life*, God was so appalled by such extremes he dried up the water each night and refilled it each morning, a creative editorial line that surely reveals a reluctance to countenance women's bodily devotions.[10] The hard reality of the landscape is and always has been a place where all people, whatever their backgrounds and beliefs, can coalesce in the face of something much greater and more enduring than any of us.

I for one don't see the primal form of spiritual expression that is labelled Celtic as a binary opposition between the two worlds of pre- and post-conversion Britain. Some of the best historians of this period are modern-day Pagan writers, perhaps because this was a Christianity that made perfect sense to Pagans, and perhaps it can work for other non-believers too. One of my favourite writers about all things sacred is Philip Carr-Gomm, a leader of the Order of Bards, Ovates and Druids. I am pretty certain that he and I are the only two people who have written books on holy places and (separately) nudism.[11] The two might not appear to have any logical connection, but from my perspective any faith that is deeply rooted in respect for the natural world will end up having to take a positive view on the human body, and somehow find a harmonious place for it within the created order. I have kept Paganism capitalized in this book as an indication of the place it plays as a formal and ongoing part of shaping the spiritual heritage of Britain, and would hope that the need to preserve and respect the environment will increasingly transcend all differences in all beliefs.

A modern revival?

Ritual interactions with the natural world form just one part of the vast culture that Celtic Christians developed in early Britain, so there are limits to the claims and discoveries presented in his book. But by the same token these are also very specific expressions of belief that can be isolated and studied, compared and – I am happy to report back – successfully copied today, should one feel so moved. As it happens I don't urge any sort of revival or new expression of Christianity, and commend no rituals to the reader. I think it unlikely that any religion suffers from a shortage of balding, middle-aged men telling everyone what to do, although opinion may be divided on the matter. My journey was an extreme exercise in the recovery of ancient ways, but in the end I found it was at least as peaceful and moving as it was difficult and uncomfortable. I do have opinions and prejudices that have coloured my work, and there is a fair chance that the theories I have developed to explain the Celtic approach to nature might turn out to be wrong. The only thing I say in my defence is that I believe they are slightly less wrong than all the previous interpretations I have inherited.

So nothing is prescribed or urged here, but rather a fresh perspective is presented on a way of believing, of regarding the natural world with a sense of reverence, awe and sympathy that will shed new light on spirituality in the landscape. There are of course many expressions of a creative approach to nature to be found in the rituals I studied and revived, rituals that offer varying degrees of immersion in the outdoors. None of these physical activities are of my own making, and I found some easier to replicate than others. You can certainly emulate any of these rituals if you feel so moved, but you would be tapping into traditions and beliefs that are vastly larger, older and deeper than anything I could invent, not to mention rather more feral than the average act of worship. Even the most faithful followers of Celtic evening services in church might find some expressions of this spirituality rather stark and unexpected. One very passionate advocate of a native spiritual revival had this to say in *Celtic Christianity Today*: 'Celtic saints . . . stood up to their necks naked in the cold sea reciting the psalms. While mortifying the flesh might have been considered heroic then, people would think anyone doing such things today was psychologically deranged.'[12] To which I can only reply: it's lovely once you're in.

It is the 'today' bit in all of this Celtic revival that has caused me most concern, and I have tried to push back well beyond contemporary anxieties and modern agendas, to push through inhibitions and embarrassment to stand again at the threshold between sea and sky and wonder at the vastness of creation and the smallness of the human body. It was only by copying to the letter the various descriptions of wading into the waves reciting psalms that it dawned on me what was going on, as I will explain. Some of the Celtic bathers kept a loincloth on, as it happens, and others did indeed go naked. Neither was psychologically deranged, they did it for missionary purposes to demonstrate the existence of a single Creator God capable of operating across and on all levels of creation, including that most unruly and chaotic element of all, the dark waters of the ocean. Modern anxieties about the human body do actually get in the way of a truly physical embrace of creation and greatly obscure our view of the embodied rituals of the past, but this shame was not God-given, was not part of the original creative plan.

Stripping on a windswept shore and wading into the ocean to commune with the elements might indeed seem to be as far removed as you can get from the comfort of a Sunday morning family Eucharist, or indeed from Christianity itself if you align your faith entirely with the concerns of the city, of civilization. I am willing to hazard a guess that devotional bathing rituals in the North Sea don't appear in the Alpha course. But such deep immersion was once the epitome of holiness, a devotion to be admired and copied by the faithful, immortalized in a saint's cult and praised to the heavens – before being abandoned without trace by the formal church. If you take these saints' lives as stories and role models for the lay folk to listen and look up to, then this was in fact the Alpha course of the day, spectacular and heroic tales to educate and entertain, to inspire and sometimes to emulate. It is easy to write off many of the more intense and idiosyncratic interactions with animals and the elements as fringe and marginal, but if you read the earliest texts these aspects are obviously of enormous significance. As mentioned already, the life of the great Celtic leader St Columba was a particularly rich expression of this mission to the natural world, directing more spiritual energy towards the land and lochs of the Pictish regions than he did to the people themselves. It's a fair question to ask why.

My journey to recreate such forgotten devotions might stretch credulity, but everything in it is historically documented, whether or not that makes it 'real' or 'true'. Though easily dismissed as folklore and written off as fanciful by many a historian and theologian, these intense nature interactions are among the most plausible elements in the early saints' written lives. I have broken bread with a pair of friendly birds, spent dark night vigils in remote caves, waded out many times to pray in natural water and slept alone on a hermit's island, but I have never knowingly resurrected anyone. I was following closely in the footsteps of these ancient holy men and women, the saints whose encounters with nature in the raw give us the earliest glimpses of this primal spirituality: sea, rock and tree rather than hymn, pulpit and pew. The British landscape was not a wilderness to be shunned, but embraced and won over, worked and worshipped in as surely as any parish church. As will be shown in the chapters that follow, nature itself contains the rudimentary infrastructure of a church: the sea can provide its own rhythm for praise, the rock a natural preaching platform, the sacred tree a place to sit and meet. Hymns, pulpits and pews were in short supply during a time of mass conversion, but nature provides in abundance.

There are human explanations for all of the many wonders I saw on my travels, including my own Celtic dreams and gilded visions in the solitude of the land at dawn and dusk. But then there are human explanations for God too in a Christianity that takes seriously the full implications of the incarnation. The devils and angels are what we make of them, and on returning from a deep immersion in our small corner of creation I am confident in saying that the greatest threat by far to the fabric of the cosmos as we know it comes from human intervention and disruption. I did not want to write a book about pollution, but stopping and spending time intently focusing on places marked out by nature as special, at these natural landmarks, it was impossible to ignore that the degradation of our environment has affected every one of the holy places marked out by Christian tradition. These are supposed to be non-human spaces, spaces where the spiritually minded can escape from the mundane to encounter the divine. It was a little difficult to imagine myself as a new Adam in his paradise garden while picking my way through the plastic bottles and washed-up fabrics that line our wildest shores.

Yet it was in search of such primal experiences that I travelled, and it is still possible to cast aside all vestiges of civilization and modernization to stand in unadorned wonder at unadorned creation. At best my immersion in these half-forgotten rituals and bramble-covered landscapes felt like I was encountering something of the holiest and most devout women and men in our history, glimpsing the possibility of heaven on earth and touching the garments of great leaders such as Columba, Cuthbert and Hilda. At other times, it must be said, edging my way into murky caves, across swamps and into the ruins of an ancient hermit's lair, I felt rather more like Gollum. Somewhere between these two extremes I have navigated through the Celtic mists to bring you this book.

The body

And finally a few paragraphs about the full-bodied title of this book and the very raw embrace of the natural world in many of the Celtic rituals it describes. The nakedness of the hermit's life is open to misinterpretation, but the closer I came to experiencing and reflecting on it, the more I realized it worked not just as a mirror but as an embodiment for the impulse towards nature and creation. The simplicity of the desert and the minimal possessions of nomad and monk alike are combined in this witness, an expression of humility and solitude, of vulnerability and poverty, and even of innocence itself. The spiritual lessons that began to tumble out of my encounters all emerged at the bodily intersection of humans with the rest of creation, the interplay between the soil and the soul that first moved Adam.

We are each given one small fragment of creation at birth, the human body, and there is nothing that so neatly and entirely encapsulates our complex and contradictory relationship with nature than the one we direct towards our own selves. In presenting a story in which the human body – at times the naked human body – has a positive role to play in Christian devotion, I have decided to let the examples of the early church and my own experiences speak for themselves. Ascetic nudity does work in both Christian theory and practice, but it is a discipline that I had to learn the hard way. I am and have been for my entire adult life an enthusiastic naturist, of a very traditional type that was introduced to me through my German aunts. I have written books about naturism, but this is not one of them. The nakedness of a hermit is completely different from the twentieth-century movement promoting recreational and communal nudity, and an attempt to mix the two together proved not only spiritually suspect but profoundly disturbing. Even so, this background did equip me with one thing that I found extremely useful, and that is a willingness to embrace the elements in all their Celtic rawness with absolutely nothing to protect, distract or comfort me.

St John Cassian, who more than anyone was responsible for importing desert monasticism into Western Europe around the year 400, urges hermits to practise bodily nakedness (*corporis nuditatem* are his exact words). He is being literal, because there was just such a tradition of Christian nudism in the lives of the desert fathers and mothers, one of whom was surprisingly influential in Celtic nature lore, as we will see.[13] This has vanished from our Christian heritage, and not just vanished in the sense that people have stopped doing it, but quietly edited out of the historical record. The latest translation of John Cassian is a case in point: the introduction highlights this phrase and translates it literally, but someone editing the text itself substituted the misleading phrase 'bodily deprivations', presumably averse to the very suggestion of a devout hermit's deliberate nakedness. This is nothing if not a good reminder that the human body is the site of passion, the focus of so much anxiety, guilt, shame, pleasure, disgust and celebration. It can also be, as I discovered, a vehicle to experience and understand the divine. I did dispense of all trappings of civilization in order to go in deep, breaking the ice on a river in Surrey one frozen January and eschewing any wetsuit in favour of my birthday suit to encounter nature in the raw. I managed to gasp my way through the Lord's Prayer, then paused for a moment out of time as the profundity of my condition sank in, and the cold passed me by.

Indeed, wetsuits figured surprisingly large during my academic research. The only bone of contention between me and my lead supervisor Professor Tina Beattie, the Roman Catholic theologian, was over the issue of whether a devout wild swimmer should ever wear a wetsuit. We conducted one academic supervision while treading water in the middle of the Thames. It was August and we had compromised by choosing swimming costumes for our supervision meeting, the first time I had worn anything to swim in open water for many years. Some people earn such respect. My other supervisor, the historian Dr Charlotte Behr, had an attitude towards my research that offered the balance of dry land, honed in German universities: no-nonsense, calm, measured and methodical. I've no idea what these two custodians of academic integrity make of the intensity with which I have pursued the physical dimension of my research into nature rituals, the way bodily experience pressed into the abstract theological and intellectual material. That was the more conventional material of academic research after all, a dimension that they supported, encouraged, tempered and enabled with unfailing good grace and wisdom. The running about naked bit is all mine.

I am not sure how other academics or theologians would accept this book's attempts at reconstructing early nature rituals, because in the wider academic world I detected considerable antipathy towards anything involving the body in the disciplines of the humanities (history and religion). This extends to the point where the primary source texts are routinely censored or mistranslated by modern scholars, as John Cassian's example above shows. There are several instances given in this book, and many more besides, that point in the same direction. However, I believe that taking early religious belief seriously, taking it to its ultimate conclusion wherever possible, does turn out to be a productive exercise, no matter how cold and awkward it might feel to be an outcast slipping on estuary mud on a misty winter's day. I genuinely would not have made any dent on understanding the devotional bathing practices commonly reported among Celtic saints had I not tried to copy what was described. I had originally planned to write a defence of the presence of a naked body in these Christian rituals, but it is too visceral and personal to touch, and at the final reckoning there is no point covering the reality of what I went through with words and arguments. Make of it what you will, all I can offer in return is an honest account of what I did, and what happened to me as a result. The only suggestion I would offer is that embarrassment does not need to be the overriding emotion or impulse with which we view our physical selves, even though many have argued otherwise. Shame was the first sign in Genesis that something had gone severely wrong with the human relationship to God's creation, and it was shame I left in a crumpled pile on the shore as I braced myself to meet my maker.

1

Sacred trees

———◄●►———

The clearest way into the universe is through a forest wilderness.
John Muir, personal journal (1890)

Our journey begins at the foot of a sacred tree. Pagan as such a concept might sound to some, one only needs to open the Bible and start reading for a couple of minutes before encountering two divinely protected specimens at the heart of the garden of Eden. Not for the last time in this book, the raw ingredients of Adam and Eve's paradise home seem surprisingly close at hand in the Celtic landscapes of Britain. Trees are very much part of the spiritual infrastructure of our island, shading and protecting us beneath their spreading limbs, long-lived witnesses to the most enduring of communal beliefs. Some of our oldest churchyard specimens have been growing since before the first missionaries set foot here, marking common ground where people and their beliefs could coalesce and find peaceful expression, where new religions settled into the landscapes of the old.

Ages of five thousand years and more have been proposed for yew trees beside churches in Scotland, at Fortingall Parish Church in Perthshire, and Wales, at St Cynog's Church in Powys. The Fortingall Yew is so ancient it even bears a rather far-fetched legend that Pontius Pilate grew up playing beneath its branches – yes, the same man who condemned Jesus to death. This yew was thought to be a male specimen until one branch suddenly burst into life with berries, changing sex in 2015 to the delight of arboriculturalists and nature lovers alike, not to mention one or two of us with a spiritual interest in the fabric of creation. Standing today beneath its evergreen branches it is difficult at first to take in what you are seeing, a grove of individual trees arranged in a vast circle, until you realize that these are the fragmented remnants of a trunk so ancient its heartwood has not just rotted but vanished entirely.

One thing we know for certain about Pagans right across Europe is that they were into tree veneration, the seemingly miraculous longevity of the yew tree as good an example as any of their awe-inspiring character. So many of the early records refer to tree-based cults, so it is fair to conclude that they felt this was important enough to be worth mentioning. It also rather preoccupied the early Christian church. How exactly you 'worship' a sacred tree is something of a moot point, and we will come to that as this chapter unfurls. Several books have been written on early medieval trees and their spiritual significance to both Pagans and Christians, but few have attempted to piece together the hints of ritual practices that survive in order to recreate their devotional context. Tree-based spirituality is not quite what I had expected when I set off to examine the evidence, but from what I can piece together the role of trees in religious practice did serve a truly useful function, so useful that I would say it still has relevance and agency today. In particular this chapter demonstrates how a sensitive Christian approach to nature managed to encompass the earlier ritual function of a landmark tree that pre-Christian beliefs bequeathed. Locked in their gnarled trunks and shady branches there is a spirituality that not only survived the transition to Christianity but also remains very much alive. I have stood and admired many of the great and ancient specimens growing in churchyards the length and breadth of Britain, and at the end of this chapter I describe what happened when I put my sacred tree theories to the test in a short service conducted in the churchyard of a busy, suburban high street next to a fairly young yew. At the end of my journeys to the edges and margins of our island I can't help but think that the universalism of Celtic Christianity makes it just as relevant to the urban environment as it does to rural Wales, Scotland or Cornwall, and take heart by remembering that one of the greatest Celtic Christian leaders, St Cedd, was actually Bishop of London. Sacred trees, or the potential for them, are all around us. And they still work today.

They are also close at hand, a gentle and easily accessible introduction to the wilder landscape experiences that increasingly fill the chapters of this book. In so many ways they mark an ideal starting point for our adventure into the Celtic wilderness.

Missionaries and the axe

Giant specimens of long-lived trees crop up again and again in tales of Norse and Germanic Paganism, such as Yggdrasil the giant ash or yew tree in Scandinavian sagas, Thor's oak in Germany, or a mighty evergreen that St Martin encountered in Gaul. We know this because of the stories of the first missionaries in mainland Europe, who took great delight in seeking out these ancient holy places, sitting down and talking to their Pagan guardians about religion, and then taking out an axe and chopping through the sacred trunks. Christianity and the environment, one might well tut. This is the sort of thing that so many of the church's critics are no doubt thinking of when they criticize religion as arrogant and unsympathetic to the created world. Right across continental Europe, the records are embarrassingly consistent on this point.

In fourth-century Gaul, St Martin felt sufficiently moved by the spirit to cut down an ancient evergreen tree that a local community venerated as their god. Having stood by silently while he destroyed their temple, this was a step too far and they refused to let him do it, unless he stood beneath the tree so that it would crush him for his insolence. Needless to say, in the story St Martin confidently obliges and manages to deflect the toppling tree by miracle, winning the folk round as it falls harmlessly beside him. Harmlessly, that is, for the bishop. The missionary St Boniface did much the same in Germany, where he cut down a huge and ancient tree called Thor's Oak, which local Pagans had venerated for many centuries. He then used the pile of wood from the tree to build a church, which is a good way to make a point but again not exactly uplifting from an environmental perspective. Two other eighth-century saints followed suit, St Sturm overseeing the destruction of sacred groves, and the Emperor Charlemagne ordering the destruction of the enigmatic Irminsul sacred object, which probably refers to the trunk of an oak or other mighty tree.

Everywhere you go across mainland Europe you hear the same sort of story, the ancient trees cut down, the groves burned, the Pagan temples ransacked and destroyed. Worship of nature was officially outlawed, even acts of worship set in a natural arena. The Council of Arles in 452 hints at some specific rituals involving a matrix of natural features, including trees, that had supposedly been tolerated by Christians. It does its very best to stamp out the fun:

> A bishop must not permit unbelievers in his diocese to light torches or trees in honour of fountains or rocks. If he fails to prevent this, he has made himself guilty of sacrilege. The proprietor of the place, moreover, who permits such in defiance of warning given, shall be excommunicated.[1]

And then you come to the islands of Britain and Ireland, and things start to look very different indeed. Throughout the entire conversion period and beyond there are no stories of trees being cut down, and no church decrees condemning the veneration of ancient oaks, pines or yews until the early eleventh century, six hundred years later. So while Christians all over Europe were busy deforesting sacred groves in the name of the new religion, something rather different happened when they and their faith crossed the sea. There is no record anywhere of people destroying the ancient natural landscape of Britain or Ireland in the name of the new religion at any stage during the long transition from Paganism. Indeed, the first recorded destruction of a tree in the name of Christianity occurred when St Wulfstan complained about a nut tree that was casting a shadow over a rural church. When the local thegn, a land-holding member of the gentry, refused to do anything about it the holy man pronounced a curse on the tree, which duly withered and died. While some might see faint echoes of Pagan sensibility in the thegn's protection of the churchyard tree, in reality this took place half a millennium after Christianity had become well established throughout Britain, and even post-dates the Norman Conquest by about a decade. The thegn's reasons for preserving his tree were also rather far removed from what one might consider signs of devotion: he enjoyed sitting in the shade to play dice and feast with his friends.

So it is reasonable to ask what was so different about Britain and Ireland. And it is not just that we simply don't know whether trees were cut down or not, because a wide range of surviving evidence speaks eloquently of a very different narrative, one where trees continue to play a full part in the spiritual lives of the tribes, people and religious leaders alike. The lack of any reference to the destruction of sacred trees is not simply the result of the limitations of the historical record. Far from it.

Under the greenwood tree

What did people do at Celtic sacred trees that somehow kept them safe from the axe? The answer to that question is surprisingly simple if my interpretation of the evidence is correct: they met there. The sacred tree served as a public meeting space where people of widely different backgrounds and even different tribes could assemble and discuss matters of mutual concern, including complex negotiations and serious disputes. And they were not merely convenient landmarks, but cast an aura of spiritual protection over those who gathered under the shade of their branches. They were places where violence was forbidden, taboo if you like, where protagonists could meet and discuss all manner of vexatious issues without fear of attack. My research leads me to the conclusion that they were a neutral negotiation space in a land where most inter-tribal disputes would involve hitting people with swords, a place set apart from normal human rules.

Trees, including trees formed into a sacred grove, were little enclaves of peace in a land that was racked by tribal conflict, where brutality, warfare and slaughter were very much part of daily life. Whatever peace and unification the Romans had imposed on their northern colony soon shattered following the withdrawal of the imperial army in about the year 410, a fragmentation helped on its way by the arrival of numerous opportunistic Anglo-Saxon warrior leaders. Any map of Britain in the post-Roman period shows a patchwork of competing tribes and kingdoms, mostly named after Anglo-Saxon groupings but undoubtedly including still further layers of undocumented communities of native Britons, in addition to several Welsh, Scottish and Pictish kingdoms. The arrival of Christianity greatly helped to consolidate this patchwork, the Anglo-Saxon kingdoms in particular coalescing into regional powers as alliances were forged and law codes and literacy introduced to regulate larger areas under one ruler. The profusion of kingdoms crystallized into seven, a period of relative stability known as the heptarchy, which in turn ultimately led to the gradual unification of what we now call England. My belief is that all of this required a degree of diplomacy and negotiation from the outset, as Britain became a crossroads for numerous conflicting belief systems, tribal identities and military powers. Not exactly a controversial opinion for sure, but what this chapter proposes is that this process was deeply embedded in the landscape and particularly its sacred trees, every bit as meaningful as the various other spiritual and secular interactions described in the chapters of this book.

Right across Britain there are stories that celebrate sacred trees as part of the founding legend of a saint and his or her church. In my own diocese of Southwark, hardly the most rural of episcopal sees, there are two really ancient yew trees standing alongside medieval church buildings, one at Crowhurst and the other at Tandridge, both in Surrey. I preached a sermon, about sacred trees no less, at Crowhurst one day and beforehand we went to stand inside the yew that is so vast its inner trunk has long since rotted, leaving an area inside the size of a small room. A cannon ball dating from the Civil War was once found buried in its vast bulk, and it easily pre-dates the fourteenth-century church building. How many seasons this tree has stood is anyone's guess, but figures of up to 2,500 years have been mentioned, suggesting that the church like so many others was deliberately sited beside this living companion. Dating yew trees is a famously contentious subject, but I suspect a little of the scepticism I hear on the subject is driven by a desire to disparage religion, and Christianity in particular, denying that we could ever be so sensitive and inclusive as to build a church next to an ancient sacred tree. But this modern narrative and the historical evidence will never fully tie up because there are very old references in saints' *Lives* that talk of a saint miraculously planting a yew or ash that shoots up into fully grown maturity, and then building a house of worship alongside. This is unarguably a way of explaining the juxtaposition of a very large sacred tree and a church, and such tales date from long before twentieth-century attempts to rope in 'science' as some sort of proof or opposition to religion.

There are many literary references to such miracles, including one by the monk Reginald of Durham, the finely named chronicler living in the twelfth century who wrote of an ancient ash tree at Oswestry, Shropshire. Following the death of St Oswald in battle here in the seventh century, Reginald reports that a raven carried his severed arm into the ash, which was subsequently endowed with healing powers and ageless vigour. So by the twelfth century there was an ancient tree with a Christian legend attached.

It is important to note that Bede, who wrote about St Oswald's death just a few decades after it occurred, did not seek to make any claim about a giant healing tree. This is an important point of silence in all the near-contemporary records of saints. Any legends that record a miraculous origin for any such landmark tree could not be made within living memory, for the simple reason that the local people would know immediately that it was untrue. If their ancestors had known and worshipped this very tree long before Christianity came along it could hardly be claimed as a miraculous addition to the village. By the time of Reginald in the twelfth century it was clearly safe to claim an ancient ash tree for Christianity. In similar manner Bede writes much about the miracle-working founder of Ely, St Etheldreda, but only her twelfth-century *Life* records that her staff miraculously sprang to life overnight, at a place called Stow. A lofty Saxon church in that Lincolnshire town remains a lasting testament to the respect afforded to this archetypal holy place, although the tree itself is long gone. What is clear is that these founding legends are typically written a few centuries after the supposed miracle, when the juxtaposition of church and sacred tree demanded some sort of explanation. This silence by contemporary records does not directly prove that these trees were well known by local people as pre-Christian sites of veneration during the conversion era, but it certainly adds to that picture. Communal memories last longest when they are embedded in the landscape, attached to durable natural features. The name of the River Thames is thought to be so old it dates from some sort of early Indo-European common language, because it is also the name of a river in Uttar Pradesh. In similar vein, the name of the town Oswestry (Oswald's Tree) also memorializes this founding legend for the sacred ash tree and its unfortunate royal saint.

Stories of saints planting their staff in the ground and then watching it spring miraculously into life as a fully grown tree, as the *Book of Ely* records about St Etheldreda, are found across Britain. On occasion the very tree itself is still standing, as at Congresbury where the ancient yew planted from St Congar's staff can still be seen half buried in the trunk of a vast beech tree that has grown up alongside its cousin, more or less swamping it. This legend appears in a twelfth-century *Life* that is somewhat fanciful, but there is nothing fictional about the fragments of an ancient tree still visible in the churchyard today. At Glastonbury the most famous of all our sacred trees has had a chequered history over the centuries. The Glastonbury Thorn was supposedly planted by Joseph of Arimathea, after he fled with the chalice used at the Last Supper to Britain, an island that remained outside Roman rule until a decade after Jesus' crucifixion. It's a great story, which continues to be rehearsed today; the only observation worth adding here is that it is also the scene of great conflict. The holiest of places seem to attract reverence and desecration in equal measure, something that comes across strongly in my chapters on such rocky places as caves and mountains. The Glastonbury Thorn is a late legend, dating from the sixteenth century, but the evidence of conflict is entirely real, the original tree chopped down in the mid-seventeenth century by one of Cromwell's Puritan soldiers. Cuttings of the tree continue to grow in and around Glastonbury today. When I visited the site of one of these offshoots, planted on Wearyall Hill just outside town in the 1950s, it had recently been brutally hacked by a chainsaw, its branches cut off in a modern-day version of the missionaries and Puritans with their axes. The stump stands at the time of writing, the criminal and the motive still unknown. A little gathering of Pagan women were standing around the tree in a circle, singing softly and lamenting its demise. Their leader told me the spirit in the tree was no more, despite efforts to revive it, but that a second sapling nearby, very recently damaged, still harboured faint signs of life. On many matters of nature I would trust the opinion of my Pagan friends over those who hack away at our founding legends and mythology.

A place of peace

So we return to the question about what you do at a sacred tree, and why Christians choose to adopt pre-existing specimens for their own religious stories. I could write a whole book about the evidence I have gathered on this topic, and perhaps I had better get round to that one day, but in summary my research suggests that trees and groves were regarded as safe meeting places where it was forbidden to do physical injury to another person. Their status as a meeting place is reasonably easy to demonstrate, but it takes a fair amount of contextual analysis to determine that these meeting places were, like the meetings themselves, regulated by deeply held ideas about protocol, weaponry and personal safety.

We can start with the easy part of this, demonstrating that trees were used to mark a place to meet. The first written reference is found in the writings of the Venerable Bede. The scene happens very early in the campaign to bring Christianity from Rome to the Anglo-Saxon people, the first recorded meeting between St Augustine of Canterbury with the bishops of Celtic Christian tradition. The year is 603, and this was a meeting fraught with difficulty and disagreement, partly due to the Celtic method of calculating the date of Easter but also due to the extreme antipathy felt by the native Celts towards the Anglo-Saxon incomers, some of whom were accompanying the Roman bishop. Augustine had been told by the pope he should generally be relaxed whenever he came across innovations and local expressions of belief in the churches he encountered on his journey from Rome, but the date of Easter was a red line about which no compromise would be granted. This was also a meeting fraught with the potential for tribal conflict, since the Anglo-Saxon party supporting Augustine included his sponsor and protector King Ethelbert of Kent, travelling some distance from his home territory. This is what Bede has to say:

> Meanwhile, with the aid of King Ethelbert, Augustine summoned the bishops and doctors of the nearest British province to a conference at a place still known to the English as Augustine's Oak, which lies on the border between the Hwiccas and the West Saxons.[2]

The location of this oak has gently exercised academics in recent years, and there are no definite answers to be found other than somewhere around Gloucestershire.[3] Wherever it was in that region, the bishop and king were a long way from their base in Canterbury, and this was clearly an important council meeting with much at stake. The participants appear to have found a venue appropriate for attempting to perform a balancing act between these competing parties, which means there is rather more to this oak than first meets the eye. It is clear that the tree sits on the boundary between two tribes: it was not merely a notably large landmark but a place where opposing factions could and did gather. It was already mapped and incorporated into a human scheme by the time Augustine and Ethelbert arrived for their discussions, a neutral space between two territories that neither side had under their temporal control. The text does not say explicitly that this was a ritual or holy site, but if anywhere can be considered a haven for non-human use and exploitation, outside conventional rules of ownership and control, it would be just such an enclave on the margins between two jurisdictions.

This meeting with the British bishops was far more complicated than a simple religious synod, where theological discussion and ecumenical prayer might be expected if we look at this through a modern-day lens. The mere involvement of the Kentish King Ethelbert in a meeting place associated with two other tribes is sufficient reminder that missionary work during the conversion of Britain was commonly a negotiation not just between two faiths but between different ethnic groupings, backed up by armed men. Often missionaries would travel from their base in a neighbouring tribe, or in Augustine's case from even further afield, protected as he was by an English king from the other side of the country.

The significance of meeting rituals, of protocol and etiquette, that would govern the conflicting interests and power structures is forcefully brought home by what happened at the follow-up meeting to this first encounter in the shadow of an Old English oak. At this second synod, probably held further north in Britain, the Celtic bishops had been advised by a wise hermit to note how Augustine greeted them. If he had the discourtesy to remain seated during the ritual of welcome, they should have nothing more to do with such a 'haughty and unbending' man. As it happened, Augustine failed to stand for the British bishops, and the split between Celtic Christian leadership and the Roman hierarchy was left to rumble on for another two or three centuries at least.[4] These meetings, and in particular the etiquette surrounding them, were not just important, they could be pivotal in changing the course of history.

The need to guarantee physical safety was clearly pronounced during the conversion period in tribal Britain. Not only did the threat of war hang over this second council between Augustine and the British bishops, according to Bede, but its failure led indirectly to armed conflict in which 1,200 monks were killed. If nothing else, this was not a simple misunderstanding about good manners but an indication of attitudes towards meeting spaces that were saturated in ritual and notions of the sacred, of sanctuary. There is indeed another recorded meeting that involved St Augustine and King Ethelbert, when they first greeted each other at the start of the bishop's mission, an encounter that so worried the king he insisted that they meet 'in the open air'. Bede here explains that the king was nervous about being caught indoors lest he fall victim to some sort of magical arts, so we can infer that he might have been keen to have armed men alongside him as insurance during this difficult encounter. Bede does not speak of any tree or grove but rather an unbounded space, and yet again this paints a picture of a time when meeting protocol was a matter of life and death. As we will see in the next chapter, the transition to Christianity was carefully managed and delicately negotiated at all levels in society. Sacred trees, along with other natural landmarks and features, appear to have taken centre stage in this process.

There is a little more to be said about this notion of meeting etiquette and protocol before we return to the trees and groves. King Ethelbert also wrote down the earliest Anglo-Saxon law code after his conversion to Christianity. The seventh provision in this code contains a very rare word in the Anglo-Saxon vocabulary: *mæthlfriþ* ('assembly peace').[5] It comes in a section of this code that is focused on protecting the church and clergy. Anyone violating this 'assembly peace' would be required to pay double the usual compensation. Glancing through the rest of this law code, it is clear that the greatest threat by far to an individual's safety, whether in a protected meeting or not, came from the risk of being attacked. The code contains detailed prescriptions for the compensation paid for injury to specific parts of the body, even down to two different types of damage to the nose. It is impossible to read these laws without gaining the impression of a society in which the violent use of weaponry was a prevalent and widespread means of conflict resolution. Placed in this context, the notion of a regulated space for resolving disagreement, in which the noses and other parts of the participants could emerge unscathed thanks to rules about 'assembly peace', seems unarguable.

If Augustine's Oak is an example of the sort of traditionally determined meeting place where leaders from different tribes or kingdoms could gather to negotiate on neutral territory, then it would be entirely appropriate for such sites throughout Britain to be used by missionaries too. This is the process by which I think that pre-Christian meeting sites around trees and groves acquired a Christian significance. Leading missionaries as diverse as Columba, Hilda, Wilfrid, Mellitus, Etheldreda and Aldhelm were all of royal or noble blood and would have been entirely comfortable negotiating formally with a king and his court. As has been seen, such negotiations between neighbouring tribes were freighted with matters of temporal as well as spiritual power. Place-name evidence backs up the idea that trees were used to identify meeting places. Della Hooke's excellent study of early medieval trees in England lists 46 administrative units named after a specific species of tree, and 23 others that use the generic word *trēow*, tree. These units were commonly named after their place of assembly.[6] Trees were and are a gathering place for communities.

The evidence from Ireland further corroborates the notion that there was a matrix of royal, tribal and spiritual power concentrated around trees, which has many parallels with the evidence unearthed in Britain. The juxtaposition of landmark trees with early churches is recorded at three of the most important early Irish centres of spiritual power, all of which contain the place-name element *Der*, 'oak'. The site of St Brigit's foundation was called Kildare, meaning 'church of the oak', while Columba's Irish monastery was built at Derry, an etymology noted by Bede: 'known in the Scots language as *Dearmach*, the Field of Oaks'.[7] A similar etymology accounts for a third Irish monastic site founded by Columba, Durrow, from the Irish *Darú*, plain of the oaks, ancient specimens of which survive up to the current day. From the outset the Irish set up their churches next to these ancient trees; indeed, the oak is the same specimen that St Augustine used for his first major synod. St Patrick is recorded as building a church beside the Torten tribal tree in Tírechán's *Life* of Patrick, written in the mid-seventh century.[8] Later Irish literature records the existence of five sacred trees of Ireland, seemingly the ceremonial trees for each of the island's five tribes. Della Hooke adds that the Irish annals record the destruction of the *bile*, a large tribal tree, in County Clare by King Malachy in 981.[9]

A Pagan enclave

It has been argued above that trees delimited a sacred space where early Christians could speak in relative safety before a gathered tribal delegation to discuss the merits of conversion – to evangelize, in other words. Thus they could become permanently associated with this foundational site for the tribe's new faith, and at times the location of an early church. The arguments in favour of this conclusion might seem logical enough if somewhat lacking in definitive proof, but there is other evidence that supports the idea that a ritually protected space demarcated by a tree or trees had huge cultural resonance at the time of the conversion and transition of Britain.

Remember the missionaries who were destroying Pagan shrines, including their trees and groves, across continental Europe? The same bulldozer diplomacy was originally planned for Britain. This is what Pope

Gregory the Great wrote to King Ethelbert shortly after the king was converted to Christianity: 'Press on with the task of extending the Christian Faith among the people committed to your charge. Make their conversion your first concern; suppress the worship of idols, and destroy their shrines.'[10] This somewhat heavy-handed letter was written on 22 June 601. But then the pope wrote another letter less than a month later, this time to one of his missionaries, Bishop Mellitus, in which he said something remarkably different:

> For if the shrines are well built, it is essential that they should be changed from the worship of devils to the service of the true God. When this people see that their shrines are not destroyed they will be able to banish error from their hearts and be more ready to come to the places they are familiar with, but now recognizing and worshipping the true God. And because they are in the habit of slaughtering much cattle as sacrifices to devils, some solemnity ought to be given them in exchange for this. So on the day of the dedication or the festivals of the holy martyrs, whose relics are deposited there, let them make themselves huts from the branches of trees around the churches which have been converted out of shrines, and let them celebrate the solemnity with religious feasts.[11]

Many aspects of this important letter have been picked over in considerable detail, the notion that Christianity 'stole' many of its traditions and dates from Paganism a particular favourite in current discussions about religion. There are, of course, theories circulating as to why the pope changed his mind in the course of a month, urging first the destruction and subsequently the preservation of Pagan shrines and traditions. Perhaps the second letter, being sent to a bishop, required him to adopt a diplomatic and negotiated approach, whereas the first letter, being sent to a king with military power behind him, assumed that a much more aggressive approach could be taken.

But I would like to draw attention to one passing reference in the letter that I think is of some significance: it clearly indicates that Pagan shrines had some connection to their surrounding trees. The description suggests a woodland setting for these places, with trees nearby and no other shelter to hand. These were not shrines built in the centre of a town or a royal settlement but were hedged around by living trees. Looking more carefully still at this second letter, it describes in some detail what people actually did at these sacred groves or clearings. Not only that, it then goes on to suggest that some of these sites had *already* been converted successfully to Christian use. So by the time the very first conversions led by Rome were taking place, there was a British template in existence that had proved to be a successful and sympathetic method of transition between Pagan and Christian religions. We are now firmly in the Celtic era, and have a clear reference to a system for adopting Pagan holy sites for Christianity, sites that we know from copious continental and British evidence included trees and groves. It is clear that the advice is based on quite detailed knowledge of pre-Christian religious practice in Britain, which must have been conveyed back to Rome by one of Augustine's associates, perhaps in letter form: a rare insight into that poorly documented period. Trees were so important to these new converts that the pope in Rome knew about them and discussed them himself. In a letter he wrote the year after Augustine had arrived in Kent, Gregory celebrated the conversion of ten thousand souls who had previously worshipped 'trees and stones'. The conclusion that a way had been found to harness this pre-Christian tree cult for the configuration of new places of worship seems robust.[12]

These sacred spaces, with their boundary of trees whose boughs were cut for ritual use, could have been a form of enclave, a safe meeting space. Other evidence, scant as it is, further suggests that these were places where protection was bestowed and enforced, a weapon-free sanctuary where normal human rules did not apply. When Bede describes the destruction of a Pagan shrine by its former high priest Coifi, he says the Pagan leader rode up to it and 'as soon as he reached the shrine, he cast into it the spear he carried and thus profaned it'.[13] I cannot say for certain, because there is not quite enough direct evidence to prove this point definitively, but I think one of the principal characteristics of Pagan sacred space was that it had to be free of all lethal weapons. This would therefore provide a safe space for the negotiations described earlier, meetings that were unarguably heavily ritualized in their protocol and, I would add, in their physical configuration.

In the early tenth century, much later than the conversion period under discussion, it might still be possible to see the ghosts of these non-violent enclaves lingering in the British landscape. A set of laws by King Edgar, which were drawn up by a bishop, uses the word *friðsplottum* ('sanctuaries', or literally 'peace-spots' or 'peace-places') alongside his condemnation of pagan worship of trees. These laws forbid 'worship of wells, and necromancy, and auguries and incantations, and worship of trees ... and in sanctuaries (*on friðsplottum*) and at elder-trees'.[14] This word *frið*, peace, crops up again in a similar injunction against worship in nature in the eleventh century, again referring to some sort of enclosure. The Northumbrian Priests' Law demands that 'if there is on anyone's land a peace-yard (*friðgeard*) round a stone or a tree or a well or any such nonsense, he who made it is then to pay a fine, half to Christ and half to the Lord of the estate'.[15] *Friðgeard* literally means 'peace-yard', the same meaning of 'yard' used in 'courtyard' or 'farmyard'.

While an eleventh-century bishop must have enjoyed sitting down and harrumphing about 'any such nonsense' concerning nature rituals, I think these sorts of nature configurations ran long and deep through British culture, and were at one point rather handy for bishops too. The further back we go into this early evidence, the more the clues become rich with enigmatic references to powers vested in the landscape. It is time to go back to consider the earliest surviving description of a church in Britain. It is not what one might expect.

The earliest British church

This would be a pub quiz question too obscure ever to be asked, and I expect it would test even the most avid of early medieval scholars. But I have asked it myself: what is the earliest written description of a church in Britain? It stumped me for a number of days, but I think I can offer the answer, following some intensive research. I believe that it is transmitted in a text written around the year 480, the *Life* of St Germanus, a bishop from Gaul who visited Britain during the barely documented sub-Roman period. Germanus came to bolster the British (or 'Celtic' if you prefer) Christians in their defence of the country from Saxon invaders. He also came to deal with a heretical movement that was apparently gaining traction among Britons. One of the set-piece moments in this mission came when he fortified and instructed the British soldiers, who were gathering to do battle with an army of Saxon invaders. He prepared a number of them for an Easter baptism:

> A church was built of leafy branches in readiness for Easter Day, on the plan of a city church, though set in a camp on active service. The soldiers paraded still wet from baptism, faith was fervid, the aid of weapons was thought little of, and all looked to help from heaven. Meanwhile the enemy had learned of the practices and appearance of the camp. They promised themselves an easy victory over practically disarmed troops and pressed on in haste.[16]

As it turned out, the newly baptized British soldiers went out and won the battle without striking a single blow, by yelling 'Alleluia' at the tops of their voices to strike fear into the hearts of their Pagan adversaries. The cry was echoed back by the mountains, and the enemy scattered in fear. This battle has been known as the 'Alleluia Victory' ever since, and took place in 429. There are numerous points in the story where it sounds rather more fanciful than factual, including a detail that the fleeing Saxon marauders drown in a river that they had recently crossed safely: something that sounds suspiciously similar to the crossing of the Red Sea in Exodus 14. And yet the historical context overall rings true. It was a time of warfare and invasion, and the British churches were mostly cut off from the Continent, already developing their own idiosyncrasies. It would be difficult for the author of this work, a bishop of Lyons, to fabricate the entire confrontation and expect to be believed. It is certainly true that a devout author of this era can be expected to filter what he understood as historical 'truth' through a theological lens. To us it would be counter-intuitive to believe that such an editorial hand made the text *more* truthful, but that would have been the writer's motivation, a historical event gaining more meaning and revealing a higher truth through its spiritual validation. Anyway, the point that leaps out at me from this battle is that it wasn't really a battle at all.

And there at the start of it is the earliest known description of the construction of a church in Britain. This strange structure woven out of branches is a peculiar addition to the story, indeed a peculiar configuration in any context. It sounds rather more like a demarcated outdoor space than a church edifice, and the detail that the branches used were leafy further suggests that the trees themselves lent some significance to this enclosure. Finally, if you look carefully at this short piece of text you will see that it describes the soldiers as unarmed not just once but twice: 'the aid of weapons was little thought of' and the troops were 'practically disarmed'. A sacred space, demarcated by leaf-bearing branches where weapons were absent: this sounds less to me like a 'city church' and more like the many other enclaves we have glimpsed in our journey above. The fact that the *Life* avoids mentioning any defensive purpose to the structure, even though the woven branches could in theory refer to some sort of palisade, further embellishes this scene.

The conclusion I have come to is that the Alleluia Victory was a negotiated settlement conducted under the terms of the sort of sacred, non-violent meeting space that had currency in late Pagan Britain: a space hedged around by trees. A potentially bloody confrontation was averted following negotiations led by Germanus, and credit was given to him for securing a miraculous 'victory'. This explanation requires only a minimal intervention with the text. Although it is difficult to penetrate too far into the precise detail of the encounter between native Britons, Saxons and a bishop sent by Rome, I would claim that the Alleluia Victory and the strange 'field-church' built immediately before it are intimately connected. In many ways a meeting such as this would bear uncanny similarity to the later meeting at St Augustine's Oak, which also involved native Britons, Saxons and a bishop sent by Rome, a fraught and tense set of negotiations that once again managed to avoid armed conflict.

Bishop Germanus' visit to Britain in the fifth century is just about the only documented historical event in that entire 100-year period, but it is obvious that his Christianity underwent a strange warping process as he crossed the English channel. Something rather peculiar happened when Christian mission encountered the inhabitants of Britain – and not just the human ones either. During his travels in his native Gaul, the good bishop simply went around helping people in a demonstration of humility and charity, but even as he crossed the sea to our island he introduced an extraordinary ritual that was still being remarked upon and copied centuries later. As will be described in the chapter on devotional bathing, he took consecrated oil and poured it on the waves to quell a storm. And there is more. After arriving, his journey continues to weave the landscape into his missionary work: he builds this 'field-church' out of leafy branches described above, while at the Alleluia Victory itself the river manages to drown a hostile band of Picts and Saxons that was threatening his flock of native Britons, even though they had safely crossed it when advancing. Indeed, Germanus ultimately routs this army by encouraging his soldiers to shout 'Alleluia', and, as described, the rocks of a valley echo the noise so loudly the warriors are scared out of their wits. If we are looking for the earliest manifestation of a spirituality wrapped around the land, here is a text in which nature seems to be crackling with spiritual energy at every turn, from the seething waves to the echoing mountains. I think this bishop from Gaul helped to found Celtic Christian nature traditions.

On common ground

What was going on? Why did Christianity suddenly dive into the natural world to find validation and meaning to resonate down the centuries as Christian Britain's foundations? Why did Christians adopt the groves, trees and shrines, rather than simply destroying them as they did elsewhere? One prosaic answer might simply be that the early missionaries in continental Europe simply had more firepower behind them. St Martin lived at a time when Christianity was becoming the official religion of the empire, and he and his fellow bishops were very much connected to the seats of imperial power, the cities. Indeed, the word 'metropolitan' means both bishop and city, so closely were the two elided by this stage. So it would be relatively easy to enforce new standards on the common folk. Even at the time of St Martin, living at the close of a century that saw the worst persecution of Christians at its start, the church was fast becoming a power structure, a part of the state government, an instrument used by kings and princes. It had the power and confidence of entire armies behind it. No wonder it was prepared to go and hack down the Pagan landscapes. It was powerful and successful; nothing could stand in its way.

I'm not entirely sure that is what Jesus envisaged for his church, however. And when the Christian missionaries came to Britain and Ireland they tried a different tack. Rather than hitting people and their trees with the new religion, they decided to see if they could make it work in terms the local people would understand and relate to on a very deep level.

In Britain there was no unified or imperial power structure surviving by the fifth century onwards, and missionaries were often entering uncharted territory. Throughout this book there is a consistently sympathetic narrative thread at work, stitching the story of the people and their faith closely to the story of the landscape. There was a desire to demonstrate that one Christian God was capable of reaching and redeeming every level of creation, able to operate from the depths to the heights to banish any of the shadows that lurked in the natural world. It also happened in Ireland, a sensitive and confident form of Christianity that was able to stand alongside other traditions and acknowledge their cultural power without fear. It is perhaps little wonder that Britain and Ireland lack any significant martyrs of the entire conversion period, particularly when compared to the situation on the Continent. It was an axe that St Boniface wielded against the mighty Donar's Oak in Germany to evangelize by force, and it was an axe that was wielded against him to end his life a martyr in Frisia. He is said to have held up a book of Christian texts as spiritual protection against his attackers, and to this day this slashed codex is venerated at Fulda Cathedral, alongside his shrine.

When the church in Britain finally became a part of the country's power structure, once the kings and queens had been converted and the church was operating openly alongside and often within the royal administration, it was too late to turn the clock back. Our ancient trees had acquired a new Christian meaning and were safe from attack, having accrued new spiritual narratives to complement their ancient traditions, a lingering sense of the peaceful enclave that once served pre-Christian folk so well. This book contains numerous examples of the way in which a communal memory embedded in the landscape becomes the most enduring memento of all, and remains the case even today with sacred trees and churches. You might recall that the trees used by Germanus are described as 'leafy', which suggests they are evergreens, perhaps yews. His 'field-church' was constructed for a mass baptism that took place at Easter, when there would be no leaves on the deciduous trees, the continental Easter date falling on 7 April in the year 429.

It should also be noted that this notion of a protective space hedged around by the power of a tree or grove does not appear to favour one tribal group over another, but rather the opposite. The argument of this book is that the landscape was an actor of greater power and authority than any of the social configurations that milled around its many landmarks, transcending any national, tribal, racial or even spiritual boundaries. St Germanus and St Augustine were foreign bishops, travelling to Britain with a specific mission to fulfil, and found themselves just as much a part of and participant in the landscape's narrative as any of the other tribal groups. Indeed, the Saxons themselves were also new arrivals on the island, which has seen numerous tribal groups and ethnic identities come and go over the millennia.

Pagans, Christians, and heretics, newcomers, foreigners and indigenous people all found ways to negotiate on common ground: the grove as meeting place would be the clearest physical statement possible that humans are bit players in a larger cosmology, a landmark tree standing taller and older than anyone alive. There are activists and organizations today building a global interfaith dialogue around the notion of ecological protection, seeking to harness the emotional investment that faith communities direct towards their environment in ways that will help to protect and sustain natural resources and enclaves. More acutely still, indigenous land rights offer protection for numerous threatened tribes on the basis of their long-term connection to the land, usually large areas of territory that are not currently heavily exploited for forestry, agriculture or mineral extraction, one of the last lines of defence against deforestation and illegal mining in South America. As Celtic history reminds us, none of this is new. In 1731 an Indian woman from Rajasthan called Amrita Devi, who followed a form of Hinduism called Bishnoi, which believes it is wrong to fell green trees, was appalled when she learned that the local maharajah wanted to cut down the villagers' grove of acacia trees to build his palace. She and over 300 other villagers went and put their arms round the trees to protect them, and were killed. This is where the word 'tree-hugger' comes from, now a mildly disparaging term for a do-gooder but in truth the emblem of a true martyr. None of these are 'nativist' narratives that seek out signs of exceptionalism and exclusivity in the stories woven through the fabric of the land, but rather the opposite, a shared interest in celebrating the unique elements that collectively constitute biodiversity.

If the progressive and atheist alternative is that communities and societies should have zero emotional and spiritual investment in their surroundings, then a complete disconnect between nature and culture will be the ultimate destination. This is a logic with extreme consequences that could be followed to its dangerous conclusion. The reinvigoration of society's relationship to the natural world could lead in numerous more healthy and enjoyable directions.

Forest church

As my journey through the forests of Celtic Britain demonstrated to me on repeated occasions, trees and groves are places where people have gathered. Not merely similar to a church or other community centre but actually serving as a consecrated space in Christian tradition, they were meeting places where the rituals of old and new faiths alike could be performed in relative safety, the baptisms taking place in Germanus' 'field-church' being a case in point. The only problem with this for me on my personal journey has been a minor one: it is difficult to conduct meetings and gatherings when turning up alone and unannounced at rural churches and groves in the wilderness. A hermit, naked or otherwise, has limited scope for organizing an impromptu assembly in the wild. I did once walk into a pine forest at the back of a long and deserted ocean beach, and found a natural grove in which to sit in prayerful contemplation. A gnarled tree trunk raised up as a sort of prayer stall, I knelt under the branches and watched a bird flutter down to rest high up in the canopy. Then I thought perhaps this too is a meeting place, one that befits the limitless horizon of Celtic cosmology, a place where the human can encounter the non-human. I was feeling my solitude that day, drained both spiritually and physically, and found myself reflecting as I often do on my smallness in this order, reflecting on the mustard seed. As the parable puts it, this will grow into a tree, where the birds of the air will come and lodge in its branches, a natural meeting place, perhaps at a stretch a forest church too.[17]

I did consider attempting to revive another form of extreme tree devotion that flowered briefly in the early church, although not as far as I can tell in any British or Irish context. Spending time on an island as a naked solitary seems positively mainstream compared to the outer fringes inhabited by these early Christian tree hermits, an ascetic sect known as the 'dendrites'. These were similar in a way to a group called the stylites, pillar-dwelling monks who also lived in the open air, renouncing the earth and attempting to live as birds without shelter or artifice.[18] Yet even reference books can barely come up with any named examples of this order, the most notable early example being St David of Thessaloniki who lived in an almond tree beside his monastery for three years, clinging on amid storms and the cold and heat of the seasons – and, incidentally, refusing to take up the role of abbot, which his community had tried to impose upon him. Others took literally the injunction by Jesus to follow the example of the birds of the air, one of a startling group of early hermits who believed enlightenment was to be found by living entirely like animals. In the *Lives of the Desert Fathers*, Abba Macarius encounters two naked monks drinking from a lake alongside wild animals, while another naked, elderly man is witnessed eating grass as it grew from the meadow.[19] All three are described uncritically as motivated by their Christian faith, and I am sure that they were.

In Britain, many solitaries lived in the wilderness, in caves, and particularly on islands in great number. But no dendrite apparently took advantage of any of our most ancient trees, even though some of the splintered fragments of yew are large enough to ride a horse through the centre, their inner trunks long since rotted to the ground. The closest I could find in European tradition is a seventh-century saint from Belgium called St Bavo of Ghent, who lived as a recluse in a hollow tree trunk before moving into a forest hut. So I wondered about spending a night inside one of the many hollow sacred trees I have seen on my journeys, but could not justify it as any sort of Celtic revival. Churchyards are well used by homeless people seeking a quiet place to sleep, and we have had one such resident in my own parish in recent years, a man fallen on hard times and resorting to drink after the breakdown of his marriage. There are those who pitch up still to take advantage of the age-old sanctuary provided by a churchyard and its trees, an echo perhaps from the deep forests of Celtic refuge and resort.

At the end of my journey I felt sufficiently moved by sacred trees to suggest that we hold a short talk and hymn in our suburban churchyard garden during a Sunday evening service in early summer. As I surveyed the grounds before we attempted this rather gentle exercise in nature devotion, I noticed with some concern a group of men from the local YMCA who had gathered around our benches, beer cans in hand, one of them topless. A bus motored past behind me in the road and I went inside to gather with our community, writing it all off as the sort of distractions we would have to ignore to make this service work. As I led our faithful dozen out into the churchyard some 20 minutes later, warbling along to the hymn 'For the beauty of the earth', I noticed the little group stop their boisterous talk and look over at us, and feared the worst. Then, as I began my talk, the oldest of the party shuffled over with his can and sat down on a bench beside us and listened in silence to some thoughts about the long witness of sacred trees, the churchyard as a haven, the young yew beside me the latest iteration in a timeless witness of creation making and remaking our common home.

I've no doubt that the spiritual benefits of listening to me pontificating about tree veneration through the ages are precisely zero, but I still can't think of any form of indoor church service we would ever hold in which our constant companions in the churchyard would be likely to join us. Our local churches do hold a homeless shelter each winter, but that is a different matter altogether. I don't know: I did it once and it worked once, so statisticians can pore over those figures and make of them what they will.

To say that people need to protect trees, to impose preservation orders and fines, to end logging in virgin forests, to plant native species and maintain urban street trees might seem a robust response, but our Celtic ancestors went deeper still. Today we act communally to protect our trees, but that was never the original understanding of our relationship to these sacred landmarks. It was rather the opposite, an inversion of our troubled hierarchy in the natural world: it is trees that protect the people.

2

Celtic nature theology

Our brief foray into the dark Celtic forests has already shed light on the practical, everyday concerns of the conversion period. The sacred trees of the previous chapter provide the first secure foothold for our deeper steps into Celtic lore, demonstrating that there was a hard-edged and logical purpose to spiritual interactions with the natural world. From this opening we can start to establish what else went on, what radiated outwards from those all-important missionary meetings under the branches and in the groves that had been marked out as special. As will be seen throughout this book, trees are not the only resource that the natural world provides for an amazingly productive, creative and sensitive outpouring of environmental spirituality. They are also not the only resource that had strong Pagan associations surrounding them too, something that has perplexed many a Christian over the centuries. This chapter will examine quite how the early missionaries managed to work with material that was so obviously and so deeply moulded by pre-Christian beliefs, developing new narratives large enough to encompass every part of the natural world. It took a remarkable degree of confidence in their faith to approach such a panoramic Pagan vision, and has produced some truly remarkable ideas as a result, ones that history has fortunately recorded.

The impulse to push Christian ritual into the landscape crops up repeatedly in early stories about the conversion of Britain, celebrated by all early British religious communities, whether or not one classifies them as Celtic, English or Roman. But it took the great historian and theologian Bede to reduce this down to a simple formula, and doing what all theology does by grounding it in Scripture. It was the garden of Eden and the book of Genesis to which Bede turned to explain the enduring discomfort humans feel in the natural world, a lost harmony that the missionaries of Britain tried so hard to reveal and to restore. In the first half of this chapter I will explain what the conscious theological argument was to support the hermits' deep immersions into nature, and in the remainder I will present the reason why I think this was so important at the time.

This contains the basic narrative that could be used to support a modern Christian theology of environmentalism, one that is reasonably simple to explain.

Writing about the seventh-century abbot and bishop St Cuthbert of Lindisfarne, Bede attempted to make sense of a whole series of spectacular nature interventions that had been attributed to the saint. Birds would obey the holy man's instruction, the waves would carry building materials to his island retreat, fire would subside and storms abate at his command. All good stuff to prove the credentials and charisma of a great monastic leader, to create a folk hero whose authority extended to inanimate objects, to depict a man able to produce what appeared to be miracles in the natural world. Nothing particularly educational or instructive about such obvious tales, one might think. And then Bede gives an entirely unexpected reason for the saint's ability to manipulate nature. 'It is no wonder', he wrote, that Cuthbert could do all this because an important witness of a holy man or woman was to put right the relationship between God and his creation. 'For the most part,' Bede explains, 'we have lost dominion over the creation which was made subject to us, because we ourselves neglect to serve the Lord and Creator of all things.'[1] Bede is quoting verse 28 of the opening chapter of Genesis, when God gives 'dominion' over all animals to Adam and Eve. Cuthbert is able to reactivate the initial state of unsullied creation. This is not just a passage about a single holy abbot and his remarkable spiritual powers, but a profound statement about the innermost workings and essential character of the entirety of the natural world. This is not just about how great Cuthbert was, Bede is saying, but rather his presence in the landscape reveals a fundamental truth about creation.

Above all, Bede is reminding us that humans had originally been endowed with a harmonious way of connecting to the environment at the dawn of our spiritual history. As the Genesis story goes on to say, this happy state of affairs was lost at the Fall, when we were locked out of the forest, forced to rely on human ingenuity and invention, to eke out a living through pain and hard work. 'Cursed is the ground because of you,' the Lord admonished Adam, 'through painful toil you will eat food from it all the days of your life. It will produce thorns and thistles for you, and you will eat the plants of the field. By the sweat of your brow you will eat your food.'[2] As the story of Adam and Eve makes plain, this antagonistic relationship with our environment was not part of the original design, it came about because of our sin. To put it another way, there was once a harmonious chain connecting all of creation to the Creator, with humans occupying a pivotal role in the middle. The moment that human link was broken by disobedience, disorder tumbled down through the rest of the created world: everything became tainted by human failing.

This notion of a paradise lost is of course not even remotely innovative – it is a mainstay of the Bible and also reflected in other religious traditions. But what is truly remarkable in Bede's formula is the notion that a devout human being is capable of turning the clock back and reverting to this initial state of harmony. And he does not mean this as any sort of supernatural feat, finding a way to get back through the gate of Eden by sneaking past the guards with their flaming swords. He means that this lost paradise is actually right here. The ground beneath our feet, the wind that brings storms and the waves of the sea bear within them a latent imprint of the primal perfection. It can be reactivated by someone who reverses humanity's first sin of disobedience. As Bede puts it: 'For if a man faithfully and wholeheartedly serves the maker of all created things, it is no wonder though all creation should minister to his commands and wishes.'[3] This is quite some claim, and it is this that gives Celtic Christianity its uniquely heightened sense of the potential of the natural world, a realm bursting with promise and fulfilment. The innate beauty and benevolence in creation is just waiting to break through and reveal its Eden-like origins in response to a devout and sincere approach to it, something the early saints epitomized.

Despite the best efforts of scholars far better read than me, there does not appear to be a direct match for this bold claim in any early Christian theological writing. Bede's ideas are an extraordinary stretch back towards the environmental harmony of Eden, a remarkable innovation but one he almost presents as being self-evident. Indeed, the restoration of this harmony is so natural, in every sense of the word, that Bede goes so far as to categorize Cuthbert's spectacular nature interventions as simply examples of creation revealing its original complexion. 'It is no wonder' means that he did not even consider these occurrences to be miraculous. 'For the most part' means he believed there was occasional evidence that Eden could be glimpsed in everyday life. At the touch of a saint, nature would demonstrate its fundamentally benign character, and Bede clearly believed this to be a reversion to the norm. Perhaps paradise reveals itself to everyone from time to time if they spend enough time outdoors.

The degradation of creation

The first part of Bede's formula, that creation was damaged at the Fall, has many precedents and parallels in early Christian writing, and is known as the theology of universal corruption, the idea that the whole created fabric of the cosmos was marred by human action. It is easy enough to justify by looking at Genesis: immediately after the Fall, the ground sends up its thorns and becomes a place of toil, the snake and the human share mutual enmity, and the garden paradise is closed. It could be further said that humans suffer extreme alienation from their own bodies too, an interpretation that certainly reflects the trajectory of this book. Many early theologians looked back at the happy state of Adam and Eve before the Fall and recognized there was a cosmological condition that had been lost, that the damage was universal, precipitating a degradation that left no part of creation untouched. This might seem far-fetched when you first encounter it, but it was once a common teaching in the early church. Common, that is, until a certain theologian took over the narrative and turned his attention remorselessly to just one facet: all of this was entirely focused on proving the innate sinfulness of human beings.

St Augustine of Hippo initially went along with the idea of universal corruption in his younger years, agreeing that the earth had been cursed at the Fall.[4] But his focus in later life switched, narrowing dramatically to argue with single-minded determination for his concept of original sin, which has overshadowed Christian thinking ever since. Creation, he concluded in his later works, was entirely unaffected by the Fall and remained inherently good. All that changed was the relationship between humans and the natural world: thorns were simply repurposed to prick the conscience of us sinful mortals. Everything is about us. Even the invention of clothes, according to Augustine, was to hide this visible reminder of our unruly, sinful nature. Far from any desire or impulse to restore a state of lost harmony, Augustine regarded our sorry state as entirely deserved, a spur to remind us of our sinfulness: it was God and nature serving us right.

This highly anthropocentric form of Christian theology has gained a lot of traction, and certainly flatters the importance of human beings in the divine purpose. Augustine fought his corner valiantly and very successfully, but his argument was an innovation at the time, and it was developed as part of a furious barrage of intellectual defence against a heresy that sought to downplay, even deny, the existence of innate sin altogether, to claim that humans could work their way into heaven by their own efforts and talents. In this campaign St Augustine was success-ful, and the briefly popular ideas of the monk Pelagius were routed. But this theological battle came at a cost; it created some consequences that are not entirely helpful in Christian tradition. The notion that each baby is so mired in sin at birth that she or he will end up in hell unless baptized is one of the least defensible notions arising from Augustine's intellec-tual tactics, and the blame lies firmly at his door for that.[5] So too is the notion that Adam and Eve's alienation from their bodies was entirely to do with sexual awakening. Much has been written on Augustine and ori-ginal sin, but for now it merely need be said that Augustine regarded every part of the degradations and deprivations that happened at the Fall to be focused on underlining the individual human's inherent sinfulness, without stopping to consider if there was any collateral damage.[6] And if there was no damage done to creation itself by human disobedience, there was no need for reconciliation either. If you are looking for a theologic-al route map to find your way to some sort of environmental sensitivity, St Augustine's arguments on this point will ultimately lead you to a brick wall. I have a suspicion that this is why the church generally has had more difficulty than it ought in articulating a positive response to our many ecological crises, and why some branches of Christianity are very un-interested indeed. He was no doubt doing his best, but Augustine had a very urban view of Christianity, and it is no coincidence that his greatest book is called *The City of God*.

Compare all that to the argument by the great theologian St Basil, repeated enthusiastically by Bede, that in the 'first creation' of Eden there was such harmony in the cosmos that even lions and wolves did not hunt for prey but were originally vegetarians, something implied in Genesis 1.30. 'Nor did the wolf search out and ambush around the sheepfold . . . but all things in harmony fed upon the green plants and fruits of the trees,' writes Bede in his commentary on this happy state of affairs.[7] Several chapters later in Genesis, after the Flood, humans are given permission to start enjoying all types of food, a dispensation that was understood to extend to the whole of creation, the point at which predation began.[8] To claim that creation was fundamentally unchanged, as Augustine does, but merely repurposed to focus on pricking the conscience of sinful humans is a much narrower perspective on the Fall, all but ignoring its effects on the non-human environment, giving scarcely a passing thought to the collateral damage that this newly antagonistic relationship had caused. Perhaps ironically, Augustine's over-refinement of the concept of sin has ended up greatly reducing it.

This notion of an innate harmony and universal vegetarianism might sound absurd when applied to fully evolved carnivores. Yet the underlying principle of some sort of primal unity, and in particular a common origin for all living creatures, is not entirely out of the realms of what is our genuine natural history. The experiences that make up this book, of heading deep into the landscape and minimizing any trappings of civilization, make for a feeling of particular connection and co-dependence between humans and the rest of nature, and one can be entirely scientific about that or hopelessly misty eyed. Certainly the early church theologians did not mean anything like our modern understanding of evolution in looking at a convergence between species as one moves backwards in time, yet the parallels are interesting. And the notion certainly reflects a broader purpose to the fate of creation at the hands of humans than a mere backdrop to the grinding gears of Augustine's anxiety about our wickedness.

Augustine's opinions did not dominate fifth-century Europe in the way they later came to do, and my detailed reading of Celtic Christian ritual and liturgy has detected at least as much evidence of another powerful theologian at work, St Ambrose of Milan. I have avoided the more technical aspects of this in my search for our missing 'first creation', but some of Ambrose's fingerprints on Celtic spirituality are fairly obvious and will come out in the chapter on devotional bathing. Ambrose certainly had a more cosmological view of baptism than Augustine, turning his attention to the water in the font in an unusual pivot towards the elements as an active participant in the generation of a new Christian. Nature and our effect on it does not need to be a mere incidental detail in a story focusing on the darkness of human sin, and even amid the minutiae of theological debate there is a big narrative here that touches on fundamental truths about the human condition. Human sin from the outset caused damage to the environment, and it is the mission of a faithful man or woman to put that right. There is of course no sense that Adam and Eve were responsible for any form of mass environmental destruction of the type we see today, but rather that the imposition of human values on a naturally balanced hierarchy introduced harmful changes that cut both ways.

The notion that humans should seek to restore any lost 'dominion' over nature might sound dangerous to anyone who longs for a more sensitive relationship between us and our environment. Yet it is also unarguably true. We are at the top of the tree, in evolutionary terms, and we are entirely capable of altering our planet's natural resources, to the extent of destroying pretty much all of them. We might as well accept that our actions and choices are absolutely pivotal when it comes to the health of the natural world around us. 'Dominion' does not mean fighting and overcoming, in any case; it means the original harmonious and orderly coexistence. Adam and Eve in the garden of Eden lived without hunting or exploitation, a time considered absolutely peaceful and non-violent. In his commentary on Genesis cited above, Bede mentions Cuthbert and his friendly birds again as a living example of this 'first creation', a time of primal simplicity that he remarkably suggests should be the default position for everyone. We will look at what Cuthbert did with this pair of ravens in more detail, but the upshot was that his 'dominion' extended no further than offering them a safe place to build a nest.

When the first Christians wove their rituals into the natural world, these were not the vestiges of British Paganism or the folkish yarns of a primitive age, but something that penetrates to the very heart of the Judaeo-Christian story. This is a template that can be applied to pretty much all the varied and colourful stories about spiritual encounters with nature, even the wilder ones that appear as this book goes on. Celtic spirituality reflects a faith that spilled across all creation with a message of redemption and an actual restoration of the original, innocent harmony that people could see with their own eyes. This story is the oldest of all: human sin at the Fall had not merely disrupted our relationship with God, it had precipitated disorder through all of creation. The Celtic instinct was not just to accept enthusiastically that humans had played a pivotal role in violating this natural order, but to add that they also had a pivotal role in putting things right.

The implications of this are profound. If one agrees with this trajectory, as it was passed from Scripture through the work of the patristic writers before finding its full expression in Celtic practice, one is left with the conclusion that sin is inextricably bound up with our relationship to the environment. The evidence is there that humans have had and continue to have a deleterious effect on the natural world, in physical and spiritual terms alike. To deny something such as global warming, and even more obviously the plastic pollution of our seas and waterways, is to deny the message of the Bible, from the first book onwards. 'For by the sin of man the earth was cursed,' to repeat Bede's understanding of Genesis. If you put that at the heart of your faith, some very interesting consequences will follow.

But why did all of this come out so starkly in British and Irish spirituality during the fifth to the eighth centuries? It is all very well to muse theologically about a damaged relationship between humans and nature, and idiosyncratic but not beyond the realms of speculation to suggest that this relationship could be put right. But what is really unusual is to find an entire cohort of missionary leaders who set out into the wilderness with the express purpose of demonstrating that the Genesis story was physically true. The notion that disharmony was caused by human sin is easy enough to find in theological tradition, but in Britain and Ireland what is innovative is the idea that it could be resolved by human sanctity, indeed that it even needed to be resolved. Apart from anything else it is quite hard to walk into the wilderness with the minimum of protection and equipment and demonstrate that the experience will be entirely harmonious and peaceful. Bare legs and brambles are as painful a combination now as they were when God first sent up the thorns, as I discovered myself. So why did they pick up this notion of universal corruption out of hundreds of patristic and biblical threads and put so much weight on it? Bede used it to develop a unique theological formula to justify the astonishing amount of energy that was being thrown at the natural world across all parts of Britain, and one might add in Ireland too. But to what end?

The answer turns out to be wrapped up with the missionary work that Celtic Christians were directing towards the folk of Britain, a coherent and strategic attempt to lay foundations for the new faith that were more stable and reached deeper into the earth than the old beliefs it supplanted. I would love to say I discovered this context through a careful process of deduction, but the truth is I stumbled across it by chance. Once I had finished my studies into the theology behind intense nature rituals, I decided to take a break and look at the wider context of the period, to conduct a little research into the way in which the transition from pre-Christian to Christian beliefs was being managed. Having set aside all thoughts about Genesis 1.28, the lost dominion that Bede wrote so passionately about in his vision of a first creation, I was more than a little surprised by what I found when I looked at the way in which the conversion negotiations were handled.

A mission to the cosmos

It was seemingly a separate question I had in the back of my mind for a year as I pondered the start of the Christian story in Britain: what exactly did the missionaries say to their potential converts, the tribal folk who were doing perfectly well with their lives when Christians turned up? To answer that I needed to know what beliefs the missionaries were trying to grapple with, to understand how they attempted to persuade the Pagan people that Christianity offered something better than their existing answers to life's big questions. There is not a lot to go on, if truth be told, since the culture of pre-Christian Britain is remarkably poorly documented. And that despite 350 years of rule under the Roman Empire, a literate society that generally gives a good account of the same period in continental Europe. Not a lot to go on when it comes to this side of the English Channel, but just enough to point us in the right direction.

The earliest reference by a Christian writer to what might be genuine Pagan beliefs about the natural world is both brief and rather surprising. Writing at some point in the depths of this poorly documented post-Roman period, anywhere between 480 and 550, the British monk St Gildas produced a passionate declamation about the state of his country. Harried by the waves of Anglo-Saxon invaders, Gildas partly pinned the blame on his fellow Christians and the clergy for failing to provide moral leadership. He does, however, have one positive thing to say about the lasting benefits that Christianity had brought. It comes down to the relationship between humans and the natural world: 'I shall not set out in detail those mountains or hills or rivers, once so deadly, now so useful for human needs, on which in those days a divine honour was once heaped by a blind people.'[9] I ignored this scrap of evidence when I first read it, because it didn't seem to make a lot of sense. Was Gildas seriously suggesting that pre-Christian beliefs towards the natural world were in fact negative, that rivers and high places were once considered 'deadly'? Everything I thought I knew about Paganism, partly through several good Neo-Pagan friends, was that these religions revere nature to the point of worshipping it. Why would anyone claim that this relationship had once been hostile, antagonistic, even 'deadly', and that Christianity had eased this and made these natural landscape features 'useful'? The thought nagged at me infrequently as I turned to study the scant records of missionary negotiation that have been passed down to us by Christian writers, hoping to find a more plausible or comprehensible account of the terms in which pre-Christian and Christian discussed matters of belief.

I decided to look in a systematic way at a number of accounts that describe the conversion process, using a method that would allow me to glimpse beneath the propaganda so often presented by the Christian record. In order to do this, I focused only on texts that include negative attitudes towards Christianity, worth poring over in some detail simply because they are likely to be believable. A devout writer would be highly unlikely to make up critical comments about his or her faith, particularly when they were usually so keen to present a completely air-brushed picture of the conversion process. The transition is bound to have been bumpy and unpredictable, painful and erratic, and I found just three accounts that met my strict criteria of including some faint traces of the inevitable resentment and hostility that the missionaries faced. These three accounts pass what is known as the 'criteria of embarrassment' test for historical authenticity: they record attitudes that an author would probably prefer not to record, but is required to write down because of the sheer weight of evidence, context and popular memory. When it comes to certain events, as it were, you literally couldn't make it up. As I say, it is only on rare occasions that the Christian writers of this early British period let slip a hint of criticism through the net, but the three I offer here fit the criteria admirably. These are just three accounts among a very large number of other texts that blithely claim the process of transition was entirely smooth and orderly.

For reasons that baffle me, many historians seem remarkably willing to take these simplistic accounts of the transition period at face value. Indeed, many historians of the conversion of Britain, and even Europe, claim there was no need for any programme of mass conversion whatsoever because the common people were entirely compliant: missionaries went to the king and queen and convinced them to convert. The royals then barked out a series of orders to the common folk, who quietly acquiesced without further ado. I'm a Christian and even I think this is nonsensical propaganda, but it is surprising how historians seem willing to go along with the idea of royal prerogative pushing all objections before it.[10]

Perhaps it is only understandable when you consider just how biased the historical record is, and I can give some hard evidence for this. Bede's *History* contains 25 'conversion' incidents, in which a tribe is persuaded to convert to Christianity, often with the king present. Only one of them, examined below, includes explicit criticism of Christianity. All the others indicate at worst indifference ('we have no need of it'[11]) and usually a brief indication of complete acquiescence, sometimes before the missionary had even started preaching ('people flocked together with joy to hear the word'[12]). I don't think these simplistic accounts can be taken at face value, not least because we know from elsewhere in Bede's own writings that there was long-term ambivalence towards Christianity in seventh-century Britain, including a few incidents of apostasy.

More sensitive writers have started to question this unlikely story of easy transition. The shrewdest recent observer when it comes to the negotiations between Pagan and Christian is Professor Ronald Hutton, who points out that there is just enough evidence creeping through in the texts that offers a glimpse of a resentful population, prone to disobedience and disrespect towards the new faith, and sceptical of its benefits.[13] So I picked up this thread and assembled my small collection of incidents where just such hostility has made it through into the historical record. When I read them closely, the lights on the dashboard lit up in red, as it were, and some of the mist that shrouded the landscapes of conversion-era Britain cleared before my eyes. You might already find it easy to spot some of the terms and biblical passages that jumped into focus for me once I had sifted out these three passages.

The first incident appears in a Latin *Life of Gregory the Great*, which was written by a monk at Whitby between 704 and 714. The author was a contemporary of Bede, but neither writer seemed to know the other's work.[14] That fact alone gives this text great prominence as a witness to the conversion process, particularly because Bede dominates our understanding of this period. Most of the action of the *Life* takes place in Britain as a result of Pope Gregory's decision to send a mission to the people here, no doubt reflecting the fact that the author had only limited information about events in Rome. And so he records the conversion of one royal household, that of the Northumbrian King Edwin around the year 627.

The story goes like this. The people had been won over by the preaching of Bishop Paulinus and had agreed to enter his church to start receiving formal instruction in the faith. But as they set off a crow started croaking in a way that signalled ill omen to Pagan ears. Disturbed by this portent, the mood of the crowd turned against the bishop: the song of this strange new church was not divine in origin but 'something false and useless'. St Paulinus, in an unusual missionary manoeuvre, ordered one of his men to shoot the bird dead. He then turned his intellectual weaponry on the Pagan hostility confronting him. First, he said, the bird had clearly proved unable to see into the future because it had not sensed an arrow flying towards it. Second, he continued, the Christian Bible taught that humans had been given dominion over all the animals, as his bowman had just demonstrated. In other words, he rebutted Pagan scepticism by preaching Genesis 1.28 at them and then proving it in action.[15] Remind you of anything?

The argument used to convert the common folk to Christianity rested on precisely the same verse as the lonely nature rituals of Celtic hermits.

The second incident was recorded by Bede around the same time, and appears in his two versions of the *Life of St Cuthbert*, a verse and later prose composition. Not only does it record popular resentment against

Christianity, it also mentions that people still talk about the incident described: you couldn't fabricate that sort of detail because your readers would immediately know you were lying. So this story has a double seal of authenticity to it. A group of monks were carrying timber on some rafts across the mouth of the River Tyne when wind started to blow them offshore. The young Cuthbert, then still a member of the laity, was appalled when a crowd of locals started jeering at the holy men. He turned on them and urged them to follow the virtues of Christian charity, receiving a pretty robust response from the angry crowd: 'Let no man pray for them, and may God have no mercy on any one of them, for they have robbed men of their old ways of worship, and how the new worship is to be conducted, nobody knows.'[16] Cuthbert's appeal to mercy, loosely based on the beatitudes and a classic of Christian teaching, was clearly falling on deaf ears. So what Cuthbert did next had to cut to the chase to make a connection with his deeply sceptical companions. He fell to his knees and prayed that the wind would change direction, which it promptly did, to carry the monks home. Such unexpected control over the elements not only shut down the critics, it won them over entirely:

> When the countryfolk saw this, they were ashamed of their own unbelief, but forthwith they duly praised the faith of the venerable Cuthbert, and thereafter never ceased to praise it. A very worthy brother of our monastery, from whose lips I heard the story, declared that he himself had often heard these things related in the presence of many by one of those same folk, a man of rustic simplicity and absolutely incapable of inventing an untruth.

I half wonder if the entire scene was set up using the flow of the estuary mouth to demonstrate a point, particularly if the locals were not so knowledgeable about seafaring and currents. The last 14 miles of the river are tidal, and would wash a raft in and out of the mouth with predictable regularity. But it was clearly a story that received popular acclaim. You can be as rational and scientific about the miraculous elements as you like, therefore, but there was still something going on here that passed into local lore. Bede also wrote an earlier, verse rendition of this story, which makes explicit the significance of a Creator God in this event, Cuthbert saying: 'Let us pray to the Lord, who created the winds and the waves, that He may grant a safe journey.'[17] Once again we are back at the creation story, the first book of Genesis. This incident is used to illustrate the Christian point that there is one divine being who has power and authority across all levels of the cosmos. The idea that the sea and wind might be a 'no-go' area for such a God and his followers was disproved by observable reality.

Cuthbert was taking on board the country folk's view that nature was capricious, unruly and capable of hostility towards humans, accepting and validating it while at the same time offering a bigger narrative to absorb it into the Christian story. Scholars debate whether the jeering onlookers can be called Pagan or Christian in this story, since they are obviously familiar with the church and its incomprehensible Latin services ('how the new worship is to be conducted, nobody knows'). It is worth repeating here that Celtic spirituality was an expression of Christianity that made sense to Pagans, to people steeped in the pre-Christian cultures and landscapes of Britain. The overall point once again is that Pagan hostility towards Christianity was overcome by turning to the natural world to demonstrate its truth. Traditional preaching methods based on moral instruction failed.

Most commentators regard this story as designed to bolster Cuthbert's credentials as a monastic leader, to demonstrate his personal authority within his immediate community. But I think the story is bigger than that, especially when one compares it to the demonstration of power over the croaking crow. Cuthbert had been something of a killjoy when he told the folk to stop laughing, but they fell silent when he moved to confront the unseen forces of nature. Cuthbert and Paulinus could have called on dozens of conventional arguments to persuade people to convert – St Augustine wrote a whole book of them – but on both of these occasions their winning tactic was to demonstrate a degree of control over the natural world.[18] These tales were not written down purely for monks but were used to inspire the common folk, a point that is overwhelmingly obvious when you read the stories themselves, popular witness and acclaim playing a pivotal role.

And so I briefly offer the final historical incident which records Pagan hostility towards Christianity, where there was no happy outcome to be found. In this story, one of the convert kings of the East Saxons, Sigeberht, ends up being murdered by two of his retinue because they complained that he was 'too ready to pardon his enemies, calmly forgiving them for the wrongs they had done to him, as soon as they asked his pardon. Such was the crime for which he met his death, that he had devoutly observed the gospel precepts.'[19] This is recorded in Bede's *History*, which he finished around 731. The murder itself took place around 660. I have no idea why this devout king has never been recognized as a saint by the early church. The conversion of Britain took place with next to no incidents of martyrdom, and it is curious that a king should be murdered on account of his Christian virtues in a period of otherwise bloodless transition but has somehow missed being highly honoured. It seems likely there is a lot more going on in this story than we can fully appreciate. When Bede comes to explain the real reason behind this murder, which he suggests was an act inspired by the devil, he switches topic entirely. One of the murderous thegns, it turns out, had entered into a marriage that had been condemned by the church, and the king had been warned to keep away from such a wicked man. The king ignored this advice, and so Bede seems to position his killing as somehow deserved. We know from other sources that Christian rules about marriage between blood relatives were one of the biggest obstacles to the acceptance of the new religion, particularly among Anglo-Saxon tribes.

Without being side-tracked into such broader topics, it is clear in all of these stories that instructing the laity by teaching them Christian charity, morality and rules on marriage appears to have received reactions ranging from prevarication and scorn to outright hostility, violence and murder. Physical demonstrations of control over the natural world gained a uniquely positive reception, particularly among the common folk. This book looks at a wide range of these sorts of ritual interaction with the natural world, and it would appear from a study into the context of the conversion period that they had a hard-edged purpose to them. They were a way of cementing the new faith into the public's affection. The fact that the same biblical story – indeed the same single verse – was used both in preaching to crowds and in lonely nature rituals suggests there was a conscious missionary strategy at work, one that had been designed to win over a fairly difficult audience.

In addition to these lonely nature rituals, further evidence continues to demonstrate the common folk's enthusiasm for a belief system that can bring a beneficial influence over the natural world. Prodigious displays of missionary showmanship using modern technology appears to have done this same trick too. A short distance along the coast from the unfortunate Sigeberht's kingdom, at Bosham in West Sussex, Bede records the existence of an Irish (i.e. Celtic) monastery that was struggling to convert the local people. A rather dejected-sounding abbot called Dicul, along with his monks, attempted to win over the locals to Christianity, but 'none of the natives cared to follow their way of life or listen to their preaching'.[20] Along came the powerful and wealthy northern bishop St Wilfrid, who apparently arrived during a three-year drought that had left the people starving. The resourceful missionary baptized the people, and immediately it began to rain. In the same passage, Bede records, he also taught the locals how to fish successfully. And so Wilfrid introduces the technology of fishing with nets, and on the same day a three-year famine miraculously ends. How lucky is that? An attempt to teach Christian morality to the common people by the monk Dicul had yet again been unsuccessful. Technological advantage gave the impression that this new faith offered an unprecedented degree of control over the environment, a factor that Wilfrid was not shy to exploit.

Christianity had at its disposal more sophisticated systems of coastal navigation, fishing technology and perhaps even archery too, all of these tools for advancing human control over the environment. Science and human progress were part of the missionary mix, an interesting contrast to the notion that religion is automatically regressive and against reason. It must be said that not all interactions with the natural world were entirely sympathetic in these stories. They record a grinding of gears between different beliefs, visceral moments in the transition of the life of an individual and of a tribe, when passions ran high, and are to be cherished for the fact that these precious few records appear to let slip some of the hostility that inevitably followed.

So I believe there was a very serious and urgent point to all the nature rituals that fill these pages, which was the conversion of both the people and their landscape to Christian tradition. The early evidence turns out to be consistent on this point: missionaries to the British margins found that the usual forms of preaching did not resonate with the natives. Ethical arguments that had been honed in the Roman Empire to convert an educated and literate audience simply did not wash in a tribal, non-Romanized region. Demonstrating a degree of control – of dominion – over nature was the best strategy missionaries could devise in order to win over the sceptical folk of Britain. Finger waving about their sex lives and marriages, denunciations of their moral failings and harsh lecturing on the fate of their unbaptized ancestors turned out to be surprisingly ineffective, when one studies the evidence. A great shame for preachers everywhere, but terrifying, shouting at and hectoring people have their limitations. The missionaries needed a new approach that would resonate with the Pagan sensibilities that had developed over thousands of years. It appeared to work in sixth- and seventh-century Britain, and I have a feeling that not a lot has changed when it comes to the likely success that moralizing and judging people continue to achieve as a means of promoting the virtues of the Christian faith.

The missionaries discovered they were pushing at an open door when they promised the lay people a reordering of creation to tame and explain the forces of nature. Unfortunately for them the door turned out to swing both ways. It was easy enough to maintain when leaders such as Wilfrid had superior technology on their side, but there was the risk of a reversal too: the arrival of drought, plague, crop failure, severe storms and the like would all undermine the tenuous claim that being a Christian will make harvests easier, boat journeys less hazardous and animals more compliant. Ironically, this argument that humans are in an antagonistic relationship with nature almost works better today than it did in the early medieval period, when the disbalance in this relationship has swung so far in the other direction. Our own shortcomings and misuse of resources have left ecosystems the world over straining under human use, while the climate is undergoing irreversible changes due to human activity. But in the time of the Celtic Christians these were not the problems that motivated a more sympathetic and engaged relationship with the natural world. The theology of Bede's formula was not a modern, ecological one: it was the people who felt most threatened by the mutual antagonism between humans and the natural world, whereas today it is the environment that is most threatened. It is not a major difference, since extreme weather events and the unsustainable loss of natural resources are already making the devils and demons who hurled their storm-ridden fury at our Celtic ancestors look like a picnic. But it is good to be clear exactly what the motivations were for this valuable piece of improvisation in a culture that was highly attuned to the vagaries of nature.

A final connection between these different scraps of evidence comes down to another word that you might have spotted more than once: a conversation about whether religious beliefs were 'useful'. This was the term that Gildas used to describe the landscapes that had been exorcized of their Pagan meanings, the hills and rivers rendered 'useful' by their rehabilitation through unspecified Christian ritual and narrative. And the Pagan subjects of King Edwin, disturbed in their journey to the font by a croaking crow, expressed reservations about Christianity in identical terms, worried that it was 'false and useless'. This seems to be a term in which the two forms of belief, Christianity and Paganism, could be evaluated and contrasted in a meaningful way. There is also a third conversion account that uses the same concept, a newly converted Pagan turning on his abandoned beliefs as 'useless'. Coincidence or not, this is Bede's version of the conversion of King Edwin's tribe, a rather different account that bears very little relationship to the story of the croaking crow.[21] In his version Bede claims that the Pagan high priest Coifi states without any apparent reservations that he considers his own spiritual tradition to be 'powerless and useless' and decides to desecrate both his priestly authority and the tribal temple by riding a horse and casting a spear into it.[22]

So it would seem that the most meaningful way in which the two entities of British Paganism and Christianity could be compared was in terms of how 'useful' they were. I would hesitate to describe these two as 'religions' in the same breath, because they were not really rival organizations operating on the same terms. On this point scholars have expressed considerable doubt about Bede's claim that Paganism had 'high priests', which perhaps reflects his desire to set them up as opposing systems competing on a level playing field. Whatever the truth of the underlying history, what we have is three independent accounts of the transition from Paganism to Christianity that all use the same phrase to evaluate the best one: 'useful'. In other words, people wanted to see agency in their religious practices, they wanted to see that it was functional, that it had a physical effect that measurably improved their lives. Abstract theological and philosophical arguments do not appear to have been so successful, at least not when it came to the common folk.

Piecing together these rare fragments of history from the conversion period, it is possible to gain some idea of the missionary theology that was pursued by Celtic Christians, consistent enough to be considered something of a strategic approach. Yes, the missionaries said to their pagan converts, the natural world is capricious, it is hostile, we are in antagonistic relationship to it. There are certainly spiritual powers lurking in the wild and in the depths, and some of them are indeed dangerous – but the Christian faith explains and puts all of that right. The evidence turns out to be consistent on this point: missionaries to all parts of Britain found that the usual forms of preaching about personal morality, charity and the afterlife simply did not resonate with the natives. The Celtic missionaries had to draw on deeper reserves within the Christian story, and what they came up with is astonishing in its originality and scope: it offered a new relationship with the natural world, a faith that was practical, useful even, in accommodating the very real landscapes of Britain within a new framework of ritual and belief. Although it looks like environmentalism to us, and certainly offers a benign theology for approaching nature with sensitivity and respect for its original pristine state, I would say that it was motivated by the more immediate context of a vast missionary enterprise to convert the tribes of Britain. When I first perceived this outline of a missionary strategy, and then realized that it matched the hermits' wilderness rituals, I thought it all seemed a fairly obvious and plausible explanation for the nature aspect of Celtic Christianity. Maybe it will seem that way to others too, or maybe other arguments will come along, but this does at least tie up some of the threads in our patchy understanding of this era.

Ireland and beyond

Having decried the notion that finding religious connection to a landscape needs to be an expression of nationalism, patriotism or any other sort of non-spiritual impulse, I am aware that the focus of this book is Britain. I believe there were good reasons why Christianity had to find new ways to express itself on this island, because historical, geographical and cultural circumstances conspired to create a unique challenge to the missionaries. And much the same could be said of Ireland, whose Celtic history is always within touching distance of events that took place on its neighbour. The close parallels to be found on either side of the Irish Sea during the long conversion period demonstrate by themselves the ability of Celtic sympathy towards nature to transcend boundaries. Delving deep enough into British history to figure out an explanation for nature rituals took me three years, but I am certain that a similar study into the conversion of the Irish folk would yield just as much, if not more, for someone with the time – and knowledge of the Old Irish language. What I did read, however, threw up repeated parallels and similarities from the writings of and about St Patrick in the fifth century onwards.

By way of illustration, one story that kept coming to mind during my travels was that of Ireland's patron saint and his encounter with two princesses standing beside a well in Ireland. These young daughters of King Loíguire had come to a well to bathe one morning when Patrick held them in a conversation that speaks eloquently of the way in which Christian mission wove itself into the landscape. If the record of this spontaneous sermon is accurate, included in the writings about St Patrick by the Irish bishop Tírechán in the 660s or 670s, this is perhaps the first time we can see where the stories that have guided my own travels took hold of the imagination of our ancestors. Even if this tale were a seventh-century concoction, that still places it squarely in the middle of the Celtic golden age. The central place that nature plays in negotiations between Christians and Pagans could not be more clear:

The first maiden said: 'Who is God and where is God and whose God is he and where is his dwelling-place? Has your God sons and daughters, gold and silver? Is he ever-living, is he beautiful, have many fostered his son, are his daughters dear and beautiful in the eyes of the men of the earth? Is he in the sky or in the earth or in the water, in rivers, in mountains, in valleys? Give us an account of him; how shall he be seen, how is he loved, how is he found, is he found in youth, in old age?' Replying, holy Patrick, full of the Holy Spirit, said: 'Our God is the God of all men, the God of heaven and earth, of the sea and the rivers, God of the sun and the moon and all the stars, the God of high mountains and low valleys; God above heaven and in heaven and under heaven, he has his dwelling in heaven and earth and sea and in everything that is in them; he breathes in all things, makes all things live, surpasses all things, supports all things; he illumines the light of the sun, he consolidates the light of the night and the stars, he has made wells in the dry earth and dry islands in the sea and stars for the service of the major lights.'[23]

It hardly needs to be said that once again the primary missionary text is Genesis 1. The story itself becomes increasingly far-fetched, and this perhaps distracts from the important and serious-minded presentation of a missionary theology. In the bishop's account, the two women are baptized by Patrick, receive communion, and promptly drop dead in order to fulfil their wish of seeing heaven. Yet as a record of the intellectual rather than specifically historical content of the conversion period it is the most articulate early expression of the same missionary argument later developed by British writers, and summed up by Bede with his theological formula about the original condition of the natural world. Patrick's argument for a single Creator God was expressed to engage with the beliefs of two Pagan converts, whose faith can best be described as polytheism: many different gods. The most significant difference is that the landscape of pre-Christian Ireland seems rather more benign than the demon-infested peaks described by Gildas. Perhaps the conversion of the Irish landscape was less of a war than the missionaries in Britain had to wage against the elements. Patrick's response is an example of a Christian theology known as 'panentheism', which means 'all-in-God', a model in which all of creation is suffused with the divine presence of a single Creator God. It is, in other words, a perfect bridge to ease the passage of a Pagan culture to a Christian one. The whole of creation is suffused with a spiritual presence, in Christian and Pagan schemes alike, but in Christianity there is one God who is in every place, whereas in the Pagan universe it seems to be that every place could have its own divine being.

Lessons from the desert

Simply looking at the witness of the missionaries in Ireland is a reminder of the wide-ranging ambitions of Celtic Christianity. One can continue the trajectory further still to consider its connections and achievements in continental Europe, particularly in Gaul which provided surprisingly fertile territory for Irish missionaries to work. Many of the building blocks of Celtic Christian theology were developed by church leaders and writers who came from Gaul or spent time there in study, and they in turn were consciously inspired by the desert monasticism of the East. The debt that Bede's theological formula about nature rituals owes to the great church writers of the East has already been discussed – the witness of the goodness of creation and its universal corruption at the Fall. Time and again this book bumps into examples of desert dwellers going to extremes in order to experience God in unadulterated wilderness – including one who managed nearly half a century without wearing clothes in the process. These are the original hermits who pioneered what became a mainstay of Celtic Christianity: outcasts, cave dwellers, anchorites, nomads and simple communities all driven by the desire for solitude in the unadorned beauty of creation. Above all else, this impulse has bequeathed to the church one of the most notable of all its many institutions: the monastery, established by the intrepid adventurer Antony of Egypt in the fourth century. It is almost impossible to overestimate the influence that these desert traditions had on the history of Christianity, and connections between the wilderness spirituality of the East and a wide range of Celtic practices have been discovered and documented by numerous modern writers.

The linchpin of this connection was a man called St John Cassian, who more than anyone built the first bridge between Eastern monks and their Western counterparts. His works on monastic life were well known and emulated in Celtic circles, and closer to home he inspired the establishment of a monastery on the island of Lérins, near Nice in the south of France, one of the first and most influential outposts of desert monasticism in Western Europe. Thanks in part to this establishment, Gaul became a remarkably well-used training ground for British church leaders. The founder of Bede's monastery, Benedict Biscop, trained on Lérins for two years, and it is possible that this is the Mediterranean island where Patrick studied, mentioned but not named in chapter 1 of the text quoted above by Bishop Tírechán.

A fourth figure who will crop up repeatedly in this book is the missionary bishop St Germanus, Bishop of Auxerre in Gaul, who is also sometimes linked to Patrick. He led the mission to regularize the British church in the year 429 and, as argued in the previous chapter, left his fingerprints on Celtic Christianity with his extraordinary desire to prove that the British landscape was on his side. My fifth and final son of Gaul is a writer called Sulpicius Severus, whose tales of tame wolves and kindly lions in the East fired the imagination of monks living in the altogether colder and wetter climate of Northumbria.

The extraordinarily rich and creative outpouring of nature devotions in Britain and Ireland were themselves adaptations of a faith that first put down roots in the harsh landscapes of the East, and was transmitted from there via Gaul. I spent some weeks reading through tales of desert hermits to see if there was any sense that they too sought to restore the original harmony of the first creation, to regain that 'lost dominion'. The writings come close on several occasions, but there was never quite the sense of a natural world pregnant with the promise of a return to paradise as Celtic Christianity depicts. The closest I could find was contained in the writings of a fifth-century theologian called Isaac of Antioch. The parallels offer inviting similarities: he talked of holy hermits able to tame wild beasts, the animals recognizing the 'same scent that exhaled from Adam before the Fall'. Invitingly similar, one might think, as Isaac explains how the hermit took advantage of this friendliness when it came to creepy-crawlies. 'As soon as the feel of his hand comes near and touches their body, the virulence and the harshness of their deadly venom ceases; and . . .' – just as we prepare to concede that there is really nothing new under the sun when it comes to a mutual love between hermits and the natural world – '. . . he crushes them in his hands as if they were locusts.'[24] Celtic missionaries did at times befriend their animal partners, and at times shoot them too, as we saw with the croaking crow, but they never tamed pets in order to kill them.

The connections between the arid deserts of the East and the green valleys of north-west Europe perhaps demonstrate above all that Christianity tends in certain directions when it develops away from a hierarchical and sophisticated society: both of these two places were on the very fringes of Roman influence. In Britain, Christianity was moulded not on to the trappings of power and the administrative hierarchy of the empire, but on to the contours of the landscape itself. Just as bishops and basilicas aligned the imperial church with the centralized, metropolitan structures of the Roman Empire, so too did the faith need to adapt to the unfamiliar topography of non-urban and tribal cultures in Britain and Ireland. The period of imperial rule in southern Britain never quite Romanized the territory as intended. When Augustine of Canterbury arrived with instructions to resurrect the old Roman administrative centres of York and London for his archbishops, in practice he found Canterbury a more suitable seat of royal power. So too the deserts of the East were a place of active escape from the cities, initially during times of persecution, and then as a movement away from the institutionalization of the church once it gained imperial protection and patronage.

Britain's northerly improvisations of a hard-won campaign to incorporate the wilderness into Christian tradition have bequeathed a goldmine of powerful spirituality and precedent every bit as rich and inspiring as the parched visions of their counterparts in the East.

3

The naked hermit of Mount Sinai

Man is the sole animal whose nudity offends his own companions.
Michel de Montaigne, 'Apology for Raimond Sebonde' (1743)[1]

Halfway down a cliff face on the south coast of England, I stumbled across the hiding place of a modern-day hermit, and a naked one at that. Invisible from a coastal path above, and well camouflaged from the beach below, it was only by chance I spotted his lair one afternoon in late July. I had been scrambling along this remote stretch of shore in East Sussex, pursuing my own thoughts about solitude and wilderness, when I noticed a clump of dead bushes in the distance on one of the crumbling cliffs' broad ledges. Thinking little of it, I pushed on noisily over the shingle until I looked up as I drew near and noticed that these brown and withering plants had been cut and carefully stacked in a row. Somebody clearly had a secret they wanted to hide out here in this rocky landscape. My mind raced at the possibilities, heart thumping at the suggestion of something illicit, smugglers and contraband stashed above a beach where nobody walked. I slowly crept backwards to hide behind a boulder, acutely aware that anyone sheltering in this hideout would be highly unlikely to welcome intruders, hardly daring to shift my feet on the stones, hardly even daring to breathe. I didn't know it at the time, but I could have spared myself the bother: I had already been spotted.

Looking back along the mile of deserted shore behind me, I remembered that my mobile phone's signal had long since passed into eclipse beneath the cliffs. Up ahead I knew the shoreline eventually tapered into an impassable headland. I was also acutely aware that my skills as a hunter-tracker were non-existent, even if I could think of a way to crawl to a higher vantage point to perform an impromptu stake-out. I would be very much on my own if it came to any sort of confrontation, but my curiosity was getting the better of me. I decided in the end that my best option was to head down to the beach and nonchalantly pass this strange configuration, out of sight and gazing out to sea as if lost in my thoughts. After a couple of minutes of trying to tiptoe over the noisiest shingle imaginable, I climbed up the bank and peered over the top to gaze upon the most unexpected of sights.

Standing next to what appeared to be some sort of ramshackle hut, a naked man with a huge bush of black hair and tangle of beard stood staring directly at me, hands on his hips, clearly alert to my presence. I wanted to show him I meant no harm, that I brought no trouble to disturb his simple retreat from the world. I did the least threatening thing that I could think of, climbing to the top of the shingle bank and pulling out a bottle of water to take a long swig. I put the bottle back in my bag and began to walk back down to the shore, turning to offer a parting smile and wave at this singular man. I noticed that his body had been deeply tanned by the East Sussex sunshine, a darker colour than any casual sunbather could achieve. I have only once seen such a mahogany tan on a European, a German man who had lived in an abandoned Spanish fishing village without clothes for ten years. His British counterpart returned my gaze, then raised a single hand as if to say 'Welcome . . . and goodbye', before turning to disappear through a narrow opening in his makeshift wall. A broken wheelbarrow resting on the end of its handles suddenly appeared in the gap through which he had vanished, pushed by his unseen hands to mark an end to our brief interaction. The structure of this enclosure seemed to be composed of mud, plastic bottles and driftwood bleached by the waves.

I did not meet the naked hermit that day, but soon I had cause to think of him again when later that year my studies led me to another naked hermit, living in a distant land a long time ago. This ancient figure turned out to be a key that helped me unlock the secrets of Celtic Christianity, as this chapter will explain. Separated though they were by vast distances in time and space, as I began writing this book I felt that I should go back to speak to my modern-day hermit to see if the lessons I had gathered from the ancients still rang true today. After all, the basic requirements for such a life had remained entirely unchanged: his was an authentic and time-less witness if ever there were one. So I returned to this lonely stretch of beach to see what I might glean from actual contact with a real-life, bona fide naked solitary, living out of contact with civilization and commu-nity. He is not the naked hermit of this book's title, and nor am I for that matter, since both of us are following the footsteps of a very long tradition, quietly forgotten by the Christian record but every bit as authentic and copper-bottomed as my silent friend on the Sussex coast.

My meeting did not go entirely as planned, as you can read at the end of this chapter, but in all my travels, both literary and coastal, I did eventually discover what I was looking for. None of my hermits gave up their secrets easily, but when they did it proved entirely worth the patient pursuit.

A long-forgotten source

I only discovered the much earlier naked hermit of ancient church history after spending two years picking my way through a rather different but equally challenging terrain: the writings, histories and saints' lives that were composed during the first centuries of Christianity. In the end I stumbled across something that would change my entire understanding of early spirituality, a lost source for nature rituals that shed more light on Celtic Christianity than anything else I discovered in three years of systematic research.

A throwaway comment in the *Life of St Guthlac*, written by a monk called Felix, first alerted me to this possible lost source of inspiration for Celtic nature rituals. It set me off on a literary detective trail that ultimately opened up the entire world of natural wonder that is set out in this book. Guthlac himself was a slightly alarming wilderness figure from around the year 700, a hermit who went to live in an abandoned tomb in the Fens, chasing away demons with a whip and gathering the birds of the marshes to nest in the eaves of his hut. When asked the eminently reasonable question why, his response was cryptic: 'Haven't you read ... that someone who is frequently visited by people can't often receive visits from angels?' As it happened, I had not read that, and there wasn't much surviving material from the period that I had overlooked. One of Britain's most important and nature-loving early hermits was quoting a well-known text to justify his existence, but I had no idea what he was on about. You can visit the haunting ruin of a vast monastery built to commemorate Guthlac's extraordinary life today, in the town of Crowland in Lincolnshire, an altogether tamer place than the stories of old suggest but a monument to a truly epic life in the wild. All of this was based on something older still, an ancient text of the ways of the solitary that was now missing, perhaps lost for ever.

Whatever the mystery source that inspired such a colourful life, it was famous enough to be cited without being named, which of course made it even more difficult to identify. By the time I read the oblique reference to it, this source had been forgotten for over a thousand years, an ancient literary puzzle that became something of an obsession of mine to solve. A couple of centuries after this comment was first written, an Anglo-Saxon translator got to work on the Latin text and rewrote this phrase: 'Haven't you read *in holy scripture . . . ?*' The translator clearly didn't know what Felix was talking about either, and filled in the blank as best he could. I have read the Bible from cover to cover and there is no passage that explains how to increase your chances of meeting angels. Two years of painstaking detective work and an enormous number of false leads later, I finally stumbled on the answer entirely by chance, sitting in the dusty corner of a research library in central London. Much of this book hinges on the extraordinary trail of research and discovery that this tiny but vital clue revealed, a trail that ultimately led me from the damp Celtic forests through conversion-era Gaul to the desert cave of the most unlikely Christian hero you are likely to meet: the naked hermit of Mount Sinai.

It was already clear when reading through the early British tales of spectacular nature interventions that at least three writers were working and reworking the same raw material: obedient birds, tame animals and control over the environment. An anonymous monk on Lindisfarne, then the Venerable Bede, and finally Guthlac's hagiographer Felix all told of hermits who enjoyed a special relationship with elements and animals alike, particularly with the many birds that flocked around their homes. Emerging first from the Celtic monk on Lindisfarne, these themes had been picked up enthusiastically and even amplified by the two English writers. It was this relationship with nature that moved Bede to write his theological formula about our 'lost dominion' over creation, described in the previous chapter. Guthlac's hagiographer copied this formula and added two of his own reasons why nature rituals were important: the method of meeting angels quoted above, and a rather touching suggestion that a true Christian is united with every other creature in communion with God.

I knew that this missing source could rewrite the history of Celtic Christianity if it turned out that one of its main features – a devout regard for nature – was actually borrowed from elsewhere. My best guess was that the British writers had indeed borrowed from overseas writers but that the missing text was likely to be Irish, reflecting a nature-loving literary culture where angels were often depicted as birds.[2] This little grouping of nature rituals to me epitomized the fabled Celtic spiritual connection to nature, with the added bonus of a theological justification that seemed convincing enough to counter Pagan beliefs about the landscape. Powerful stuff, and I was fairly hopeful its source was to be found in the Celtic heartland of Ireland. It turned out I was wrong.

It was just two words in Felix's text that led me to believe this single missing source existed. '*Nonne legisti*', wrote the eighth-century scribe, '*Have you not read* that if a man is joined to God in purity of spirit, all things are united to him in God? He who refuses to be acknowledged by men seeks the recognition of wild beasts.' A true hermit, the writer continued, shuns human society because 'he who receives frequent visits from men can not often be visited by angels'. So the first thing that had drawn my attention was that intriguing suggestion that we should already know what he was talking about: 'Have you not read . . . ?' It is true that the bit about friendly animals is fairly standard stuff, and there are even passages in the Bible that would just about fit the bill at a stretch. Alternatively, Felix could simply be alluding to the tales of Cuthbert that had already been well circulated, and from where he borrowed copiously. But a hermit who avoids men in order to spend time with angels? This simply did not fit anything I had come across before, and was not among Cuthbert's many well-documented exercises. Clearly Felix thought that his readers should nod knowingly at this point. I had never read an early Christian text, including the Bible, that set out a ritual formula for en-countering angels. I was quite interested to know how one goes about that, and having discovered the answer I did go and copy it myself, on top of a mountain in Wales. I discovered to my surprise that it sort of works, after a fashion, as my chapter on mountains at the end of this book explains.

In the end it was another topic that led me to the mystery source by complete accident, while I was sitting in a research library reading the tales of the Eastern deserts written by Sulpicius Severus in the early fifth century, a man we met in the previous chapter. And so I came to the description of a hermit who lived naked for 50 years on the slopes of Mount Sinai. Half my mind was wondering about what the climate must be like there, since I tend to read these descriptions in terms of bodily sensation and practicality. Then the words leapt out of the page at me. This hardy hermit explained the reason for his intense solitude thus: he who receives frequent visits from men can not often be visited by angels.[3] I checked the Latin and it was the same slightly awkward wording as Felix's text. I had a match: Felix was clearly alluding to this book written by Sulpicius Severus. He was one of the few authors at the time who could genuinely be called famous, and his book was full of stories of hermits and their animal companions. It seemed to be the Eastern deserts after all that had inspired the Celtic heroes in their battles and friendships with the animals and angels of the wild – Eastern deserts as filtered through France, a corridor of transmission that has already been noted.

A Roman citizen of Gaul, Sulpicius is best known for his hagiography of St Martin of Tours, the late Roman saint who was and remains an enormously popular figure in Christian tradition, a bishop who eschewed the finery and trappings of high office and maintained the simple lifestyle of a monk. Sulpicius was devoted to Martin, whom he knew personally, and was no doubt fascinated by the hermit origins of the bishop's monastic calling. And so he wrote a book, known as his *Dialogues*, the first volume of which is full of tales of solitaries living in the Egyptian deserts. I was reading it because I had heard that it contained this rare example of early Christian nudism, an expression of the ascetic life that was once regarded as a sign of great holiness. It felt like a considerable breakthrough to know I had finally tracked down the original formula for meeting angels in the wild. Whether I would be able to copy it was another matter entirely, although in some respects the formula is rather minimalist.

The naked hermit is not named in the text: 'He used no clothing. Covered only by the hair on his body, he was enabled by divine grace to ignore his nakedness. Every time religious men wanted to visit him, he fled to some inaccessible place and avoided human contact.' He granted an interview just once, near the end of his life, when he explained about his conversations with angels.

And so in many ways my Celtic hermit journey begins in the shadow of this minimalist witness, a man so focused on worshipping God without distraction that he lived without clothes for the best part of 50 years in a mountain cave. He is without doubt one of Christian history's most devoted nudists, a field with rather limited competition it must be said. For many reasons he is a figurehead for my voyage deep into the wilderness, not least because he led me to the raw material out of which many of the British nature rituals were constructed. He is also the naked hermit of this book's title. It is helpful to have precedent in Christian tradition, even though the naked hermit of Mount Sinai has been quietly forgotten. No amount of editorial reworking, euphemism and censorship can deny his existence, however, and perhaps more importantly his one-time acclamation as someone to admire. His was a devout, high-minded and spiritually authentic existence, reaching almost back beyond our sinful condition to touch the very purity of the first-created man himself, placing the body and soul on a level in unadulterated service of the divine.

All of this sounded like a great model for my own journey of discovery into the echoing vastness of the Celtic landscape, until I ran into the Scottish midge.

Celtic adaptations

For all my joy at solving this literary mystery, it became clear that it takes more than a cut-and-paste job to transplant something as alive and rooted in the soil itself as a hermit's life to another climate and culture. Cold, hunger, solitude, limited provisions and a lot of climbing and walking were all taken in my stride during my expeditions into the wilderness, but it was on my very first night attempting to sleep in a hermit's cave that I was beset by a swarm of stinging monsters. My attempt to map the devotions of the Eastern deserts on to the British landscape clearly needed some creative adaptations to work. That is in essence the driving impulse behind the development of Celtic Christianity, as I was about to find out the hard way. If you've ever heard the joke about being spoiled for choice like a mosquito in a nudist colony, I was in danger of inventing another: a nudist in a midge colony. Most of that night I even kept my hood fastened tight around my ears, and resolved to work ever more closely with the land and its traditions. Having found a powerful source for Celtic nature devotions, the most fascinating lesson of all was looking at how they were reworked in Britain. Knowing the original, in other words, it became possible to see this process of adaptation in action.

The midges and many other creatures form the cast list for my own book. Relearning how to live alongside all the flora and fauna of creation in some sort of harmonious order occupied much of my own thoughts and efforts. The more I looked at the lives of the desert hermits of the East, particularly those in Sulpicius' colourful tales, the more I realized that they too were very much aware of the vagaries and foibles of their fellow indigenous creatures. The most immediate participants were the desert and its inhabitants, the animals of the Egyptian desert forming a colourful backdrop to those otherwise living in solitude. The wolves, goats, lions and nudists would roam the landscape in a generally benign way, befriending hermits and on occasion providing some sort of help. These stories were not just copied by pen, but actually copied in the caves, forests and valleys too, and the Celtic tales reflect their authentic adaptation on the ground. Britain and Ireland turn out to be rather fertile land for such devotions, both physically and mentally.

The biggest adaptation I found, though, was just how these stories became somehow spiritually supercharged once they crossed into Britain. The main point of the creatures of the Eastern deserts was to help the reader marvel at the obedience and endurance of the monastics. When the early texts do stop to make a bigger theological point out of all this, the reader is encouraged to contemplate in turn the charisma and power of the Saviour. A she-wolf who has stolen some bread, for example, returns later to a hermit to be forgiven, and is said to perceive the mercy of Christ when she has her head stroked. In Britain, these same stories are reworked in a way that is almost magical – not just more intense but taken to a completely different level of interaction. The animals and elements become active participants in liturgies and rituals that touch a cosmological scale of importance. The next chapter will demonstrate just how far the mission of a hermit to the whole of creation can extend when Sulpicius' tales of a wolf and a lion were reworked in a British context, with birds substituted as the hermit's animal companions. There are other examples of this intensification of ritual with the natural world throughout my journey.

Again and again Sulpicius stresses the obedience of monks living under community rules. As I argued in my previous chapter, the monastic scribes of Britain had rather bigger fish to fry. Monastic obedience is all very well as a theme, and it is entirely logical that any monk would wish to celebrate it. But I don't agree with others who believe that this was the main or primary purpose of the *Lives* of the saints and other spiritual tales. Monastic obedience was already there in the original source material from the East, and needed no reworking. There is nothing new or original about urging monks to listen to their abbot, and that aspect was simply carried across. The British and Irish writers added a new twist that revealed the 'first creation', the lost dominion over nature that had given Adam and Eve a harmonious life and that could break into everyday life at the wave of a holy hermit's hand. There is little hint of this regained paradise in any of the Eastern desert stories, including those of Sulpicius, who fails to describe his naked hermit as a latter-day Adam.

In recent decades writers have noted a growing awareness of the similarities between Celtic spirituality and the lives of the desert hermits. Some months after making my discovery, I learned that one scholar in the mid-twentieth century had noted similarities between the desert *Dialogue* of Sulpicius Severus and some of the other nature rituals of early medieval Britain, but nobody had investigated this systematically, and crucially had not spotted the elusive naked hermit. It is only when you begin to dig deep into the way in which this desert material was reworked that things start to become very interesting indeed. I began to make what felt like real headway into understanding what makes Celtic Christianity unique by looking at the many tales that surround this story of the naked hermit on Mount Sinai. This entire collection of desert writings turns out to be a treasure trove of raw material on which Celtic Christian culture worked its magic. The chapters of this book demonstrate consistently that the Celtic and Anglo-Saxon way of adapting this raw material was to heighten the ritual and spiritual interaction between humans and the rest of creation. Their ambition was to reveal a sort of hidden paradise lurking behind every bush and bird, nature brimming with the potential of its first creation, not just overflowing at the touch of a saint but actually moving towards church liturgy and ritual as if it were the most natural thing in the world. All of this fits precisely with the missionary strategy I had uncovered through my study of Pagan attitudes towards the new religion, as outlined in the previous chapter. Having made my discoveries from the comfort of a library, I had a theoretical model to work with. But it only truly came to life when I put it into practice, when the bare theological bones were fleshed out into a living and breathing witness.

You can follow the progression of many of these tales in the chapters of this book. Where Egyptian monks once stood in a well to subdue their flesh, in Britain the Celtic saints strode into the seas and lakes casting the sign of the cross, exorcizing the primal substance of the cosmos in a ritual of boundless liturgical power. Where obedient wolves get a pat on the head for saying sorry after stealing food, in Northumbria the reconciliation suggests that not only has an animal committed a sin but it can receive formal absolution from a priest. In the Eastern desert, demons are confined to haunting abandoned human structures, but in the mountains, islands and waters of the islands of Britain they roam freely on an epic scale. At every turn the stories become wilder, larger, more urgent and also more sacramental in their resolution. You do not need to go into the harshest of desert landscapes to experience spiritual extremes after all, as the midges in their own way taught me. If the struggle between humans and their environment can be seen in rarefied glory here, in the temperate and gentle climate and countryside of Britain, it can surely be seen anywhere. There are universal lessons to be found here, lessons that happened to be sharply expressed for reasons of historical and cultural coincidence, but lessons that echo through the cosmos.

Ultimately this theology and its practice are incarnational, the essentially embodied nature of what might sound like a spiritual and theological concept entirely encapsulated by the entry of our Creator into that which he has created. What it does require is a recognition that the divine purpose had rather more to it than a way of tackling the rather feeble and uninspiring collection of sins that is humanity's lot. Jesus might have 'died for my personal sins', as the saying goes, but he also reminded us that God was entirely concerned with sparrows too. The ritual insertion of Christ and the Christian body into the physical landscape precipitates a chain of reconciliation and participatory devotion that cascades through the entirety of creation.

Enter the hermit

Mine is a journey from the city to the wild, but it is also a journey from text to action, from the page to the field as I moved to inhabit the long-abandoned homes of hermits and demons that had been documented so earnestly in times gone by. The list of landmarks and other natural features that have drawn generations of devotion is a long one, and the diversity of places is entirely matched by the range of stories and experiences to be had at them. The most notable sites that have been marked out by nature as separate and hence capable of special meaning are obvious ones: mountain peaks, islands, caves, springs and ancient trees. A number of times in this book I stopped to think that the view, the setting, the sound, the scent and the physical sensations alike were unchanged since our illustrious ancestors led the way into this embrace. The sea particularly haunts the imagination, a vastness of possibility and scale that produces some of the most innovative Celtic nature rituals to be found. My exercises in devotional bathing encountered all the savagery of the primal element of chaos, against which the human body is both utterly powerless and insignificant, and yet pivotal and purifying. It was on a windswept Northumbrian beach where Cuthbert once prayed that it first struck me how timeless the original naked hermit's witness can be considered, how removed from any trappings and context, from any fashions that date and fabric technologies that advance. I am certain most people with faith would agree that one of the big comforts of going to a formal service is to take part in age-old ritual and connect to patterns of a bigger and longer human story. This turns out to extend to physical as well as conceptual matters, to the bodily expression of a spiritual impulse. Rituals on the furthest shores take you to the edge of space and time alike.

I was very surprised how quickly I would engage with the places and actions that made them holy, although some took more time than others. Devotional bathing in the depths of winter is quite difficult, as you might imagine, and it took me a while to combine transcendent psalm-singing with the feeling that my body was being showered in broken glass every time an icy wave broke over me. But on the whole, holy places give up their secrets quite easily, as easily as somewhere more conventionally given over to worship, like an ancient country church. Just as you can feel the centuries of prayer and the weight of a community's loves and losses as you walk into the village parish building, the same can be found in the raw outdoors. It doesn't take years of solitude to start feeling connected closely to the natural world, and I hope it comes as no disappointment that my research for this book did not involve spending 50 years naked in a desert like the hermit on Mount Sinai. I began to feel the story of the many sacred enclaves I visited within minutes, if not seconds. I did worry that my exploration would be little more than a pastiche, but it felt increasingly authentic and more personal than any of my other forms of travel and historical writing. I speak only for myself, but I think these places are the most accessible and universally appealing facet of religious culture and belief, and I wonder on a daily basis why we don't make more of this. The Church of England was surprisingly unhelpful when asked to take part in my media campaign to promote this dimension of our faith to a national television audience for my previous work on holy places, but I owe an eternal debt of thanks to the leaders of the Roman Catholic and Orthodox Churches for their immediate support and enthusiasm. The Anglican bishops of my area have been unfailingly helpful to me person-ally, I should add, which has enabled my engagement to go deeper on a local level, but a wider dimension has been lacking. My own church as an institution is remarkably cautious when it comes to pronouncing any sort of public message, but being defensive and reactive is not even a successful way of minimizing risk, let alone growing and inspiring people's faith.

For all the accessibility of the divine in a whole range of places in Britain, as in other countries, Celtic nature rituals themselves require careful preparation. My first encounter taught me that I was playing with fire to a certain extent, that spiritual discipline was and is intense and demanding on a physical and mental level. Celtic ritual is very specific and single-minded; it is on a different level from simply going for a walk in the countryside, swimming in the sea, admiring an old tree or – and you will have to take my word for this – attempting to live like a naked hermit for a week as part of a beach holiday. My first plan for researching this book had been to camp by the Atlantic ocean for a week at one of the most peaceful and good-natured naturist centres I know, a place where being naked is completely normal and laid back. I had just the previous month uncovered the naked hermit on the slopes of Mount Sinai and was keen to emulate him in the simplest way I could quickly devise. Need-less to say, conducting a nudist lifestyle in the depths of southern Egypt would present one or two logistical hurdles at this point in time, so I opted instead to go to my favourite resort, called Arnaoutchot, in south-west France. Nothing could be simpler, I assumed, as I packed away my clothes on day one, and prepared myself to spend as much time as possible in the sea and walking along the largely empty shore and in the silent pine forests behind to commune in elemental simplicity. This turned out to be a woefully unsuccessful attempt at devotional living, a misunderstanding at a basic level of what the pioneering hermit was doing. For one thing, solitude when set alongside human company becomes an exercise in loneliness, and not at all a hermit's withdrawal for silent contemplation.

On my first day at the beach I set off to the north, into the miles of undeveloped natural simplicity, and discovered I had a rash on my thighs after driving for 12 hours in 40 degrees of heat. Over the next days it worsened and spread, the remorseless sun beating down on me wherever I turned, the nights passing without sleep. I needed a doctor, a pharmacy, antibiotics, air conditioning, a bedroom, the car . . . but none of this was possible unless I got dressed. And then it occurred to me that this sort of nudism, when practised in a devotional context, is in fact a physical expression of solitude. It makes real the lack of company, guarantees it even; it is an absolutely extreme form of self-exclusion from other people: putting off clothes means putting off society. I had imagined this would be a rather relaxing spiritual discipline whose purpose would naturally reveal itself to me, but the only lesson I learned here about nakedness was how physically limiting it is in terms of interaction with other people. The life of a hermit was in no sense a holiday or even a temporary retreat from the cares of the world, but an entry into a different space entirely. Nakedness when pursued for ascetic and spiritual reasons is in fact the embodiment of being alone. For the first time it struck me that this was also the experience of Adam – his solitude and his nudity were more intimately connected than I had realized. The character who begins the Judaeo-Christian story bears more than a passing resemblance to a real-life solitary, a wilderness dweller of the most rarefied kind. I had never considered Adam as a prototype hermit before I began to experience a tiny fraction of this most singular life, but I would now say that he is. Perhaps Eve is too, her Genesis encounter with the serpent indicating that she spent time by herself.

My attempt to treat this high-minded calling as an adjunct to a holiday was something of a false start. Naturists are lovely company, a world apart from what an active imagination might think, but this is essentially a form of leisure and socializing that emerged in the twentieth century, a reaction to urbanization, mass travel and the imposition of swimming costumes. Naturist communities are happy and functional, and therefore one of the worst contexts in which to seek out any sort of isolation. I have spent years of my life enjoying the outdoors without clothes, but none of that was even remotely the same as communing with the elements as a form of spiritual discipline. It certainly made me open to the idea, enthusiastic even, in a way that enabled me to pursue this journey in the first place. But I had to relearn how to be naked.

Nudity in the wilderness can be considered a sort of working uniform that some of the hardier hermits adopted, a bodily expression of the desire to shun all human company and the trappings of society. My hero on Mount Sinai was alone, and he was naked: these are two sides of the same coin. The aching solitude of someone who is truly cut off from society is briefly expressed by St Paul: the groaning of the body for clothing.[4] This touches a universal experience because being naked is part of the human condition, for everyone, even when it is a brief daily encounter. I've never groaned for clothing myself, quite often the opposite, but I did long to head into town as my health worsened during my sojourn in France. After four days I relented, put on my clothes and drove to see a doctor, who promptly told me to take them all off again. The medicines worked on what turned out to be a mundane form of folliculitis that I could have safely ignored, but at the time it felt like some sort of Old Testament plague under the remorseless, unblinking eye of the sun. As I drove back slowly with a bag of antibiotics, I could not help but think what lakes and forests there were to explore, what shopping I could do, and what absolute pleasure the air-conditioned surgery had afforded. The following day the grey torrent of a sudden coastal storm washed away any lingering illusion I might have had that this planned week of high-minded prayer was going to be in any way uplifting. The storm broke when I was an hour's walk from the campsite, so I sheltered in a hollow among the sand dunes and began to worry that one of the lightning bolts fizzing into the sea and sand would have my name on it. I suppose in hindsight that was also another lesson the week gave me: how to pray very hard for something.

On all my subsequent expeditions I cared less and less for comfort and safety as I went on, reducing my possessions with each subsequent trip, but I was never more than a very transitory visitor to the wilderness. Ironically enough, in terms of journey time the longest I travelled from all trappings of civilization, including any item of clothing, was in Surrey rather than the west coast of Scotland, or France for that matter, on a watery adventure to the inaccessible ruin of Newark Priory, which Turner once painted. When I finally reached my destination by swimming along the River Wey, I pulled myself up on to a grassy bank and sat amid reeds and dragonflies until the water had dried on my skin, and watched the river pass by a monastic settlement in silent flow unchanged for centuries. It is true that church liturgy puts us in timeless continuity with our ancestors, but my pilgrimage that morning had been in some ways more primal still, my bathing experience unchanged in every detail since the birth of the human race.

From book to body

All of the nature rituals in my source texts are known only in their literary forms, in stories written down and told. They may well fit the conversion milieu outlined in the previous chapter, something I could figure out in a library, but to truly understand the Celtic cycle of experience and wisdom combined I needed to push this trajectory onwards. It is a story that drives these encounters from their origins in biblical theology, through tales of the Eastern desert, through Gaul with its lightning-lashed beaches, to British writers telling their wondrous nature stories, and from there into the landscape itself as hard, observable evidence that this new faith was useful in moderating relationships with the natural world. The lives and actions of the saints were intended as just such a handbook for how one should behave. So although they are stories, and as such could be entirely made up, using them in the way their writers intended – by copying them physically – has revealed a depth to the narratives that is not visible from the page. By asking what you do at a sacred tree, how you interact with a holy well, why you would bother preaching to birds, how to hide from the sun's gaze, and finding out the hard way how horrid it is to sleep in a hermit's cave, it is only then that the texts themselves start to make full sense.

It was impossible for me to understand what was going on with ritual bathing until I tried to put it into practice. I could read the accounts a hundred times over, and I probably did, but until I actually stripped off and waded into the sea in an attempt to copy the very precise descriptions, I had not grasped how the rituals play out in real life. And yes, this was the whole point of hagiographies: they recorded the deeds of the saints in the expectation they would be imitated by later generations of Christians. This would appear to be no idle wish either. After St Cuthbert died, Bede describes a succession of hermits living in his hut on Inner Farne, who 'rejoiced to imitate' Cuthbert's manner of life.[5] They would stand and kneel in exactly the same corner that Cuthbert had used for his prayers, even to the point of complaining about a draught that their predecessor had tried to block. Another text unrelated to Bede, *The Earliest Life of Gregory the Great*,[6] goes so far as to say that if one saint does something it can be assumed that all of them do it because they are all limbs of the same body, sharing common purpose and practice.[7] It is a rather cunning line by the anonymous monk of Whitby Abbey who wrote this text, since he is trying to justify borrowing details from one saint's life and copying them into the life of another.

But we have to wonder what has become of this powerful motivation that drove Bede and the cheerful plagiarist of Whitby to assume that the actions of the saints would be followed so meticulously, because it clearly fizzled out in the long run. Obviously the Reformation and the Dissolution put an end to all things monastic, but there were other reformations before then, a wave of Anglo-Saxon injunctions against outdoor rituals around the start of the eleventh century chief among them.[8] The last hermit to live in Cuthbert's hut on Inner Farne died there in 1246, while across the country the remorseless gravity of the church and its infrastructure drew all into its churchyard walls. Hermits did not exactly disappear in this contraction, but morphed into the harshest of all medieval vocations, the anchorites, who were usually very devout women. Their cells were built into the walls of a church like a sort of doorless porch, a gateway to the building that had no entrance or exit. As the anchorite entered her tiny cell for the first and last time, it would be walled up behind her as the priest intoned a requiem Mass, the funeral rite. To call this semi-existence paradoxical is something of an understatement: a living person buried inside a church, a solitary hermit in the heart of her village, and a prisoner willingly incarcerated, set free in a cell to roam the spiritual uplands. Lady Julian of Norwich is the most famous of our anchorite visionaries, the site of her cell now a peaceful side chapel at her church, a place redolent with powerful emotions and memories. On one level anchorite cells feel a lot more inviting than the dripping hermit's caves I inhabited, but at least these natural caverns have the distinct advantage of not being designed as a living tomb.

Over the next few pages I will give two historical reasons why I think wilderness hermits, and particularly those with bare behinds, were ushered off the stage. These remain valid as two modern reasons why some people might still find some of the impulses and ritual actions of this book difficult to accept. Authenticity and antiquity are good credentials for any form of ritual and devotional action, but they are not perfect defences in the face of a restless desire for reform, at one end of the scale, or a desire for an entirely buttoned-up form of high liturgy at the other. That is not to say

I would discount any of the views of Christians from any dimension, but I think a connection to the landscape is one of the few things of sufficient scale to cut across divisions that so often separate people of different religious traditions, requiring only a spiritually sensitive and reasonably open-minded attitude towards the natural world, quite literally a way to find common ground with others. I was delighted to bump into George Fox at various points on my journey to ancient sites of landmark spirituality, the founder of the most reformed and liturgy-free of any Christian movement in the shape of the Quakers somehow unable to break free from the magnetism of the hills.

In Celtic Christianity these sites of spiritual resort have been called 'thin places' ever since a minister at Govan Old Parish Church was inspired to restore the monastery on Iona in the 1930s. George MacLeod coined the phrase to describe where heaven comes closest to earth, where the gap between this world and the next narrows, or thins, in revelation of the potential of creation's redeemed state. MacLeod had an ecumenical soul – a Presbyterian minister criticized by one peer for being halfway between Roman Catholicism and Russian Orthodoxy – so he would not mind if I quoted the Englishman Bede on this point. Articulating what was so special about Ireland, Bede's vision is of a paradise tantalizingly close:

> Ireland is broader than Britain, is healthier and has a much milder climate, so that snow rarely lasts there for more than three days … No reptile is found there nor could a serpent survive; for although serpents have often been brought from Britain, as soon as the ship approaches land they are affected by the scent of the air and quickly perish. In fact almost everything that the island produces is efficacious against poison. For instance we have seen how, in the case of people suffering from snake-bite, the leaves of manuscripts from Ireland were scraped, and the scrapings put in water and given to the sufferer to drink. These scrapings at once absorbed the whole violence of the spreading poison and assuaged the swelling. The island abounds in milk and honey, nor does it lack vines, fish, and birds.[9]

Ireland's place on the edge of Europe leaves it perfectly balanced between this world and the next, ancient stories abounding of sailors setting off for the west to find paradise islands and wondrous lands.[10] But this notion of thin places works even better to me as a transferred epithet, by which I mean that it is we who are thin, we who are stretched and made malleable in the embrace of something that overwhelms us, something that predates us and will outlive us. Beaten to the edge between the sea and the sky, the absolute smallness and frailty of the human framed within the cosmos is nothing if not a reminder of our gossamer-like being, suspended and sustained by the whole realm of nature. It is extremely easy to insulate ourselves from this tenuous condition, in fact so easy that it has been our default position since Adam and Eve first covered their newly mortal bodies.

My most profound conversations on a ten-year journey into Britain's sacred heritage were with George MacLeod's eventual successor at Govan Old Church – perhaps a coincidence, but perhaps not. I sat with the Revd Moyna McGlynn among the ancient monuments and grave-markers of this most ancient of all ancient holy places and we reflected on its latent power as a cohesive community centre, almost lost in an urban neighbourhood that ranks in the bottom 3 per cent in terms of social deprivation in Scotland. Govan Old Church is full of stone monuments marking one of the oldest Christian sites in Britain, strange hybrids of unknown Pagan symbols mixed crudely with the first inklings of Christian culture, a writhing pair of serpents tucked up against Celtic knotwork on the enigmatic Sun Stone. There was nothing thin about George MacLeod's former church in terms of its layers of history: Pre-Christian then Christian, followed by further layers of industrial heritage and then harsh decline. So many stories have been and gone, but left their mark, and made Govan's church a place to identify with, to be proud of. Moyna told me how she had opened the church to a local school one day and introduced them to the hidden history behind their high street, and then watched the following Saturday in wonder as child after child came in dragging their disbelieving parents behind them, a sense of pride and identity taking shape before her eyes. I haven't met anyone who has loved and understood holy places as well as Moyna, and still grieve at her untimely death in August 2016, on the very day her beloved church was handed to a trust. It was her idea to safeguard the church in this way, her story another layer of devotion that will remain permanently marked on the heart of a community.

Holy places are thick with layers of significance, rich with traditions and memories that coalesce around a site set apart from mundane human affairs. They are places where the stories of the saints are told, where the tales of the tribe find focus, where a community's memories are treasured. But they are more than just words, they are physical places that need to be touched and felt, seen and used, multi-layered experiences that I now consider completely impossible to understand through simply reading about them. So much more than a product of the texts alone, Celtic Christianity is at heart not just a textual but a textured spirituality. To fully appreciate its sympathy with the natural world we need to feel the weave of physical sensation and visceral emotive responses within the written and spoken stories that make its places special.

Christian inhibition and the fabric of creation

There are certain layers of inhibition and reserve about the very physical expressions in Celtic spirituality, and hence in the practices that this book seeks to replicate. These are attitudes that have built up over hundreds if not thousands of years and might seem too deeply engrained to notice, but it is possible to trace their emergence if we look back far enough. As mentioned, I will rehearse two of them briefly here. The first of these is a strong reservation about engaging with the natural world due to a suspicion that getting your feet muddy in the name of religion strays too close to Paganism. The second of these relates to inhibition about the human body, some of which has been introduced above. Perhaps in spiritual terms these two anxieties are not entirely unconnected.

There is a wealth of nature spirituality in Judaeo-Christian religion that has somehow failed to leave a lasting mark on both Jewish and Christian practice today. Numerous references to spiritually significant landmark trees dot the Pentateuch, the first five books of the Old Testament, starting with two sacred trees in the garden of Eden, accompanied by a talking snake. There are suggestions of cultic worship in 'high places' and in groves, the appearance of miraculous springs of water and of course a sacred river in the form of the Jordan. Genesis is full of eye-catching precedents for all manner of nature rituals, leading some to speculate that it contains artefacts of some very ancient and primitive religious beliefs. When Jacob lies down and has his famous dream of a ladder between heaven and earth, recorded in chapter 28, no end of great artworks, stained-glass windows and devotional texts have been created in praise of his transcendent vision. But what he does afterwards as an immediate ritual response has been entirely forgotten. He takes the rock that was his pillow, sets it up on a pillar, and anoints it with oil, declaring that the place itself is intrinsically holy, 'the house of God and the gate of heaven'. As far as I know, nobody in any Judaeo-Christian culture performs such rituals with sacred rocks today. As for the trees and 'high places', not all of them are Pagan sites, since Moses ascends Mount Sinai to see God's energy in the burning bush and to receive the Ten Commandments. The entire setting of the Old Testament speaks of a three-way relationship between the children of Israel, God and their territory – indeed, it is called the Holy Land. Pagan religions often have an 'animist' character, with spirits and unseen forces operating in different parts of the natural world, 'animating' it, and it is hard not to see echoes of such enchantments in a religion that so tightly binds people to place.

Christians have been shy and embarrassed about this Old Testament landscape legacy from the start. The fourth-century scholar Jerome, who systematically translated most of the Bible into Latin, was usually careful about accuracy, until he got to a famous passage in Genesis 18 which describes a meeting between Abraham and God in the form of three angels. As the original versions of the Bible state, along with every translation since, this took place at 'the great trees of Mamre' (Genesis 18.1). Or rather, nearly every version of the Bible. If you happen to have a King James Version you might be a bit confused if you look up this verse, because Jerome's translation renders this as 'the steep valley of Mamre'. And it was clearly no slip of the pen: a few chapters earlier in Genesis 12.6 he used the same mistranslation for the great tree of Moreh at Shechem, where Abraham went so far as to build an altar under its sacred branches. Some scholars have charitably suggested that Jerome was dealing with an ever-so-slightly unclear passage when he chose this translation. If that is the case, it is remarkable how far Jerome's Hebrew had improved a few pages later when Jacob hides some foreign idols 'under the oak at Shechem', a story where an unambiguous association with Pagan cults perhaps had something to do with Jerome's new-found precision as a translator of the identical Hebrew word for tree (Genesis 35.4).

When a devout Christian does not merely misinterpret the Bible but actually rewrites it, you know you have a serious issue on your hands. At least one authoritative Bible commentary suggests that Jerome did this in order to avoid the Pagan connotations of a sacred tree.[11] A lot of my book is concerned with connecting the dots of evidence we have on this issue of nature and religion, and it turns out Jerome's anxiety about sacred trees reflects precisely the situation in Europe at the time he was working on his translation into Latin. Just a decade or so before Jerome was picking his way judiciously through the Bible, Bishop Martin of Tours was nearly killed by a group of villagers when he insisted on cutting down their sacred pine tree, perhaps a yew, described in the previous chapter. A little part of me can't help feeling rather sorry for this venerable pine. As our look at trees has demonstrated in some detail, there were thankfully more sympathetic ways of incorporating Pagan sacred trees into Celtic Christian lore. And worship amid nature need hold no fear in any case. The landscape's spiritual function is in no way erased or supplanted by the ministry of John the Baptist and then Jesus, but rather made new, the

Evergreen companion: the ancient yew at Dunsfold in Surrey sits by the south entrance to St Mary and

All Saints, an archetypal churchyard tree that greatly pre-dates the thirteenth-century building

Room for one: this well-disguised shelter sits on a remote stretch of coast to the east of Hastings in East Sussex, home to a modern-day naked hermit until 2017

Faithful companion to numerous early hermits, a house martin beadily eyes the latest inhabitant to sleep at St Ninian's Cave, Galloway

Carningli, Pembrokeshire: members of the crow family attracted considerable missionary energy in early medieval Britain, and continue to keep hermits company today

Between worlds: the pristine beauty of St Herbert's Island, on Derwentwater in the Lake District, offered 'draughts of the heavenly life' to the seventh-century hermit who made it his home

Holy Isle, nestling in Lamlash Bay on the east coast of Arran, once served as a place of retreat for St Molaise, and is now home to a friendly Buddhist community whose retreatants spend three years in solitude at the southern tip

Celtic England: the monastic ruin on the tidal island of Lindisfarne is a prominent reminder that seventh-century Britain was a crossroads, where Irish missionaries pursued their ministry alongside Roman bishops to convert numerous tribes to Christianity

On the side of a shady valley in Denbighshire, the holy well of Fynnon Fair flows undiminished into the overgrown ruins of a well chapel, a place where nature wins against human artifice

An icon by the author's wife Anna depicts the hardy Saxon abbess
St Ethelflaeda bathing in the river Test near Romsey Abbey

St Cuthbert's full-bodied embrace of the waves at Coldingham in the
Scottish Borders illustrated in a twelfth-century manuscript from Durham
Cathedral. The saint is depicted twice, bathing naked and having his feet
dried afterwards by otters, while a nosey monk watches from the cliffs

River Jordan the scene once again of a watershed moment in the history of God's people. The mountain too is a place where the light of God is revealed, as it was to Moses in the burning bush, and when Jesus is transfigured to shine like the sun.

In a way, the relationship with the landscape is just a dress rehearsal for the real focus of so much intense religious anxiety and activity: the human body. I am increasingly convinced that these two are linked. This is our own personal sliver of physical creation, given to us at birth, and it hardly needs to be said that we have at least as complicated a relationship with ourselves as we do with the rest of the environment. We dress, adorn, modify and augment our bodies – the site of so much anxiety and so many layers of meaning and emotion, miniature landscapes that are worked and reworked, shaped and cultivated, all but impossible to accept as they are. The human body is as much a part of creation as a tree or a rock, and you only need to look at the Bible to understand that these two can be used for the worst and the best of human activities, the rock that Jacob anointed as his 'gateway to heaven', the rock on which Jesus built his church, and the rocks used to stone the first martyr St Stephen being a case in point. One thing I would say is that no part of creation is there to be despised or abused, and that includes our own bodies.

It was easier for me than for most to overcome certain inhibitions about using the body in outdoor devotions, but I would not dismiss the barriers between us and nature lightly. There is a reluctance by scholars and high-minded Christian leaders and theologians alike to take the embodied implications of such Celtic Christian devotion to their logical conclusion, and this can again be traced back to early biblical alignments and realignments. In what is known as the 'Great Commandment' of Jesus, where he instructs us to love God and our neighbours, there is one word that is conflicted, and it relates to the human body. Mark and Luke list four vehicles for expressing this love: heart, soul, mind and physical strength. The original formulation, in Deuteronomy, lists only three of these: heart, soul and physical strength. But Matthew inexplicably deletes altogether the suggestion that the physical body plays a role in worshipping God.[12] For him it is the heart, soul and mind. I doubt that Jesus can be used to justify any sort of recoil from our physical beings as easily as so much religious culture might hope. While preaching to a crowd that included some very pedantic Pharisees and scribes, he talks about the process of going to the toilet,[13] something I have never heard repeated in such detail during a lifetime of listening to sermons. I did once see a Presbyterian minister hold up a roll of recycled toilet paper in church, to the astonishment of my Russian Orthodox wife, who had recently moved to Britain and was visiting Scotland for the first time – but why not?

It is hard to think of any facet of human existence that compares to the body as a focus of conflicting emotions: desire and disgust, shame and showing off, pain and pleasure all find their most intense expression in bodily sensations and impulses. It is something of an understatement to say that this relationship is problematic: eating disorders, bullying, depression, poor nutrition and a burgeoning market for cosmetic surgery indicate a detrimental and at times lethal unhappiness about our very selves. It is worth investigating if the ancient wisdom of our ancestors offers fresh perspective on some very modern problems, problems that are embedded in secular culture and have not exactly faded away as religious observance declines in Britain. There is much body-positive imagery to be found among some of the earliest church writers and theologians, perhaps most starkly expressed by Symeon the Studite and particularly his follower St Symeon the New Theologian (d. 1022). In one of his hymns he claims every part of his body for Christ, mentioning by name the penis, and then exhorts listeners to accept ourselves as we are, and to worship Christ who made us in our entirety. Symeon pushes this celebration of the incarnated nature of Christianity far beyond the matter of shame to touch on other areas of devotional activity, arguing that the discipline of fasting was not designed to punish the body but to help it, that it was meant to be good for you, designed to enhance rather than deny the place of the physical – perhaps closer to what we might call a detox. Symeon is well aware how viscerally people will react against the ultimate bodily implications of a fully incarnated faith, and warns people not to accuse him of 'blasphemy' for embracing the body so wholeheartedly.[14]

Symeon was perhaps the last clear voice on the matter, in theological terms at least, as the church, along with secular culture and society, has moved remorselessly in the other direction to deprecate and contain the body. It has spilled out in artistic expression of the spiritual: Michelangelo at the Renaissance, and later particularly William Blake, whose belief in the wholesome integrity of body and soul inspired him to take up nude sunbathing in his suburban London garden. As described in the Introduction, 'bodily nakedness' was a discipline that the monastic leader John Cassian listed among the practices for a devout monk, though censored in the most recent academic translation with the misleading euphemism 'bodily deprivations'. In my three years of research I came across so many examples of scholars changing and editing texts to remove references to nudity in the early church, right up to the modern day, that I gave up compiling a list. It is one reason why my time in academia has left me with mixed feelings about its claims that scholarship treats its source texts with rigour and accuracy. If I were to remove words from original texts that I did not like, introduce misleading euphemisms, or simply censor whole phrases altogether in translation, I would have expected to fail my PhD. But it seems you can when it spares scholars the sight of a bare body; a veiling has been going on for rather a long time without being seriously challenged. It was a Dutch scholar, Gisbert Cuypert (d. 1716), who began by suggesting that all references in classical literature to nakedness should be taken to mean 'lightly dressed'.[15] That was the ancient Romans and Greeks sorted. Perhaps the impulse seems relatively unimportant, but it has the effect of obscuring the view of the physicality of Christian ritual at the time of the early church, in contexts such as asceticism, devotional bathing, and particularly baptism. The body certainly has a place in modern academic discourse, with conversations about gender and sexual identity increasingly common in universities, but these are not the only ways to articulate the universal condition of having a body through which to experience the world. Aversion to our physical being and functions, and particularly shame about nakedness, are so deeply engrained they are difficult to argue against. People assume their attitudes are normal, not just for themselves but for everyone else, and clothe the world around them accordingly.

In terms of theology and church history, actual nudity is clearly seen as slightly dangerous and undesirable by many commentators and translators, inappropriate and unsuitable for mainstream characters, marginal and slightly scandalous – which to my mind more or less elevates it to the perfect dress code for a prophet. Indeed, no fewer than five of the Old Testament prophets are associated with public or outdoor nakedness as part of their witness. Isaiah says he was personally instructed by God to go naked for three years, which he did, even to the point of avoiding sandals. Translations and glossaries frequently attempt to get round this rather arresting detail, but the Greek and Hebrew repeat the word 'naked' three times, and in case there is any lingering doubt, God compares him to Egyptian prisoners with 'buttocks bared', demonstrating if nothing else that God is also perfectly happy mentioning intimate parts of the body by name. Micah, Job and Saul talk about going naked as part of their prophetic witness too, and if you consider Adam to be the first of the prophets that makes five.[16] Stepping out of the conventions of society clearly makes people uncomfortable, but prophets were prepared to put their bodies on the line, in addition to shaking up the attitudes and beliefs of their day. This is all a matter of personal comfort zone, but in Christianity it is impossible to argue that the human body is inherently or intrinsically indecent, or that nakedness is essentially sinful or shameful, because there is Jesus at the moment of his incarnation demonstrating that it clearly isn't.

So put all other thoughts about what the naked body means out of mind and reflect on my discoveries described in this chapter: nudity is one of the uniforms of a hermit. The naked body provides the working overalls for a solitary life, because it is an embodiment of the impulse to be entirely alone. It is quite literally a way to remove all trappings of civilization, society and human company, a way to express physically what is a spiritual and emotional reality. You are unaccompanied and unadorned, absenting yourself from the most basic physical attributes of communal living and human artifice. In the end I discovered there were two other even more powerful lessons to be learned from such full-bodied exposure to the Celtic sea and sky, both of which I write about in my concluding chapter. Both of them are entirely consistent with Christian tradition, one having biblical precedent but the other being a complete revelation to me: the way in which one can enter into the divine in a way that takes the Celtic theology of 'thin places' into bodily experience.

The naked hermit of Sussex

At the end of my travels across Celtic time and space, I could not shift the image of my own encounter with a naked hermit on his isolated platform, amid crumbling cliffs and crashing waves. I would have kept his location secret, but I discovered as I was finishing this book that he died in 2017, suffering a heart attack while back in town during the winter months. When I returned to find him in 2018 his enclosure was untouched, the rusting wheelbarrow that served as his gate still in its place. I walked around the outside for ten minutes hoping to see him, marvelling at the simplicity and robustness of the construction, a circular wall that enclosed a small patch of grass, a fireplace and an oven made of clay, a tent whose opening flapped in the wind. A washed-up plank had been formed into a bench, but after peering closely I could see that the fresh grass growing at its foot was untrodden. I slid the wheelbarrow from its socket and walked along a narrow passageway into his home.

Untouched for a year, the hermit's complex was already a fading memory on the landscape, the mud of the walls and oven starting to melt in the rain. His tent was still mostly sound, but the mattress had a scattering of green moss growing across it where rain had blown in through the flap. I prodded the end and was surprised that it was an airbed, still inflated. It was only by picking up a plastic noodle pot and looking at the expiry date that I could see he had been gone for over a year. A dusty bottle of olive oil and a few items of cutlery in a bowl were the best indications that his life had been interrupted. I thought of the most remote hermits said to live unseen on Mount Athos in Greece, secluded for decades, a plate of food left out for them each day, an empty plate collected each evening – until one day the meal is found uneaten and arrangements can be made for the gentle soul's funeral.

I have a friend who has visited this Sussex shore for many decades. It is a walk east along the coast from Britain's first official nude beach at Fairlight Glen near Hastings, and I thought if anyone might know it would be Colette, who is full of sparkling tales of the naturist characters who make up her community. It turns out he was called Tony, nicknamed Tony the Viking due to his wild appearance and almost seafaring life, an amiable but solitary figure whose motivations for such a deep retreat were never fully expressed. Colette drew a blank when I asked if she thought Tony had been moved into the wilderness by something spiritual, any expression of religious impulse. Few people pass this way, but even those that do had not touched his former enclave, so powerfully demarcated is this archetypal configuration. Back home I managed to identify the shelter on satellite images. It first appeared between three and five years previously, and judging by the way the landscape shifted between images it was clearly built on unstable ground, a shifting miasma of mud that washed around his home.

I knew what I was looking for when I entered this abandoned home, amid the modest collection of personal belongings stained and fading in the wind, sun and rain, but found it nowhere until I looked up suddenly from the tent opening. There on a pillar, wound carefully in weatherproof tape, gazing beatifically at his empty bed, was a statue of a gently smiling Buddha.

4

A company of birds

This was the best of May, the small brown birds
Wisely reiterating endlessly
What no man learnt yet, in or out of school.
Edward Thomas, 'Sedge Warblers' (1915)[1]

The quieter the sound of humans, the louder the birds. It was only by going deep into the forest alone and stopping that I began to notice the sound and presence of so many winged companions to this otherwise solitary life. These animals feature prominently in the lives of hermits, but it was only by sitting still in the places where they had prayed that I realized how much these stories simply reflect their daily experience. It takes no exaggeration, no literary or theological convention, to raise the significance of these feathery characters to the point where they become participants in any life that is far removed from human society. Yet what participants they become.

Read the stories of ancient holy men and women immersing themselves in the natural world, and the sound of birdsong will often break through. And it turns out they were providing far more than mere background music to the psalm-singing of their Celtic neighbours, but became the targets of a sustained campaign of what can best be described as ministry. And by this I mean ordinary birds, the sort that hop around a woodland encampment or a suburban garden alike. I knew before I began my project that there was a carefully observed and greatly treasured relationship between hermit and bird, but nothing prepared me for the spiritual depths it was capable of touching. What follows in this chapter reveals a reciprocal relationship between humans and the natural world that strays far and deep into the territory of ritual and liturgy, so intense were the actions that bound birds and saints together, singing in one voice a song of praise to their mutual Creator. As a guide for a more considerate way to treat and respect the natural world, following the gaze of hermits towards the heavens offers a thought-provoking perspective on our place in the order of things.

On my own journey into the forests and shores of Britain, birds were an ever-present part of the devotional mix, alighting in a clearing beside my tent, gazing down at me from the mouth of a cave, sharing breakfast, and on one occasion sending me packing from a wild stretch of river where cygnets were nesting in the reeds. They were my fellow creatures and I learned quickly to appreciate this fellowship, to observe and respect their patterns of behaviour with just as much curiosity as they were beadily observing mine. I was enchanted by them on many occasions, learned to value their song and to await their arrival with joy when I had some food to hand. Which made it all the more difficult when I realized the time had come when they were obliged to listen to one of my sermons.

Os it turned out, I learned far more from the experience than my feathered friends. The remarkable discovery that I present in this chapter is what I can only call a priesthood to all creation, a human ministry that seeks a fundamental realignment of all created beings back towards God, placing us on a continuum with nature. If we need a long word to describe this theological attitude, the best I can offer is 'creatureliness', a term that puts us and the natural world on a level, a term to encompass the condition of all creatures united under the one Creator. It is a solidarity revealed again and again by Celtic ritual performed in the outdoors that is more or less modelled on practices and procedures that are familiar from everyday church life, patterns of worship and even liturgy offered and gratefully received by the widest possible congregation. It is certainly why my faith in church-based religion ended up mostly stronger rather than weaker on my journey, although somewhat more colourful as a result of this revelation of the depths to which liturgy can reach. By turning to their fellow creatures with a desire to share and show God's grace in action, hermits believed they could turn the whole of creation with them to face the divine. As described in previous chapters, the early church taught that we humans precipitated a catastrophic pivot away from order and harmony at the Fall, degrading all of creation with us. But that pivot still moves, and with it we are able to reorientate creation back towards God. The depth to which sacramental engagement with the natural world can go is almost giddying when you first encounter it: ritual that strays far beyond the confines of the church walls. Yet at the same time it remains firmly rooted in absolutely conventional and mainstream practice. This is not a faith breaking away from Christian tradition but rather a recapitulation of its small acts of worship and reconciliation on a cosmological scale, an extension rather than a repudiation of other devotional activities.

Preaching to the flock

Delivering a sermon before a congregation of birds is one of many interactions recorded by our holy ancestors, perhaps most famously with Francis of Assisi but stretching back to the lives of the early hermits. If truth be told I didn't actually subject birds to any sort of attempt at moral instruction or exhortation, wave my finger at them, or threaten them with fire and brimstone for their perverse and wicked ways. I get more than enough opportunity to do that to humans in my local Anglican church. When I stood in front of a flock of seagulls for the first time I simply said what came immediately into my head: 'I'm just so sorry.'

I was standing ankle-deep in water on an Atlantic coast in front of this gathering of birds, pecking their way across a sandbank as it emerged from the receding tide. They did not respond to my presence or my voice, and I was not expecting them to either. As I came to understand it, this exercise was a lesson for me, a way to refocus my thoughts and change my attitudes towards the non-human world. It takes greater faith than mine to move a bird's tiny heart. I had no expectations and no plans at all as I waded into this rather damp pulpit and simply said the first thing that came to mind. As soon as I had expressed my sorrow to this flock for what we have done to degrade and pollute their beautiful ocean and beach, I felt a gentle bump against my leg, a nudge at the surface of the water. I looked down in hope of some miraculous connection with one of the sea's creatures, and saw only a discarded length of green nylon rope floating about in the swell, its ends frayed and bleached from years in the waves and sun. I fished it out and saw that it was tied in a loop, to my eyes at the time more or less the shape of a noose. There was nothing further to be said to the birds as I silently removed this piece of flotsam from their home and made my way back to my towel and bag, too embarrassed to continue. As I set off towards my camp I decided to pick up every piece of plastic I found on my way, my seashore ministry switching from preaching to penance in the space of a minute. Within 100 metres my arms were entirely full of plastic bottles, and I realized I had at least half an hour longer to walk. Unwilling to place a single bottle back on the sand, even though I could pick up just as many as I neared the campsite and its bins, I clattered along the beach deep in thought. It was no great hardship, but there are difficulties when confronting and dealing with the aftermath of our mistakes. I thought of Robert De Niro's penitent soldier in the film *The Mission* heaving his armour and weapons in a rope net up a cliff to atone for killing his half-brother. There are deaths for me to atone for on the shore and in the sea too.

By coincidence, and it was just a random if strange coincidence, I was reading *The Brothers Karamazov* that evening and got to an unusual passage where the elder Zosima says that his young brother would go into the forest:

> 'The youth who was my brother asked forgiveness of the birds; that might seem foolish, and yet it is true, for all is like an ocean, all flows and is contiguous, and if you touch it in one place it will reverberate at the other end of the world.'[2]

Dostoevsky here too was concerned with primal notions of sin, that by going into nature we are surrounding ourselves with the sinless ones, whose very presence alone can help alleviate our burden of failings, can put us on track for redemption. These notions of sin, pardon, absolution and forgiveness turn out to be precisely the same spiritual colours that painted the Celtic birds as they fluttered around the early hermits of Britain.

Many months later I turned to the writings about St Francis of Assisi, wondering if history had recorded what he said to his feathered flock. I was surprised to find that it had, and even more surprised to notice many echoes of the sentiments expressed by the Celtic saints, including hints at the same theology of a pure 'first creation' that Bede developed. Perhaps most surprising still was to read that his first interaction with birds also took place in a missionary context. As he wrestled with the dilemma of whether to lead a solitary life of prayer or to go into the world and preach the gospel, word came to him from St Clare and his friend Brother Sylvester that he needed to go out and engage. Francis immediately took to the road, and before long his first missionary encounter happened beneath a tree. Spotting a large flock of many different species, he rushed over and began to preach:

> My little sister birds, you owe much to God, your Creator, and you ought to sing his praise at all times and in all places, because he has given you liberty to fly about into all places; and though you neither spin nor sew, he has given you a twofold and a threefold clothing for yourselves and for your offspring . . . He has given you fountains and rivers to quench your thirst, mountains and valleys in which to take refuge, and trees in which to build your nests; so that your Creator loves you much, having thus favoured you with such bounties. Beware, my little sisters, of the sin of ingratitude, and study always to give praise to God.[3]

You can almost scent the purity of the first, unblemished creation, the beauty of a creature in absolute harmony with its habitat. It was Jesus in Luke 12 who talked of the natural splendour with which creation has been clothed; for decades these have been my favourite verses of the Bible, the reading I chose for my wedding in 2004. Yet even St Francis can see a cloud on the horizon, a warning of the 'sin of ingratitude' that shadows the hearts of those created so well, those who can move across all levels of creation from water, land and air. I think that cloud has long since passed, for the birds at least: my seagulls were in no danger of taking the purity and purpose of their environment for granted. At this point in time it is hard to think of any species of animal that is still revelling undisturbed in the pristine splendour created for it. I did not want this book to be all about plastic and pollution, but they have seeped into the very fabric of the material with which I was working. If there is one practical result I can hold up as a result of researching this book it is the amount of rubbish I collected on my journeys. Afterwards I wrote almost every chapter, including this one, in my back garden, a small suburban haven of solitude, picking all the artificial objects I could find out of the grass and soil and placing them in a corner. Thin shreds of blue tarpaulin, a collection of plant ties, fragments of balloons, green coated garden wire, discarded toy parts . . . the pile was still growing as I finished the book.

A pleasant company of birds

My first ritual encounter with birds took place during an abortive effort to live as a hermit for a week, on the edge of a family resort set amid pines on the French Atlantic coast. As I described in the previous chapter, an attempt to shoehorn Celtic simplicity into this three-star camping holiday turned out to have unexpected limitations. Despite the rather unnatural setting for my attempt to recreate Eden, I had at least managed to find a pitch entirely removed from other people. My view down towards the sand dunes was an uninterrupted vista of bracken, bushes and tree trunks, which bore a passing resemblance to the undeveloped landscapes where hermits pursued their calling. Yet I knew within hours of arriving that there was little to be learned from combining my journey into unvarnished Celtic spirituality with a holiday. And so it would have remained had it not been for two birds who came to visit one morning.

Sitting at my breakfast on the second day, I noticed a pair of plump brown birds had hopped into my clearing and were pecking the sandy forest floor near the wheels of my car. Here at last was something for a Celtic hermit to do. Hastily grabbing a biscuit from the table, I broke it into crumbs and gently scattered them in the direction of the two birds.

I hazard a guess that these were wrens, but one thing I can say for certain is that whatever the species they are not particularly interested in eating biscuits. A few exploratory pecks and they were off again, retreating into the bushes in search of more suitable fare. And so it happened on the next day when I had a cereal bar to hand, the birds' indifference to my gestures of hospitality feeling increasingly like a deliberate snub. On their third morning visit, by chance I had a stick of French bread on the table, and broke some into crumbs again when the birds returned. Whether or not they were the same birds as before I will never know, but this time they set about my offering with enthusiasm. I broke them some more, and it again disappeared quickly down their hungry throats. They hopped closer and eyed me as I reached for the loaf a third time.

It must be said this event is hardly the greatest breakthrough in terms of human–animal interactions, but it cheered up my morning to think my meal had been shared, to find company in my forest clearing, and a purpose for my lonely and hitherto uneventful observations of creation unadorned. I had fed the birds, not quite out of my hand but in close proximity, and with a sense that I had done something positive with two of God's creatures, enjoying for a moment this company of birds in my clearing. And so they had been: a pleasant company of birds. This was a phrase I could not get out of my head all day, it had a ring to it and was silently on my lips that evening when I ate alone again at dusk. Then it dawned on me why. I suddenly remembered that the very word 'company' derives from the Latin *cum pane*, 'with bread'. The original way to describe a group of close associates was those with whom you shared a meal. The birds and I had become companions: we had broken bread together.

One of the benefits of spending so much time alone with only the natural world to contemplate is that you do end up chewing over such small interactions. The ensuing train of thought kept me busy all evening as I realized how those who lived entirely in the wild felt as they shared bread with their animal companions. And it is so often bread that unites humans and animals in spiritual narratives, a two-way exchange that first finds biblical expression with Elijah and his ravens in 1 Kings 17. Even the ravenous wolf in Sulpicius Severus' tales of the Egyptian desert chose to steal a loaf from her hermit friend. In our churches it is bread that we break together at the altar to mark our incorporation as the body of Christ, and in the forest it was bread that had turned two indifferent birds into my companions.

There is something primal about feeding bread to birds, a thought that resonated with me long into the evening as I watched the stars come out through the whispering pine leaves. Many years earlier I remembered one of the first things I did with my daughter Alexandra, before she could even talk, was to take her to the park to feed the ducks. Sitting in her pram and pushing the crumbs away from her in delight as the birds responded greedily to the shower of food, her happiness was complete. I have numerous pictures of her in the pram surrounded by a variety of birds, often with bits of crust in her hand and always an intent look of delight. If you don't have a pet, I would imagine this is possibly the first substantial interaction many children have with animals. New parents often complain that their horizons narrow dramatically when they have a little one to look after, when a walk in the park with a stale loaf is the only scheduled outing in the day. But I treasured every such moment, vaguely aware of some sort of peaceful simplicity to it without stopping to think about the primal interaction taking place. It is an interaction, just like my own in the forest, that is entirely positive for every participant, and not a bad place to start contemplating what positive things humans might bring to the table when it comes to the planet's shared resources and habitats.

Bread is a common currency between us and the animals, yet deeper still went my thoughts as I wondered through the many biblical incidents of bread's place in spiritual transaction. Jesus talked of the harvest that gathered in and processed the wheat, and the thought finally struck me that what I and the birds were sharing that morning went one step further back still: we were effectively eating grass together. I had followed the trail of breadcrumbs all day and ended up back in the garden of Eden, entirely due to a chance encounter with my two feathered companions. What we had in common was our shared roots as grass eaters. I thought at once of the early church fathers described in Chapter 2, whose comments about Eden had seemed so far-fetched – the notion that we had all once been herbivores. In a forest clearing in twenty-first-century France, a shaft of light broke through from that harmonious time and revealed the birds and me as fellow creatures. As we both tucked in to our meal of grass, we were sharing more than just a loaf, we were sharing one of the oldest stories in the book.

It was surprising to consider that only a broken loaf was able to reveal such a depth of kinship between different species, just as it reveals between humans in their own company around the table. I remember once reading a book that asked at which point the Lord's Prayer becomes 'alive' for you, and I thought at once of 'deliver us from evil', the last of the petitions, important to me because at the time I had a toddler to protect. But after my encounter in the clearing it has become 'give us today our daily bread'. It means more than merely satisfying my own physical and spiritual needs: it is a reminder of a shared meal in a shared forest home.

As I say, these transactions have shifted my perception about the nature of all church liturgy. What happens at the altar with the gifts of bread and wine looks to my eyes increasingly like a model rather than an exception for what sacramentally charged action can precipitate. There was nothing consecrated about the bread I gave to my wrens, but it did strike me that the notion of a spiritually charged feast involving animals is not entirely divorced from traditional Christian practice and teaching, much as the idea might alarm some of the more high-minded believers. As we will see with a striking example of Celtic interaction with birds, the extent to which Christian ritual is cosmological, a way of binding Creator and creation together, has consequences for how we approach the natural world. It would be a mistake in any case to think that participating in a ritual such as the Eucharist is all about you: the bread is also involved.

There is no need to discuss here what actually happens during the consecration of the elements at the Eucharist, or during their blessing when they take on symbolic value for the less sacramentally focused. The only point I wish to make before moving back out to the birds and trees is that the bread brought to the altar is not merely changed for the benefit of the communicant, but the bread itself has been transformed (insert preferred theological qualification here), and matter itself has been lifted slightly higher towards the divine in the process. Sacraments are good for every participant in them. This notion that ritual action radiates a 360-degree blessing to the created world was something I encountered even more sharply during my bathing rituals in open water, as I will explore in Chapter 6. There is a real sense that any ritual action in the landscape radiates out a blessing towards every part of the created world, an entirely benign way of interacting with the environment that causes no harm. Indeed, with the well-fed birds and the imperceptibly cleaner beach and ocean after my own ritual interactions it went beyond merely innocuous coexistence to become actively beneficial.

The notion that I was sharing any sort of sacramentally shaped relationship with these birds might seem far-fetched, but bear in mind that this is following Celtic spiritual tradition. As the rest of this chapter helps to demonstrate in specific ways, the birds of Britain were not merely keeping hermits company but took an active part in their ritual and in their community lives. An exhausted heron that landed on the shores of Iona in a storm was welcomed into the monastic community by St Columba himself as a 'pilgrim guest', a term used for monks in his *Life*. Fed with great care for three days, the bird recovered and set off back to the saint's own homeland of Ireland, a kindred spirit to Columba at the most profound level.[4] My musings on the spiritual significance of bread and grass-eating are nothing compared to the other wonders that befell Britain's birds when they came into contact with holy hermits, who used a potent mix of formal Christian rituals and sacraments on them. We have seen some of the building blocks for this already in the early evidence – the notion that ravens, crows and jackdaws were tainted with malign intent, one of the legacies of our Pagan forebears. There was, for example, the croaking crow which distracted the entourage of King Edwin on their journey towards the font, but it was not the only one of its species to draw the attention of a missionary. Fortunately some of these other interactions speak of a rather more subtle method of restoring order and harmony to the natural world than that provided by a bow and arrow.

A penitent thief

Various black and blue feathered birds of the *corvus* family get a bad press in a wide range of Celtic tales of the natural world. St Patrick was so exasperated by a flock of black birds on the top of his holy mountain in County Mayo he ended up hurling his bell at them.[5] A rather more gentle and thought-provoking solution is presented in this section, as I recount what happened when some ravens stole thatch from St Cuthbert's building on Inner Farne, which is off the coast of Northumberland, a few miles to the south of Lindisfarne. A close consideration of what the patient saint, and the birds for that matter, did to restore a sense of order demonstrates just how far a devotional attitude towards the natural world can stretch, the remaking of previously antagonistic relationships with the rest of the cosmos.

Cuthbert had retreated to Inner Farne on two occasions, first in 676 when he raised his hand to exorcize the demons that had driven away all previous colonizers, after which he turned his attention to the birdlife, as we will see. His second retreat took place a decade later as he prepared for his death in silent contemplation and prayer. On his first visit, he built for himself a little complex and managed to plant the few acres of sparse soil with a crop of barley. A simple life in sympathy with the environment, one might think, were it not for a pair of ravens who stole thatch from the roof of a guest house that he was building to accommodate visiting monks. Chiding them for the injury this theft was doing to his brethren, Cuthbert told them to leave the island immediately, at which the pair 'flew dismally away'. Our story will focus on the way in which he approached a reconciliation with these birds – and the remarkable way in which the birds reciprocated his move towards them.

Approaching the island today by ferry from the port of Seahouses, it is still easy to gain a sense of the wilderness that greeted Cuthbert as he escaped from the pressures of life on Lindisfarne. Seals bob in the waves, the air is thick with birds and their cries, while the bare rocks are covered with a layer of white droppings. Stone, sea and sky: the simplest of elements, yet materials from which this solitary man of prayer managed to weave a tapestry depicting some of the deepest truths about Christianity and the cosmos. Celtic hermits deliberately sought out such remote places, in conscious emulation of their counterparts in the Egyptian desert – a mental map that lay over Britain's watery places, which will be navigated in more detail in Chapter 5. This is a reminder that the saints were reworking material from the East when they sought to impress on their British converts the urgency and expediency of the Christian message. So we will leave me floating in the ferry boat beside the Inner Farne jetty for a while, and look at what happened to the stories from the arid Eastern landscapes when Cuthbert transferred them to this rocky crag in the North Sea.

I have already mentioned the bread-stealing wolf who features in Sulpicius Severus' collection of nature tales, which proved to be the source material for Cuthbert's and Guthlac's intense relationship with wild animals. The primary story is charmingly simple and its resolution a happy one. This she-wolf had been a frequent companion at the hermit's mealtimes, waiting obediently until she was given some leftover bread. One day she visited the hermit's hut when he was out, so helped herself to a loaf, leaving a tell-tale scattering of crumbs. The next time the hermit saw the culprit, she had what can only be described as a hang-dog expression, unable to lift her guilty eyes from the ground for violating her host's generosity. The holy man summoned her over and stroked her head, pardoning the offence and offering a double portion of bread to mark their reconciliation. The wolf is said to have perceived Christ's mercy in the hermit's actions, to the shame of ungodly humans who fail to make the same connection when they receive charity. A fairly simple moral tale, in summary. In the following chapter, a different hermit in another part of the desert is out walking one day when a lioness approaches him and lies down at his feet. He follows her to a cave where five blind cubs lie helpless, prompting the holy man miraculously to restore their eyesight with a touch. A few days later, the lioness brings the hide of an animal to the hermit and presents it to him as a gift. Two good tales, in other words, that talk of wild beasts recognizing the Christian charity of a hermit. But look at what happens when they meet Celtic imagination and are collapsed into a single narrative.

The start of this story is not exactly a harmonious scene, Cuthbert angrily waving away the two thieving ravens from his lonely crag. Three days later, however, one of them plucked up courage to return and found Cuthbert busy digging. The bird approached him with its head hanging down and eyes cast to the ground, a somewhat bizarre image until one remembers that it is modelled on the guilty she-wolf in Sulpicius' tale. Cuthbert recognizes contrition when he sees it and offers the birds a pardon for their 'sin', granting them permission to return. The notion that animals can commit a sin is an interesting one: when Bede tidied up the first, Lindisfarne version of this story, he tactfully reworded it to speak of the bird's 'wrongdoing'. But what the birds do next remains the same in every account: they fly off and return with a gift of pig's lard, which they place before Cuthbert's feet. The stories of the bread-stealing wolf and gift-giving lion of the Eastern deserts have been collapsed into one event-filled story on a lonely British isle. The latest academic writers to study this tale have categorized it as yet another story designed to demonstrate monastic obedience, the birds showing deference to the leadership of a holy abbot.[6] On that I beg to differ.

Both Bede and the anonymous author before him explain carefully that the bird's offering was put to a practical use: for an entire year, visitors to the island would be given the lard in order to grease their boots. The purpose of this gift was therefore to aid the hermit's provision of hospitality. We can be clear that this is no literary invention, because Cuthbert's brethren had returned and told the tale within living memory of the texts' composition. You may remember the story began with the birds stealing thatch and damaging a hut – a hut that had been built for the use of these visitors. The birds had damaged Cuthbert's provision of hospitality, and their atonement involved enhancing precisely this same capacity to entertain guests. This was no happy coincidence. Rather it follows the pattern of one early Christian practice that was unarguably an Irish innovation: the formal discipline of the penitential.

One of the greatest contributions of Celtic Christianity to mainstream religious practice, perhaps the greatest of all, was this institution of the penitential. This ritual gave shape to a ministry of reconciliation, requiring a sinner to make amends for his or her misdeeds in a very specific way. It operated as a sort of tariff, and the idea behind it was that the penitent

would make some reparation for any injury they had caused. Once regarded with suspicion by modern Christians as a rigid, almost judicial
procedure for insisting on a strict system of recompense, more sensitive
study has revealed that the penitential was actually a rather thoughtful
procedure that sought to restore harmony in damaged relationships.
Where there was a victim, the victim would gain restitution, but for the
sinner there was the double comfort of an absolution combined with a
feeling that he or she had taken steps to undo the damage that had been
caused. It was another monk from Gaul, John Cassian, who had first developed the idea that sin was to be approached not as a judicial matter
but as a medical one: penance was a cure for sickness rather than punishment of sins. Sin required not prosecution and punishment but diagnosis
and remedy. Thomas O'Loughlin's writings on Celtic theology first drew
my attention to the significance of the penitential, and he also directed
me towards John Cassian's astonishingly productive intervention in early
European Christianity.[7]

The reparation paid by the ravens fits precisely into this model. The
birds have committed a sin that degrades Cuthbert's ability to offer hospitality. Their penitential payment offers direct recompense that enhances
this same ability to offer hospitality, an object that can be used to grease
the shoes of his guests. In other words, the anonymous author's version
of these animal tales adds a completely different dimension to the original stories of wolves and lions, framing it in terms of a single penitential
transaction. The conclusion is unavoidable: Cuthbert's interaction with
the birds is articulated in terms of an exercise of priestly duty, a bold
theological innovation that frames Cuthbert as a minister whose ritual
activity and agency extend to the entirety of creation.

So I would not agree that the birds in this tale were cameo actors who
put all of the focus on the charisma of a monastic leader, great though
Cuthbert was. Many of the tales about this saint are said to reflect his
kindly, pastoral side, and surely that is the message here too. It was an
exercise in priestly ministry that flooded not just over the walls of the
monastic community but over the usual human borders of ritual activity
to touch any creature around him. To underline this point more clearly
still, the ministry of the penitential was never confined to monastic rule
for the internal management of a community's wayward members. Rather
it was a discipline specifically designed to encompass every person in society, as Thomas O'Loughlin writes of the first known penitential text, the
sixth-century *Penitential of Finnian*: 'it assumes that the one judging
the required penance – and there is no hint as to his status in terms of

Holy Orders – will meet people from the whole of society, lay, monastic, clerical, men and women.'[8]

We can now add ravens to that list. In the innovative reworking of desert tales by an anonymous monk of Lindisfarne, it is clear that the holy man's exercise of ministry was capable of touching the entirety of the natural world. This understanding of Celtic nature rituals needs to sit alongside the rather narrower dimension of monastic discipline that other writers have discerned in this incident. There is indeed obedience, but there is also a participatory engagement, a communion, with the saint's acts of worship and reconciliation that speaks of a pastoral ministry transformative of every creature it touches. As we will see, this is not the only time the natural world becomes not merely a prop, or even a beneficiary, but a willing participant in ritualized Christian activity. Of all the animals to approach a holy man or woman in the conversion era, perhaps none carried a greater spiritual significance than this penitent raven as it bowed its head and sought to be brought into the fold of the Christian church. It certainly points to the workings of a spiritual power altogether higher and mightier than the archer with his arrow who killed the black bird disturbing the conversion of King Edwin's people.

To focus on the milieu of the monastery to the exclusion of all else is to imagine that the concerns of early monks began and ended at the monastic walls. You can certainly see the outlines of an ordered community at work, but that is not the be-all and end-all of the witness and function of monasteries. British church leaders were constructing an entirely new sphere of spiritual influence, in addition to repeating something that was already part of the background noise. Monastic obedience runs through the writings about Eastern deserts already, the whole point of several stories about hardship demonstrating that a monk might need to offer years of obedience before seeing any purpose to his sacrifice. This is in the source material, in other words, but it was rewritten and extended to include something else again, a completely new dimension tailored to fit the unique circumstances of conversion-era Britain. Celtic Christians were forging a new role for themselves in society and in the wider landscape at a time before Britain had any sort of meaningful network of parish churches and priests, a time when the monasteries are best thought of as minster foundations, serving the spiritual and physical needs of a local population at least as much as they worried about their own internal affairs. Cuthbert's interactions with nature were part of his fame among the common folk, the anonymous writer and Bede even identifying those involved in spreading it widely. Both these authors also went out of their way to mention the ongoing fame of the penitent ravens. This was a story designed to capture people's attention, and it worked.

Nature rituals: a Celtic innovation

At this point it is possible to make a significant conclusion about the intense Celtic interactions with nature that I have followed to write this book: they are a unique innovation in early Christianity. It is only by looking at the raw materials from the deserts to the east, as recorded in the writings of Sulpicius Severus, that we can see what happened when they were moved into a British context and applied to the sea birds of Inner Farne. The first writer to work with this material is the anonymous monk of Lindisfarne, a beacon of Celtic Christianity in England whose imagination sheds an entirely new light on the role of nature in early religion. Bede picked this story up and was inspired to create his theological formula about our lost dominion, only pausing to tone down the suggestion that an animal might commit an actual sin. Scholars have attempted without success to find a source for Bede's formula in the writings of the early church fathers, and Isaac of Antioch with his insect-crushing hermits was the closest I could get to a match. But the search can be called off. The monk of Lindisfarne, and seemingly Cuthbert himself, collapsed two stories together to create something entirely new. There is no need to look any further for an ultimate source for early British nature rituals, because the anonymous British writer demonstrates the creative act behind them. In the previous chapter I showed how the naked hermit led me to identify the raw materials that were used to construct these Celtic stories about nature. By seeing how this raw material was subsequently reworked, we notice something that was absolutely not there in the original: the penitential model for reconciliation which birds naturally and voluntarily undergo.

But there is a big question as to what one does with all of this. I've stressed repeatedly that these stories arise from monastic culture but extend to incorporate far wider concerns and interactions. It is still not entirely clear how far this activity benefited nature itself in a wider sense: was this just a myth-making exercise designed to win over the hearts and minds of Pagan converts, looking for evidence that this new religion could reconcile all of nature to one overall God, and render the landscape 'useful' to human needs in the process? In other words, was it just a nice story that ultimately served as a cynical piece of propaganda? Or did it have practical, real-world implications that went further still, to reflect a pastoral care for creation itself? To answer this question we need to return to my boat bobbing in the waves off the jetty at Inner Farne.

As I stepped ashore from the ferry we were given strict instructions to return within an hour, and then left to explore the windswept landscape. The island is the largest in the Farne archipelago, a dozen or so rocky outcrops that are mostly barren. Inner Farne has about ten acres of grassland on it, where Cuthbert first attempted to cultivate wheat before settling for the humbler grain of barley. This is enough land for one person to be self-sufficient, although hermits were rarely entirely alone, and Cuthbert himself had supplies brought from the mainland, pig's lard included. A path runs around and across the island, giving a good idea of the extent of this isolated outpost of Celtic spirituality, and I began to stroll along the edge of the shore to imagine Cuthbert greeting all manner of visitors washed in on the tide.

Two men shouted at me for straying across a seemingly invisible line intended to separate tourists from a shingle beach. I looked carefully and saw a row of poles, flattened by a North Sea gale, through which a line of black nylon had been threaded. Obedient as the birds and monks of old, I turned and walked up the shore to these latter-day guardians of the isle, pointing out that there was no way of knowing which part of the beach was taboo, and received grudging acknowledgement that I had a point. No ritual of reconciliation suggested itself to me, so I went instead to sit in the little chapel above the dock to pray where Cuthbert once laboured in solitude. A squat tower, built as a fortification and beacon in the sixteenth century, now sits on the presumed site of the hermit's former home, a few steps along from the chapel. It is inhabited during the summer months by his rather less spiritual heirs, the wardens who had chased me from the water's edge. I thought of Cuthbert stripping and wading into the sea to pray, clutching the sea and the birds alike close to his heart and reconciling God with the wilderness.

But his spirit lives on somehow. The rangers who shooed me from the beach were trying to protect some ground-nesting birds. This and the surrounding islands are part of a large wildlife sanctuary. Inner Farne is one of only three islands where visitors are allowed to set foot. The rest is a nature reserve teeming with wildlife, one of the few places where puffins seem to be surviving reasonably well, an important breeding ground for island-loving bird life of the northern hemisphere. As I say, the spirit of our Celtic ancestors lingers on, because this island is often claimed as the site of the world's first bird protection laws, introduced by no less a figure than St Cuthbert himself. He is said to have banned the local people from visiting the islands to collect the eggs of eider ducks, of which there are still around a thousand that nest there each year.

This fact is cited everywhere in connection with the islands, but few give its source. Unfortunately it is not mentioned in any of the early writings about St Cuthbert, but first occurs in a twelfth-century text produced by the scribe Reginald of Durham. It does seem historically plausible when set against the hermit's urgent mission to the birds of his island home, and the impulse looks to us like environmentalism, but it wasn't that exactly. Rather, it would have stemmed from the same sacramental impulse that runs through all of Cuthbert's dealings with the animals and elements of the north, an approach that attempted to undo the complications that sin had introduced into the relationship between humans and the natural world. The truly sacramental theology behind these nature interactions, an attempt to demonstrate the ability of Christian rituals to undo the damaged relationship between humans and creation, radiated out in every direction. It is also quite possible that Cuthbert did not want his solitude to be disturbed by egg hunters; the hermit's desire for an enclave free from normal human activities extended automatically to his non-human neighbours. Either way, these impulses would roughly have the same sort of effect that environmental protection affords, even though they are not starting from the same premise or motivation. If this hermit's minimalist life and respect for wild animals were to be followed as a starting point there would be no need for environmental protection as a backstop.

Original sin undone

So it seems that my sermon in the Atlantic waves was not the first reconciliation between birds and humans, and nor indeed was that of the brother in Dostoevsky's imagination either as he sought forgiveness in the forest. The notion of a fragmented, fallen world and the possibility of its rehabilitation alike are animated like nothing else by the fluttering of birds around us and around the hermits of old. The ability of birds to represent spiritual extremes is uniquely pronounced among wild animals. One only needs to know that St Columba's name in Irish, Colum Cille, means 'dove of the church' to appreciate just how positive these associations can be. The Fenland-dwelling St Guthlac was so in tune with his feathery companions that a pair of swallows would fly into his hut while he was entertaining guests and,

> showing every sign of great joy, they opened their beaks and sang a song from their subtle throats, as though they had arrived at their accustomed

abode; without any hesitation they settled on the shoulders of the man of God Guthlac, and then chirping their little songs they settled on his arms, his knees, and his breast.[9]

Anglo-Saxon though he was, Guthlac bears a remarkable similarity to the Irish missionary St Columbanus, who would go in the forest and call the birds and beasts to play with him like pet cats, while a particularly devout squirrel would climb down from the tree tops to run around his neck and hide in his clothing.[10] Another great Irish traveller, Brendan the Navigator, had a particularly revealing conversation with a flock of white birds, one of whom explains they are 'fallen angels' cast down from heaven alongside Satan, not just reminders of the power of sin but relics of the very war in heaven itself. Expressing regret for being deceived by the devil, the bird is identified as God's messenger and says the only punishment they suffer is being kept away from the presence of God's glory in heaven. Demonstrating their reconciliation with the Creator in ways that fit remarkably closely to the nature rituals of Britain, the birds take an active part in the monks' Easter liturgy, singing antiphonally for an hour the night before and then greeting dawn with a chorus of psalms glorifying God.[11] Early Irish traditions about the spiritual significance of birds could fill a book by themselves.[12]

In terms of negative associations, there is even evidence that the Bible itself was subtly amended by early British Christians in order to denigrate further the already unpopular black bird species. An early copy of the Bible produced at Bede's monastery of Monkwearmouth-Jarrow faithfully copies the translation produced by Jerome, until it gets to Noah on his Ark sending out birds to see if there is any dry land. The raven, so Jerome's version goes, kept flying away and returning, backwards and forwards until the Flood was over. The *Codex Amiatinus*, the Bible produced at the monastery, actually changes the scripture to insert the word 'not': the raven flies away and does *not* return. As already seen in previous chapters, when a Christian is motivated to alter the Bible we know there is something serious at stake, and these instances relate to the role of nature in Judaeo-Christian tradition.[13] A third example will be seen in Chapter 6. It probably doesn't need pointing out that this bird, the raven, is the same bird that Cuthbert was so keen to bring into the Christian orbit, to reconcile to the one God through the exercise of pastoral ministry. There is just a single other example of a penitential transaction in Cuthbert's recorded life, to humans who are distracted during one of his long sermons and then ask for forgiveness and return to sit quietly and listen to him without further interruption.[14]

Birds formed a central part of the great mission to nurture a new spiritual narrative and absorb the natural world into Christian teaching and ritual among the pre-Christian people of Britain. The only point of difference discernible – and it is even visible as a disagreement between Bede and the anonymous monk of Lindisfarne – is whether any non-human creatures can commit any sort of sin. The anonymous writer thinks birds can, but Bede thinks not, and that argument could go either way. It is not one I want to exercise unduly here either, not when there are islands to explore and birds to feed. For the record, though, I would probably go with Bede on this point: there is chaos, disorder and harmful behaviour to be seen in the interactions between humans and nature, but humans alone bear responsibility for wilfully violating this relationship. Dostoevsky's character in *The Brothers Karamazov* takes this line further still, to suggest that nature remains in its original condition, without sin, which is why Jesus spends time in the wilderness and with animals first before he enters the fray with humanity.[15] I think there might be something in that, and I have long pondered the unusual circumstances of the nativity in this regard: Jesus born not in the place where humans live but in a stable. Apart from his parents, the first creatures to witness the arrival of the Saviour were farm animals. If ever there were a category of creation that represents the hinge between humans and nature, these domesticated animals are it, living as close as possible within the compass of human civilization and control, our first point of contact with the whole chain of creation.

Numerous tales of Celtic hermits and saints befriending animals and even adopting the most unlikely species as a live-in companion abound.[16] It has been claimed that this has left a very long and deep mark on the British psyche in particular, specifically through our love of gardening and pets. It's an interesting parallel, but it would take some doing to find evidence of continuity from sixth-century ravens to twenty-first-century cats and dogs. As argued across the chapters of this book, the context I have recovered frames all of the set-piece encounters between missionaries and the natural world in terms of original sin. The missionaries drew on biblical imagery of the garden of Eden to explain to the tribal folk of Britain why their anxieties about the natural world were entirely correct – and fully answered by Christian revelation, ritual and charisma. One thing I will say with confidence: birds, trees, sea creatures, the weather, islands, caves and many other natural features were clearly enormously important to the Celtic missionaries. Not just fun bits of colour to make these stories more enjoyable, and certainly not just little homilies designed to teach monks to be ever more obedient, they were really a very significant dimension to their ministry and witness. A lot was clearly hinging on it. St Columba's various journeys into the land of the Picts did not lead to any mass conversions, according to his hagiographer Adomnán. At least not of humans, that is. He did take time to exorcize a poisonous well, hold back a beast in the River Ness with the sign of the cross, bless a white pebble with healing powers and quell a storm caused by demons. Back on Iona his ministry among the birds and angels has already been noted: a pastor whose definition of flock had no limits.

To the cosmos and beyond

Slowly stirring my dinner over the flame at the mouth of a hermit's cave on the west coast of Scotland, I had an uncomfortable feeling I was being watched. The feeling did not abate each time I looked round and scanned the empty mile of rocky bay behind me. It was only when I turned my attention to the cliffs above that I spotted the beady eyes of my stalker, a strange-looking creature that was tucked in the remains of a circular ledge of dried mud clinging to the pink rock face. I know shamefully little about different bird species, although I was certain it was not a penguin despite having an almost identical black and white colour scheme. I took a picture and an ornithologist friend tells me it was a house martin, which I have since learned is a member of the same swallow family that nested in St Guthlac's fenland home. At the start of my journey to St Ninian's Cave, I was convinced I would be the first for many years, perhaps decades or even centuries, to spend a night here communing with the elements. Once again a bird had broken my solitude and put my attempt at early medieval revival into perspective. As I busied myself about my evening chores, this small creature began to perform a series of little flights down to a rock beside me and then back up to its roost, and I realized there was nothing new about my presence. I was not the first of God's creatures to inhabit this holy space, even within the space of a single night, but was rather occupying another cave-dweller's current home. A second of these birds flitted in and out of the cave mouth, and I turned to my bag to see if I had any bread to offer.

As my project on nature rituals moved from the library into the landscape, my understanding of Celtic spirituality shifted by the hour as the physical reality of all such interactions overtook my attempts to tidy it into a religious system. Having started out as a spectator, my first forays into the wild felt like those of a successful intruder, breaking into somewhere humans should not be, particularly those of an academic variety.

But as I shed ever more baggage and shared ever more moments with the creatures of the natural world, this perspective continued to shift. From intruder to stranger, then from neighbour to companion, I felt we humans are much more closely bound up with the planet than is apparent, even when so well insulated against it. And I don't just mean that in a negative, pessimistic sense of carbon footprints and tides of plastic rubbish, but in terms of an ability to operate and influence in other, more positive ways. It is easy enough to talk of humanity in environmental terms as a plague on the natural world, but if so there is no positive answer to that worth considering. We are also part of creation, animals ourselves despite the layers of insulation, and simply picking different parts to deprecate does not result in an all-encompassing solution to the current disharmony.

I offer very few tips in this book because I think early medieval devotions are outside the normal comfort zone for most people. But if you do plan to go into the wilderness to dwell, in any sense of that word, the most important equipment I would suggest is a slice of bread. Birds live so close to a hermit's daily life that such an offering is the happiest way to introduce ourselves as we enter their realm. Forests, beaches, mountains, water and caves are the common ground, meeting places that require some etiquette from an unexpected guest. Whenever I moved my bedroom into the wild it became more and more obvious just how far I was entering a finely balanced matrix of relationships and negotiations, accommodating not just myself but my neighbours. And the more I looked the more of them I saw. But that night there was no bread to break, so I turned to another well-disguised meal of grass and offered up some pieces of cooked pasta, which the birds pecked and shook in a series of rapid forays from the cave roof as I served my own dinner, another meal shared with companions. It was remarkable how far ritual can touch this simplest of moments. I remembered one more of Cuthbert's stories, when an eagle dropped a large fish beside a river and the saint understood the creature to be engaged in another Christian devotion, that of fasting. He returned half of the catch to this observant bird and shared the rest with some men, who responded by 'worshipping the Lord and giving thanks'.[17] It is hard to think of any way in which Cuthbert's time in the wild could be less disruptive to the food chain, causing less stress on any natural resources, since he didn't even do the fishing himself. My simple campsites were as close as I got, a trajectory I could have pushed further but I felt this wilderness vigil was already yielding up its forgotten purposes and consequences.

It is in any case completely unrealistic to hope or urge anyone to adopt any part of this rudimentary lifestyle in order to minimize our impact on the environment, and would simply end up pushing yet more human use and intervention into the wilder parts of the landscape. I start and end by pointing the finger at myself here, even though I tried to make all my interactions as benign as possible. But there is something valuable to be gained from recovering the sympathetic spirituality of an age when the relationship between us and nature was more equal. Celtic attitudes demonstrate a different mindset when it comes to approaching creation, a different starting point that in turn led on to their peculiarly intense reverence for the inherent goodness of creation. Despite being motivated by priorities entirely different from our rather large issue of environmental collapse, winning over the hearts and minds of their Pagan converts, the vision of the Celtic missionaries was absolutely limitless in its scope and ambition. It was a larger solution to a smaller problem than any of ours devised to tackle the modern issue of environmental collapse.

I no longer felt like an intruder in the birds' cave, and I wouldn't argue that we don't belong in this wilderness. Like it or not, humans are at the top of the tree in terms of the hierarchy of creation, and it is a position that we can use for good or ill. That is even more true and self-evident than it was when Cuthbert and his peers were reaching out to the birds in a bid to touch the primal harmony that connects us. In Bede's theological formula, and far more importantly in the actions of people on the ground itself, the missionary impulse was to demonstrate that this connection can be not only benign but transformative, redemptive even, repairing a relationship damaged by human failings. In these nature rituals, the whole of creation lines up in ordered manner behind the ministry of a holy person, putting right the chaos and uncertainty, precipitating a chain of worship that cascades through all manner of animate and inanimate creatures. Humans have caused the harm, and it is only humans who have the means and capacity to put that right. The witness and mission of the Celtic Christians was to offer nothing less than a priesthood to all creation.

5

A desert in the sea: hermit islands

—▪◆▪—

Any point on the infinite globe of the Earth can become a centre.
Judith Schalansky, *Atlas of Remote Islands* (2010)

Pity the monk Baithéne, but wonder too at his incompetence. This man was a pioneering hermit of the sixth century, who set out to explore the 'desert in the sea', looking for a lonely island where he could live by himself in quiet contemplation and prayer. He must have had the entirety of the west coast of Scotland to roam as he set sail from his monastery base on Iona, which lies in the heart of the Inner Hebrides, an archipelago of more than a hundred isles and islands. So it comes as something of a surprise to read that this would-be hermit 'though he sailed many miles over the windy seas, was unable to find a place of retreat'.[1] I don't like to be rude about our illustrious ancestors, but even I have managed to find deserted islands in Britain, some fifteen hundred years of intense population growth later. Baithéne gave up and returned home to Ireland, where he lived out his years in charge of a small, rural church. It is a pity he did not persevere in his vocation: living alone in prayer on an island turned out to be the most ecstatic experience of my entire journey, an intense and revealing encounter with the natural world that shook the ground beneath my feet.

This reference to the failed hermit scouring the seas is the first in British history to make an explicit link between the arid landscapes of desert spirituality in the East and the rather wetter climate of our own northerly islands. It demonstrates again how the Celtic monks consciously sought to emulate their monastic forebears in Egypt, finding new ways to map their calling on to the contours of an island topography. Britain is dotted with holy islands all the way round its coastline, some once serving as the home of a solitary hermit, others the base for a complex and carefully planned monastic enterprise to convert the people from their Pagan traditions. I have visited 20 of these islands, sometimes pushed along with large crowds of visitors and pilgrims, at other times entirely alone, with just the ruins of a rudimentary hermitage and the birds to keep me company. By my reckoning there are at least five places in Britain that bear the name 'holy island' or similar: the Holy Island of Lindisfarne; Eynhallow in the Orkney archipelago, which means 'Holy Isle' in Old Norse; the Holy Island that is off the east coast of Arran in Scotland; Ynys Gybi off Anglesey in Wales, also known as Holyhead or Holy Island; and Eileach an Naoimh to the south of Mull, the Gaelic meaning 'rocky place of the saint' sometimes rendered into English as 'Holy Isle'. These original Celtic and Scandinavian names alone are testament to the rich reworking of the island motif across different cultures and times, and are just the tip of the iceberg when it comes to the spiritual heritage to be found in our North Sea home.

It was on one such island that I spent my first night as a modern-day naked hermit, and what happened to me that night left a deep and abiding mark on my soul. Absolutely nothing about it bore any resemblance to the hopes and fears that built up in anticipation of my lonely vigil, nor indeed to my academic understanding of the comforts and sorrows of this most isolated of spiritual exercises. The scene for my attempted one-man revival of an island hermitage was in many ways the most obvious one. St Herbert's Isle in Derwentwater lake graced the cover of my last book on holy places, one of the most beautiful and peaceful of all the hundreds of sites I visited on my travels. It is named after a seventh-century hermit who was equally taken by its natural charms, a devout man of prayer who lived there in solitude, broken only by annual trips to see his close friend and monastic brother, St Cuthbert.

St Herbert and St Cuthbert were as close to spiritual twins as it is possible to be, taking up residence on small islands on opposite sides of northern England in order to spend their final days in solitude. St Herbert had the smaller of the islands, a finger of forest ringed by a grey shingle beach, about 350 metres long and 100 metres at its widest point. Inner Farne is about three times larger, a place not currently amenable to a hermit even if clothed, and I described my encounter with its modern-day custodians in the previous chapter on birds. I had also rowed out to St Herbert's Isle several times, once in the company of a National Trust warden whose sympathy for those drawn by the beauty of the place was more welcoming. There are places around the lake itself given over to wild camping, something of a rarity in modern England, and I ensured my short stay on the island itself did not breach any environmental or conservation rules. Far from it, in fact: the work of a solitary is to enhance rather than degrade the landscape.

The two hermits died on their different islands on the same day, 20 March 687, something Herbert had desired for fear that he could not bear the grief of mourning his brother, and in response to Cuthbert's prayer. No one knows where Herbert was buried, but the island bears his name.

Pulling up my own boat on St Herbert's shingle beach many centuries later, I had little difficulty in imagining what drew the monk to this enchanting island. From certain perspectives it remains entirely unchanged. Later that night I sat contemplating the shore close to where the hermit's cell is thought to have been, and realized that I could see nothing artificial in any direction: no houses, no boats, no lights and no cars. Of course, different generations of landscape use have left their patterns on the hills but essentially this was the same panorama that our devout ancestor once sat and contemplated, no doubt drawn to reflect on the goodness of creation. I wonder if his lonely watch on this island somehow acted as a missionary exercise to the local communities of the seventh century, as other nature rituals described in this book have done, demonstrating perhaps that the lake was free of demons, able to take its place under a sky created by a single God. But I wonder what minds could imagine darkness congregating in a place so naturally peaceful and pure, the lake sheltered by its surrounding peaks and often reflecting a mirror tranquillity.

Ironically, perhaps, I arrived at this peaceful vista just a few hours after a named storm had torn across northern Britain, causing damage to trees and buildings and leaving a distinctly choppy edge to the waves on Derwentwater. The winds had more or less abated by the time I unrolled my inflatable boat and set to work preparing for this voyage, but the aftermath of their passing was immediately visible the moment I stepped ashore. After hauling my possessions above the waterline, I took a brief look around and stripped off my damp clothes, certain that the cold and the isolation would encourage me to change my mind if I delayed. I spent 16 hours undisturbed on this little sliver of land, and it was here I discovered that nudity provides a perfectly viable set of working overalls for a genuine hermit, both physically and mentally. The point is probably difficult to grasp, because notions of bodily exposure are so viscerally and deeply embedded in our assumptions, but my time on the island was an exercise in avoiding any human contact or attention in every regard. It kept me alert to the prospect of an unexpected encounter, and ultimately ended my stay on the island the following morning when boats began to draw near. In my previous explorations to write a more buttoned-up guide to Britain's sacred heritage I would occasionally have to explain what I was doing as I lay on the floor of a nave to photograph some half-forgotten monument, or bashed my way through nettles to an abbey ruin in the corner of a field. Cheerfully calling out to perplexed landowners, 'Don't worry, I'm working for the church', invariably ended any doubts about my intentions, and was vaguely true too. Had a party of unsuspecting kayakers on Derwentwater stumbled upon my bare figure hopping from rock to rock, pausing to mutter a prayer or gaze into the still water at the fish, I am not entirely sure the same line would have worked. I decided that very afternoon that if anyone did cross my path I would immediately dress, pack up and vacate the island entirely: the spell would be broken and the day's enterprise a failure. But in truth I am certain that nobody came within half a mile of me that June, and on my later travels much further still. As a way of not only expressing but also assuring solitude, being naked works perfectly well. A straggly white beard would perhaps have completed the look, but we hermits have to make do with what the good Lord has provided.

I wandered inland, picking my way through the aftermath of Storm Hector, the fallen leaves and branches as fresh as if they were still growing on their trees. The violence of the storm had left the lake with low waves that made a soothing rhythm as they broke on the island's shingle flanks. As I set up my camp on a flat bed of forest leaves above a small bay, I stopped to feed a robin with bread. Clutching only an extra-long T-shirt in my hand, I carefully picked my way through the debris to the south of the island, where I found a young tree almost chopped in half by an axe, the wound and the woodchips looking as fresh as the fallen leaves. I once heard my university supervisor Tina Beattie on BBC's 'Thought for the Day' speculating about a connection between the violence we humans unleash on each other and the violence that the elements are currently unleashing on the planet. Extreme weather events have always been seen as the hallmarks of a spiritual battle: Thor the god of thunder, our Creator sending the Flood to wipe out human iniquity. After all, we fight over oil and resources, over access and influence in human affairs and commerce. War is caused by religion, so we hear, but it is oil that earns money, fills petrol tanks and damages the environment, not theology.

My own beloved Celtic era was awash with violence, some of it encouraged by the missionaries travelling with their own armed retinues, who on occasion drew their swords and bows. Bede talks of mighty battles for the soul of the nation itself in the early seventh century, long-term conflict between Christian kings, such as Edwin and Oswald, and an alliance of savage tyrants, led by the Pagan king, Penda of Mercia. Edwin fell in battle in 633 and was recognized as a saint, while the following year Oswald exacted divine revenge against this 'heathen' horde, leading his outnumbered men to a famous victory at a battle known ever after as Heavenfield. A religious war if ever there were one, and Bede spares no opportunity to glory in the divine justice meted out on the enemies of Christ. Just one tiny detail that our finest historian struggles to explain: Penda's alliance involved the Welsh king Cadwallon, who was very definitely a Christian, despite Bede's best efforts to disparage his character. When Penda's own children decided to convert to Christianity, the only response of this bristling warlord was to insist that they either took it seriously or didn't bother. Incidentally, both Edwin and Oswald were Anglo-Saxon kings of Northumbria, and their own families had been engaged in lengthy dynastic disputes. Bede himself was a proud Northumbrian with more than enough reason to show tribal bias towards these two monarchs. There are many other things to fight about besides religion, tribal loyalty and access to natural resources being two of the many constants throughout a long sweep of history.

The reason why all this passed through my mind was not just because of the great storm that had swept the island before me, but something else I felt during my vigil close to the land on this picturesque island. It was the extraordinary amount of plastic rubbish that I found. I only became aware of this by living close to the forest floor, since there appeared to be little visible litter anywhere when I first arrived. Another by-product of oil was not being washed up on the shore in bottles, or left in discarded wrappers, but had actually worked its way into the fabric of the island itself. By observing carefully wherever I stepped and sat, it became increasingly clear to me that everywhere had been contaminated in ways that were initially imperceptible. Sitting on a boulder as I boiled a kettle, I scanned the pebbles below me and slowly these little pieces of worn plastic came into focus: a discarded Coke bottle screwtop, a small straw from a juice carton, shreds of material, and a surprising number of children's toys, including a small fish made of rubber. I gathered them all patiently on my explorations across the island, wondering how far down one would have to dig to find a layer of soil uncontaminated by this assortment of rubbish. From a distance and even on the island itself it looks pristine, not a man-made object in sight, but living ever closer to the fabric of this idyll reveals a defect woven deep into it.

Do these modern concerns have anything to do with the call of the desert and the desert island? I think they do, and not just in a coincidence of scarcity and consequential rules about consumption but in a way that gets to the timeless heart of the human condition. The early Christians in Britain talked of a rip in the fabric of the cosmos, a breach between humans and the rest of creation that was the most immediate and the most durable consequence of disobedience towards the Creator. So many of the lives of our early hermits were designed to demonstrate that a Christian could put that relationship right, their dominion found not in taming and harnessing nature by artifice and force but by prayer and simplicity, moving to the margins of land and sea to reconnect with the primal wilderness, the 'first creation' as Bede so eloquently put it. This is a minimal and fragile existence, as unadulterated as one could hope to achieve.

Marginal returns

My friend Fran Hollinrake, who is custodian of one of Britain's most sacred places, once told me that nobody moves to the islands to get rich. She works at the heart of a truly holy island outpost of faith, St Magnus Cathedral on Orkney, which is blessed by the presence of both its patron and its founding saints, their bones still preserved in the fabric of this mighty sandstone church built by St Rognvald to honour his uncle. The lives of these two royal saints are a lingering witness to the holiness that can accrue to even the smallest patches of land. St Magnus was martyred on the little island of Egilsay, where a ruined church sits above a wild-flower meadow. Barely 20 people live on that peaceful reserve, the arrival or departure of a single family causing the demographics to plummet or soar. Back on the Mainland, as dwellers in the Orkney archipelago call it, Fran explained how the islands attract those who come in search of something other than the material success and comfort afforded by the city. She and her husband were called to the sensitive management of the island's heritage, their jobs as much a vocation as a way to earn a living. Fran suggested that the highest paid person on Orkney is probably the chief executive of the island council, a position funded by the state. The occupations found in these marginal places are rewarding but not exactly lucrative: this is certainly true of the artists and historians, the farmers, fishermen, teachers, archaeologists, shopkeepers, sailors and custodians I have met on my travels around Britain's small islands, all of whom expressed a profound connection to the beauty of their home. And it occurred to me later that the same can be said of the first named settlers on so many of our archipelagos, the hermits whose entire purpose was the generation of spiritual rather than material wealth. In the high medieval period monasteries gained notoriety for their economic power, land ownership and market dominance. The people of Bury St Edmunds were so fed up with their abbey's control over civic life they ransacked it in 1327 during three days of rioting. This could not have happened on Iona, Lindisfarne or Caldey, the three great island monastic missionary centres of Scotland, England and Wales.

There is a morality to the desert, and the desert origins of many of the world's religions, that I had not expected to find close to hand in a modern, prosperous and long-settled place such as Britain, but it is there in our islands. I have experienced this raw form of desert ethics elsewhere and once thought it the epitome of an alien and exotic culture. In the first year of the new millennium, I travelled for days overland into the heart of Asia to spend time among the nomads of the desert. I still don't know what drove me to undertake the journey. I was newly single at the time and vaguely hoping to find a companion, although it is hard to think of anywhere less likely to produce a new partner than the middle of the Gobi Desert. This was some years before I began my explicit search for spiritual meaning in the landscape, longer still before I began to piece together the tools for making my own spiritual connections, but it was the start of a slowly dawning realization that religion is what mediates the relationship between people and place.

What I learned on that journey has echoed back to me on so many occasions at British holy places, in particular while visiting its islands and hermitages, that I will mention it here. On my third day in the Gobi Desert, my guide and driver promised me we would call in on a nomad family. Their white round tents dotted the stark landscape of our journey, horse riders in the distance keeping an eye on their flocks grazing the sparse vegetation. In two weeks I was barely given any vegetables at meal times, the Mongolians averse to any form of agriculture that involves breaking a fragile surface in a bid to plant crops. Deserts are places where the finitude of resources is no theoretical model but an everyday reality. If you over-exploit a patch of semi-desert it will become a dustbowl and your herds will die. Nomads are shepherds, living across landscapes that will only support them if they keep on the move. We pulled up at last alongside a large ger, the family tent, with smoke rising from the chimney as our driver wound down his window and called a traditional desert greeting: lock up your dogs. The family emerged one by one in a long line of four generations and stood blinking at us in the strong sunlight. Inside their home I was offered fermented camel milk, which churned through my stomach for weeks after, and a sort of toffee they told me was made from horse milk. Everything I saw in this home had place and purpose, the entire room designed so it could be disassembled, packed on horses and moved at the changing of the season. Enchanted by this life that seemed so timeless and uncomplicated, I suddenly noticed with some surprise that behind the mother's head a plastic bag had been neatly pinned to the wall, bearing the Nivea logo, carefully placed and wrinkle free. We talked about the bag and after some discussion my guide turned to me and explained that they had already received some Western visitors. So much for my desert adventure, I thought, wondering if we would end up meeting my fellow tourists that evening at our campsite, fellow intruders disrupting the lives of these hospitable nomads for their own anecdotes back home.

'When did they leave?' I asked. It was only midday and we had been on the road for four hours, so they could not be far ahead of us. The family had a long conversation and turned to the oldest among them, pondering the simplest of questions for what seemed like an age. Finally my guide translated her answer: '1972'.

It is not just the seasonal migrations across bare desert that make a nomad. As my host family demonstrated so warmly that day, there are other consequences of living in such a harsh climate, the need to look after passing strangers being one of them. Our encounter was hedged around with ritual; their immediate provision of food and drink reflects a means of keeping communities connected and alive. It is little wonder that the morality of the desert is hard-wired into the world's major religions, rules not just about generosity to strangers and hospitality, but also about over-exploitation of the land, the accumulation of possessions, food laws, and seasons for fasting and feasting.

The morality of the desert, of the nomad, has left its mark deep within the origins of Jewish and hence other religions that have followed. The first two sons are Cain and Abel, one of them a shepherd who moves his flock across the land, the other a settled agriculturalist, who puts down roots to plant his crops. It is no coincidence that the murderer is the one who stops to cut the soil, his innocent brother the victim: God himself looks on their offerings of produce and finds only one of them pleasing.[2] Cain is the landowner, not just a prototype but identified as the founder of the first city, which he named after his son Enoch (Genesis 4.17). Some generations later, God had cause to lament Babel and its tower, a place where people focused on civilization rather than God, perhaps one could say on culture rather than nature. In the Old Testament the desert is so often the place where encounters with the divine take place, Moses and the burning bush on a mountain forbidden to others, the tribe of Israel wandering in

Sinai for 40 years before they crossed the Jordan to the promised land: 'they looked towards the desert, and there was the glory of the LORD.'[3]

Jesus himself wrapped his mission around the same landscapes of this Holy Land, preparing for his own ministry with 40 days in the desert, accompanied by wild animals as Mark 1.35 puts it. The Gospel writer's phrase *eremos topos* means literally 'deserted place', the first word providing the root for the English term 'hermit'. In a conscious echo of these Jewish wanderings, Jesus too concludes his time in the wilderness by entering the River Jordan, in his case to undergo baptism. Jesus would at other times withdraw to quiet places in order to pray, a hillside or a city garden, and ascended a mountain with his closest disciples at the Transfiguration, the moment when his face was lit up as with lightning and a voice proclaimed him the Son of God. He tells his followers that he is the good shepherd, he underscores the fact that foxes have dens and birds have their nests but he has no place to lay his head. Christian history has become rather more associated with the city than with the desert, with the bishop and cathedral, modelling itself closely on the power structure of the Roman Empire in its dying decades, clustering around imperial administrative units that were known in Roman times as a 'diocese'. Augustine's abiding image is of the City of God, an urban theologian if ever there were one, with profound consequences for the development of Christian theology. Yet my wanderings across the British landscape are as good a reminder as reading any history book to know that this development was not without its critics in the early church, powering the very instinct away from the city towards monasticism and the desert that so inspired the Celtic movement into the margins of the land. Britain had no great cities from which to flee: wilderness spirituality stands in its own right here.

Even so, there was in all places a conscious desire to return Christian devotion to a state of simplicity, hermits taking pride in their lack of possessions. Other religions and movements still have a place for the wilderness at their heart. The Prophet Muhammad went into a cave called Hira, located on the mountain Jabal an-Nour, about 3 kilometres outside Mecca, when he first received a revelation from the angel Gabriel, and heard for the first time verses from the Qur'an (chapter 96).

Although Europe is somewhat bereft of arid deserts, as has been noted the first hermits and monks found a way of making do with an equivalent island landscape. This was not even a purely Celtic innovation but first saw expression in a Mediterranean context, once again a reminder that the desert narratives of the first monks were invariably filtered through Gaul before they reached British and Irish shores. The first monastery island in Europe was on Lérins in southern France, a short distance offshore from modern-day Cannes, described in Chapter 2. A text written on this island called *In Praise of the Desert*, by a monk called Eucherius, makes explicit the connection between the desert and this island, referring to the sand that links the two landscapes and compares the sea journey from mainland Gaul to the crossing of the Red Sea. As mentioned, St Patrick is also supposed to have studied here in the fifth century before moving to another island that has been touched ever since with notions of a unique spirituality bounded by an emerald sea: Ireland itself.

The desert is a non-human space. There is something beyond human artifice and imagination, beyond the community, beyond the mundane. Judaism and early Christianity are religions forged with a very deep awareness of the wilderness, of the dangers of uninhabitable land, of the desert. The earliest instincts of religion, even a monotheistic religion such as Judaism, are to make connections to the land. As the chapters of this book explore in some detail, the vestiges of just such a religious impulse cling to the landscapes of Britain and Ireland, where fearless missionaries waded out to confront the spiritual powers that lurked in the wild, in the non-human spaces, and to show that God is found on a desert island as surely as he was found on the stony desolation of Sinai.

A place of retreat

My own stay on St Herbert's Isle was somewhat shorter than the 40 years of exile experienced by the tribe of Israel, and I did not even manage to stretch it to 24 hours. But it was an interesting question to ponder as I spent my brief vigil on that natural hermitage, whether Herbert lived there permanently, as the historical record suggests, or merely used it as a place of frequent retreat, as Cuthbert did on Inner Farne before retiring there to see out his remaining days. So although my stay was as short as it was intense, I would not hesitate to call it a manifestation of something that is popular in Christian tradition today: a retreat.

An island is the archetypal place outside normal human affairs, a natural monastery and a form of desert, but it can also serve well as a place of temporary withdrawal. In some ways this is best embodied not by the earliest of the Celtic monastery islands, Iona, but rather by its offshoot, Lindisfarne, founded by the Ionan monk St Aidan in 634. In many senses this rocky outcrop encapsulates the dual nature of a Celtic monastery, cut off by the tide for half the time, yet connected to the main on a daily basis to pursue its mission to the people, a feature that Bede keenly observes.[4]

When you study the life and work of a monastery at school, the emphasis is on the seclusion and the inner timetable of community life, the endless round of services and the internal focus of the cloister. Yet, as my Introduction and other chapters make plain, the early British monasteries are better thought of as minsters, centres of service radiating out to the people around. Early saints were not celebrated for being withdrawn and misanthropic but rather as kind and outgoing. Before Aidan the Ionan community had sent another monk called Corman to begin the mission to Northumbria, which had ended spectacularly badly in less than a year. A man of 'austere disposition', Bede wrote, he blamed his failure squarely on the Northumbrians, claiming that 'he had been unable to achieve anything by teaching to the nation to whom they had sent him, because they were an ungovernable people of an obstinate and barbarous temperament'.[5] Aidan criticized him for being too severe and suggested a better approach would be to offer the milk of human kindness to the nascent English Christians: people skills were more important than a cloistered devotion to the rule.

The role of the desert as a place of withdrawal rather than of permanent exile makes the function of holy islands easier to support in a modern context, a place not only to retreat but also to marvel at the natural landscape, to rest one's eyes and ears from the business of the mainland before returning to engage once more. It certainly helps me find a place for my own rather brief foray into island seclusion as an authentic part of the matrix of Celtic devotions that make up my decade's work. I also think this is another key to understanding the early growth of monasticism and its subsequent iteration across Britain's islands. I'm never entirely convinced that the impulse for any of the early desert dwellers in the East was to avoid all forms of human activity and ecclesiastical authority. The founder of monasticism, St Antony of Egypt, spent decades in solitude, we read, yet left his cave to enter Alexandria in great acclaim at one point, to see off the Arian heresy that was taking hold in the city.

These were good topics to ponder as I made my way to visit another evocative and lonely island site, one that I consider to be Britain's oldest retreat centre: another outcrop of rock that is blessed by the name Holy Island, beside the Isle of Arran. Nestled at the foot of this mountainous peak, where it rises steeply from the sea, lies a cave once used by the seventh-century abbot, St Molaise. Wild goats picked their way through the bracken as I stooped down to wonder at this rudimentary abode, but otherwise this small chasm in the rock remains as remote and undisturbed as it was when the hard-working churchman came here to recuperate physically and spiritually. The dusty floor is perhaps a little less inviting than the beds on offer today in modern retreat centres, although I was unable to spend the night here due to the constraints of the ferry timetable and my own busy schedule. Near to this cave a holy well trickles out from the base of the island's flank, and a large stone block known as St Molaise's table sits above the shoreline. As an advertisement for the joys of retreat this dusty cave might leave something to be desired, but the island itself could not be more appealing, a little haven of barely touched spirituality that is a ten-minute ferry ride from Lamlash bay.

There is something profoundly primal about the spirituality of islands, perhaps more than any other of the landmarks and features that provide the stage for so many Celtic devotions. There are numerous ways to demarcate an outdoor sacred space, with a circle of stones, a churchyard wall, a grove or a well. But for a truly natural form of sacred seclusion there is nothing better than an island. Set apart by nature rather than any form of human intervention, these are places of the broadest possible witness and appeal. Way back into prehistory, the people who first settled on Orkney are believed to have raised up a vast matrix of sacred buildings and complexes, as convinced as any visitor might be today that the island is full of enchantment and natural holiness. When I write and talk about my engagement with the holy landscapes of Britain, sometimes meeting a degree of scepticism, it heartens me to remember how our spiritual traditions have been sympathetically reinvented by countless generations since time immemorial.

Indeed, the point was made most eloquently to me during my time at St Molaise's Cave on the Holy Island beside Arran. This island that received its sacred title from Christian tradition is now home to a Buddhist community, known as the Centre for World Peace and Health, a religious settlement that offered the sort of gracious hospitality that would do any desert dweller proud. The centre is split into two sites, with a community centre at the northern end where visitors of any religion or none are welcome to visit. And in a pleasing echo of St Molaise's holy purpose, there is a long-term retreat centre for women at the southern end. It is not possible to visit this end of the island, such is the sanctuary here, the sort of place that puts something of a perspective on my own brief sojourn on various holy islands. Here the nuns and retreatants undertake a programme of complete withdrawal that lasts an astonishing three years. On my visit to the monastery in 2012 I shared my lunchtime table with a chance companion who told me that she had undertaken this very retreat. She waved her hand breezily when I said that three years seemed a long time to be literally and metaphorically isolated from human contact. 'Oh, the entirely silent part of the retreat only lasts for six months,' she explained. When she returned to the mainland world, the hardest thing to come to terms with was seeing things that moved quickly, disorientated by cars and even bicycles.

Later that day my friend Ifor asked the leader of the Buddhist community whether islands had any particular resonance in the Tibetan tradition from where his faith was derived. He immediately responded in the negative; Tibet is a landlocked country with no sea and no sizeable lakes. But then he thought for a moment and added that they had instead a tradition of sacred mountains, and it began to dawn on him even as he spoke that Holy Island is of course a mountain rising up out of the water, a peak of land set apart from its surroundings. Here in every way was a place in Scotland as naturally holy as a mountain in Tibet. Britain's landscape has been written over by countless ritual and sacred narratives over many thousands of years, and continues to serve as a beautiful and ever-beguiling canvas for us to spill out our collective dreams, our hopes and our fears as a community for time immemorial to come. Holy places can teach us – can teach anyone from any tradition in any corner of the world – to love the land beneath our feet.

I believe this to be as much a part of authentic, biblical Christian tradition as the many other dimensions that are preached so vigorously today. The notion that Jesus abstracts and excuses us from living a spiritual life close to the land, shunning any presumed similarity to the Pagan or the wild beast, is fanciful if remarkably stubborn – the idea that holiness somehow adheres primarily to the elegance of robes and ceremony, the status of a social hierarchy and a gilded church built in the name of the divine. It can be there for sure, but there is another side to our incarnated religion that is not exactly hidden in the Gospels. I doubt those who ask the question 'What would Jesus do?' might consider spending 40 days living without shelter in the wilderness, accompanied only by wild animals. But that was and is the model for so many Christian cultural expressions, monasticism the most acute but not the only rendition. In a gentler way too, it is also the biblical impulse to go on retreat, something that has been growing in popularity over recent years as an authentic expression of spiritual simplicity. The notion of spending time outdoors in nature as a form of 'green therapy' is also one that can be elided with the ancient spiritual wisdom of withdrawal. My own time in the middle of the Lake District offered an intense feeling of connection to the natural world that ran through me like a lightning bolt pinning me to the soil, as I will explain at the end of this chapter: it felt like a glimpse of paradise on earth. I am not sure how far the modern retreat movement in Britain fully exploits these riches of the wilderness traditions that once formed the platform for our island's spirituality and mission. I have been to a few retreat centres in my time, monastic, evangelical, Roman Catholic and Anglican. It is nice to sit drinking tea quietly while gazing out in silence over a neatly mown lawn, surrounded by other good people who are forbidden to talk for long hours at a time, but this is a vision of heaven as a middle-class retirement home.

A pilgrim calling

Islands were far more than a convenient way to be alone, to be literally isolated, but worked rather well to express a number of dimensions inherent in Judaeo-Christian spirituality. They were and are of considerable interest to the Pagans of Britain and the narratives that clung to so many landmarks. There is more to this wilderness calling than can simply be described in connection with islands, outposts of faith that are the most acute but not the only manifestation of the instinct to shake off the comforts of civilization and head out into the desert.

As so often, Bede does an admirable job explaining the purpose of such a calling to life on the outside, a life detached from the distractions of the town, and he is in no doubt that this is an authentic expression of Christian devotion. In his commentary on the book of Genesis, Bede admonishes those who are too preoccupied by the comforts of technology, claiming that elaborate gadgets are artefacts of our fallen state, and are not strictly necessary. Commenting on the attractions of the city founded by Cain, he writes:

> Anyone who truly contemplates all the works that are made with skill from brass and iron clearly learns that if the human race kept the natural law correctly, even after being driven from the joys of paradise by the sin of the transgression, it would not have any need for any of these things at all.[6]

To clarify this point, he adds that we need to avoid being 'entangled beyond measure in things of this kind'. By way of contrast, he writes, Abel and his youngest brother Seth 'led a simple life as strangers on earth'. Bede's arguments do not go quite so far as to urge a return to nomadism: he does ponder the idea that Cain's offering was rejected by God because it was the work of agriculture, but ultimately decides against it. The overall message is that technological progress has its limitations.

One academic has referred to this passage of scriptural exegesis as representative of Bede's 'primitivism', although I'm not entirely sure if that would ever be the right word for an intellectual who advanced human knowledge in a wide range of fields, including scientific study.[7] Taking the early hermits on their own terms, rather than our rather precious reaction against the physical reality of such a life, we can get closer to the impetus that sought to make sense of the desert origins of Christianity and Judaism. Bede was far more in tune with the Celtic spirit when he wrote about the conflicting pull of the city and the pasture, yet again demonstrating that the Celtic and the early Anglo-Saxon Christians had more in common than the specific and somewhat tedious problems that they argued about, such as the correct haircut for a monk. In any case it is absurd to suggest that Bede lamented human progress and civilization, but merely spoke of misuse and an over-reliance on technology for its own sake. His commentary on Genesis quoted above also acknowledges the useful function of metalcrafts in the form of musical instruments for accompanying songs to the Lord, and ploughs and sickles for putting food on the table. The sense of wonder he conveys when he talks of the introduction from the Continent of the technologies of stone architecture and stained-glass windows into an English church is palpable, evoking the gasps that such a spectacle must have provoked from the common folk.[8] Some of the world's oldest stained glass is on display in the Bede's World museum, next to the venerable writer's monastery in Jarrow where these marvels had been introduced.

Islands became the most obvious form of desert for Celtic hermits and monks, seeking out lonely places to pursue a calling perhaps better suited to the sunny landscapes of the nomad. But they also found other ways to uproot themselves from communal living and wander across the land, ways that have also left their mark on our spiritual attachment to the landscape. They developed a sort of precursor to pilgrimage, although in truth the Celtic pilgrim was somewhat different from our modern understanding of the term. To us this word 'pilgrimage' means leaving home, travelling to a specific holy destination and returning again, suitably refreshed and uplifted by the experience. A pilgrimage typically follows a set route, the journey as much a part of the experience as the shrine at the end, perhaps more so for those uninterested in shrines. Read any book on the early Christian period in Britain and Ireland and it won't be long before you read of 'pilgrimage' as an inherently Celtic practice, the road rising up to meet them, the wind at their back and the sun warming their face, to paraphrase a traditional Gaelic blessing. It is true that the Celtic pilgrims were certainly on the move, like their modern-day counterparts, but there the similarity ends.

The term that is most closely associated with pilgrimage is *peregrinatio* in the early medieval Latin. It does not, however, mean travelling to a specific holy destination and returning home again, and would be better translated as 'wandering' or 'travelling'. Bede's use of the words *peregrini* and *peregrinatio* in their literal sense never applies to individuals travelling anywhere within the island of Britain, but only to those who travel overseas.[9] As the same writer says of Egbert, an English monk who went to study in Ireland: 'He also made a vow that he would live as a pilgrim [*peregrinus*] and never return to his native island, Britain.'[10] Here the word can only accurately be understood as meaning 'in exile'.

From the earliest times this was a discipline of dislocation, of being uprooted, made uncomfortable, a voluntary outcast from the comforts of home, family and community. It would be misleading, however, to think that this meant a pilgrim had no earthly connections, that the first pilgrims were simply rejecting and rising above all mundane distractions. Already in early medieval Britain and Ireland it is possible to detect that this notion of the pilgrim and the wanderer is shifting, perhaps caused by cultural anxiety over exactly what should and should not be the relationship between the Christian and the created world. The abbot of Iona, Adomnán, who wrote the *Life of St Columba*, uses the word pilgrim in a slightly different way from his contemporary Bede, as a way of referring to monks or to very long-term guests who stay put in a monastery. As already quoted in the chapter on birds, Columba takes in a heron that had been blown to Iona on a gale and predicts it will spend three days 'as a pilgrim' with the community.[11] In similar manner are the many pioneers who deliberately sought out the wilderness, the Egyptian desert and the Scottish island alike, as a landscape to be embraced in its own right, rather than as a symbol of alienation. It is difficult to stand at dawn on St Herbert's Isle as the mists clear over the still waters and regard this as any sort of rejection of place. Negative attitudes towards what we term the natural world have obscured the way in which early nature rituals in the church were a genuine and theologically measured expression of finding meaningful connections to creation. Going into the desert or to an island and living an ascetic life makes for a more acute relationship with the physical world, not less.

In Ireland this condition of being a wanderer was developed into an explicit system, referred to as green martyrdom and white martyrdom.[12] White martyrdom is mentioned in the early monastic text, *Columba's*

Rule, probably written by a follower of the great saint, along with its more obvious, blood-letting variant red martyrdom. White martyrdom involved enduring the pain of yearning for home during a pilgrimage for Christ. The green martyrdom is an interesting addition to the colourful mix of embodied devotion, possibly referring to the colour that one's skin goes when enduring all manner of physical hardship.[13] All three colours of martyrdom first appear in a single scheme in a text known as the *Cambrai Homily*, written around the year 700. By the late eighth century there were texts discouraging monks from undertaking pilgrimage outside Ireland, while allowing travel within the island and its western isles, most notably the monastic rule written by the Abbot of Tallaght, Máel Ruain (d. 792), a text that is considered the founding document of the *Céli Dé* ('companions of God') monastic movement, known as the Culdees in modern English.[14]

Very few words that I have come across have such a shifting meaning in the early church as this concept of 'pilgrim'. The direction of travel seems to be a steady move away from the notion that Christianity should be a connection with place. This process of what might be called the 'desacralization of nature', the withdrawal of ritual and spiritual interaction with the landscape, has considerable bearing on this search for early Christianity. The reluctance to accept that Christians could be so deeply attached to the landscape for their own theologically sanctioned reasons is one that seems to have grown imperceptibly. Perhaps it reflects an endless discomfort with the legacy of the Pagan faith, of the animism that saw spirits at work in the natural world. But this inhibition ends up disassociating us from the land, and that was never the early hermits' calling, and the exact opposite of what their distant prototype the nomad was about. The word 'pagan' means 'of the countryside', bluntly used to refer to someone who was rough, uncultured in the way we might use the term 'rustic' pejoratively. In like manner the word 'heathen' refers to the wild, uncivilized people who live on the 'heath' rather than in the town. We have already considered the visceral rejection of worship around landmark features that can be seen as early as the writings of Jerome in the fourth century, in the Council of Arles of 452, but only relatively late in medieval Britain in the eleventh century under Ælfric and Wulfstan.[15] All these outdoor devotions were steadily supplanted by the enclosure, ownership, management and promotion of shrines and the corresponding shift of focus towards pilgrimage as it is currently understood over the course of many centuries.

The dislocation of holiness is a problem for Christianity – the notion that holy places are by definition somewhere else. I used to give regular talks about my last book, and would ask people for the first word that came to mind when I talked about holy places. Invariably the answer would be 'pilgrimage', the idea that you need to travel to find somewhere spiritually significant. I think there is also a redemptive potential that is around us, in the middle of our home communities. I cannot think of a single holy place that was not originally founded and carefully tended by local people, at the immediate centre of a cohesive community. The shocked monks who gathered around the slain body of St Thomas Becket and arranged his burial were not at that moment motivated by a desire to bring people on foot to their cathedral. If you are lucky enough to live in Durham, you probably don't consider yourself a pilgrim when you go to Durham Cathedral for a regular service. But the dangers of only associating holy places with pilgrimage seem very real; to confuse the journey with the actual function of the holy place itself is to somehow miss the point. Holy places are sites where local people originally gathered their thoughts and prayers to celebrate, commemorate or mourn a community event: to cohere, in other words.

There was a debate about the merits of pilgrimage in the earliest centuries of the church,[16] although it was steadily drowned out by the relentless growth of pilgrim trails and shrines, only to be resumed around the time of the Reformation, when the church pushed holiness even further away from the material and physical. It might seem like this was a major break from the past, but holy places had already been moving from here to there in physical terms, and it is in some ways logical that they should ultimately be shifted temporarily too, from now to the hereafter. The point stands that Christians did find ways to connect in meaningful and ritual fashion to their own landscape, and to animals and the elements. The Christian's sense of belonging has been inexorably turned away from earthly concerns and towards a world that is absent, albeit impending, even though this is an artificial dichotomy. This impetus gained much of its urgency from the fact that it was perfectly elided with a simultaneous rejection of Paganism: the Pagan is connected to the land, the pilgrim is supposedly detached from it.

Offshore demons

The mist lay thick over the surface of Derwentwater on my first visit to the island some eight years ago, a breathless Friday morning when the peaks around were lit up in autumn sunshine. I was the first on the lake, my oars splashing into dayspring tranquillity as I wobbled away from the jetty. 'Just row straight and you can't miss it, tallest island on the lake,' the boatman called after me, clearly deciding that my nautical abilities required a bit of encouragement. 'And if you don't come back we'll send out a search party for you . . .' I turned and glanced at the white bank ahead of my prow, and resolved that I would at least row in a straight line as he finished his exhortation from the shore, '. . . after the weekend.' As it happened, the boatman's gracious offer proved entirely unnecessary, for the mist began to clear around me as I made my way across the water. I did nearly capsize the boat when I turned round after 20 minutes of rowing and saw my destination perfectly reflected in a shimmering mirror of the deepest blue, as if my hermit's island was floating in the ether between heaven and earth. Mist still clung to the lake's shores, fading any traces of human settlement to nothing, and I realized I had the perfect image for my book on holy places.

So I am pretty confident I know in part what drew a hermit to this island. But I am equally certain that there was a hard-edged purpose that also drove these fabled expeditions into the wilderness, the missionary campaign that gives real meaning and resonance to Britain's hermit archipelago. When Cuthbert landed on Inner Farne the first thing he did was to expel some of the island's inhabitants, 'phantoms of demons' that had previously made it impossible for anyone to spend a night there alone. What demons they were is hard to discern, the anonymous author suggesting that they were 'put to flight', while Bede makes clear that the chief mischief maker had been there with a 'whole crowd of satellites'.[17] Neither writer makes clear exactly how this ill-fated brood was forced out, although both juxtapose the exorcism with the establishment of a hut, to mark the hermit's new sovereignty over his domain. Perhaps the ritual is as basic as the one I followed on St Herbert's Isle, sleeping the island towards sanctity simply by spending the night alone there.

It is a curious feature across every part of Britain and Ireland that there was this intense missionary drive to clear the landscape of all traces of demonic possession during the long conversion period. I would say it is one of the most striking features of the whole Celtic era, this notion that the land was somehow infested with shadows that clung to marginal places. These phantoms are usually interpreted as an allegory for the tainted legacy of Pagan shrines and buildings, their expulsion a symbol of the victory of Christianity over the druids. But to my mind all these demons appear to behave much more like an indigenous species of animal, especially when compared to tales from elsewhere. When the monastic pioneer St Antony went into the Eastern deserts for his epic confrontations with devils, it is notable how they clung to the remnants of human activity. In all of that vast, echoing wilderness it was an abandoned fort that proved to be the scene of his most intense spiritual warfare. Immediately after cleansing this building, he turned his attention to casting demons out of people themselves who came to visit him.[18] When Antony meets a desert dweller even older than himself, a man called Paul who is the first recorded Christian hermit, the two share bread and figs together and tut over the fate of cities far away, places where demons gather to be worshipped by the citizens. At one point Antony receives directions in the middle of the desert from a satyr, a man-goat hybrid, who makes the astonishing claim that the fauns, satyrs and incubi of the wilderness have converted to Christianity, in stark contrast to the city-dwellers who continue to regard such supernatural creatures as their gods.[19]

Once again, when you map such tales on to Britain's own desert spaces, the islands, the shift in emphasis reveals some sharp differences between these two spiritual terrains. Again and again in continental Europe and the desert, the focus of exorcism was on people, and by furthest extension on some of their buildings. The confrontation between exorcist and devil was typically inserted into a saint's *Life* at the moment when their authority was being questioned, a demonstration of their saintly charisma that was meant to be observed in the middle of a bustling town. The scholar Peter Brown observes with customary insight that such set-piece events were modelled on the language of judicial inquiry, the saint judging and condemning the demon before releasing its unfortunate hostage by performing the actual exorcism.[20] In Britain the demons seem more like an annoying and at times deadly species of bird or reptile, by way of contrast. Their preferred habitat appears to be in the watery places, in the seas, lakes, rivers and springs and particularly on islands, with a few sub-species lurking in caves and on mountains. The legend of St Patrick casting out the snakes of Ireland is well known, but was a later addition to his cult first mentioned in the eleventh century. I suspect this embellishment was partly inspired by Bede's description of Ireland's curious ability to render harmless the venom of serpents, quoted in my chapter on the naked hermit. St Patrick's pest control is again interpreted as an allegory of his victory over the Pagan druids, but I'm a little uncomfortable with any such elision of demons and the relics of Paganism in a Celtic context. These possessed animals always seem to live as far away as possible from human society or artefacts, islands being one of their preferred haunts. There is a similar story told of St Columba and the snakes of Iona in Adomnán's *Life*, which has nothing to do with any sort of Pagan contamination. Shortly before he died, St Columba climbed a low hill on the western coast of Iona, probably the Hill of Angels that we will visit in the chapter on mountains, raised both hands in the air and pronounced that all snakes would be rendered harmless on his monastery's island so long as Christians remained there.[21] I rather suspect that both Pagans and Christians alike found common purpose in this mission to the islands and waterways of Britain and Ireland, a story representing not hostility to old traditions but help in dismissing lingering fears of the wild.

Another fabled creature of the north shows this story in perhaps its starkest form of all, a beast that continues to light up the imagination of the general public today: the Loch Ness monster. It makes its first appearance in the *Life* of St Columba, the first of countless sightings, but one that has an altogether darker outcome than the sort of wobbly, low-resolution videos that surface on the internet today. One day, Adomnán recounts, St Columba and his companions were walking at the top of the loch when they came across a funeral service for a man who had been killed by a beast in the water. Columba instructed one of his men to go for a swim, whereupon the monster reappeared, bearing down at great speed with jaws open ready for the kill. Columba – and I take note of these ritual actions carefully – made the sign of the cross in the air and after invoking God's name shouted: 'You will go no further. Do not touch the man; turn backward speedily.' I would imagine a good Scot today would find a shorter and pithier way to express this sentiment so politely expressed by the holy abbot, but it did the trick. The creature fled in swift retreat 'as if pulled back by ropes'.[22] And so the monster sank back into the cold waters of its loch, to reappear ever after when the mood takes it.

The detail about ropes pulling the monster back was one of those tiny little asides that nag away when trying to figure out what was going on, suggestive of some sort of theatrical prop, a rather elaborate hoax designed to catch the attention of a mainstream audience. But it seems unlikely this was any sort of precursor to today's 'Best Loch Ness Monster Sighting of the Year' award, now sponsored by the bookmaker William Hill rather than the church. My supervisor Charlotte told me to keep chewing it over, and eventually it occurred to me what was going on when reading tales of other exorcisms in this period, more conventionally performed on humans: I am certain these ropes reflect the common practice of binding the possessed. There is even biblical precedent in the Synoptic Gospel account of the demoniac at Gadarene, who repeatedly broke out of his chains until his devils were expelled into a herd of pigs. Closer to our era, the ever-dependable Sulpicius Severus describes an incident in which a possessed human being is tied up.[23] The Loch Ness monster was treated as a genuine animal that had been possessed by a demon, not entirely without precedent given the Gadarene swine either. And so the picture continues to develop that this mission to the landscapes of Britain was a genuine attempt to drive demons out of their natural habitats in the wilderness, on islands and indeed in certain wild animals too.

Was Britain as a whole purged of any infestation? It is a large island for any such cosmological intervention but it would appear that there might well have been at least one attempt to cleanse its surrounding waters from the clutches of demons, in what is the oldest narrative account of British Christian mission. It is an exorcism story that runs long and deep in the tales of the tribes, further back even than Nessie in the sixth century, and is to my mind the starting point of the entire Celtic mission to the natural world. The *Life* of St Germanus has been quoted previously, an account written in the depths of the scarcely documented fifth century about a Gaulish Bishop of Auxerre, who visited in 429 to shore up the British church. At the time it was facing a two-pronged attack from Saxon invaders and a heresy arising from the teachings of the monk Pelagius. Before he even arrived, Germanus reached deep into Christian liturgical tradition to perform an absolutely remarkable act of exorcism on our coastal waters. A storm on the English Channel had been whipped up by the action of demons and threatened to prevent the bishop's arrival, at which point Germanus intervenes:

> He, all the more steadfast for the very immensity of the danger, in the name of Christ chided the ocean, pleading the cause of religion against the savagery of the gales. Then, taking some oil, he lightly sprinkled the waves in the name of the Trinity and this diminished their fury.[24]

From Germanus onwards, the evidence of early Christian writers and missionaries of Britain continues to demonstrate that many forms of water, including the sea, rivers and wells or springs, required similar rituals of exorcism. Germanus came to pour oil on troubled waters, literally and figuratively, when he crossed the English Channel to help the church. His ritual to soothe the demons seems to have set an astonishing precedent, which was cited and copied by the main writers of the period, including Bede and Adomnán.[25] This was a ritual purification of the landscape that in many ways marks the start of the Celtic fascination with the cosmological reach of Christian liturgy, and it echoed for centuries in the texts of this conversion period. Just about the first glimpse we have of Britain as it emerged into the Celtic era, even before the good bishop had set foot on the land itself, was that it was crying out for ritual exorcism to be performed on the environment. We will continue this trajectory into the waters of Britain in the next chapter, bracing ourselves for the chill. So many of these acts of exorcism turn out to be a mere precursor to the shockingly physical witness of devotional bathing.

Draughts of heavenly life

The hermits' lives were certainly simple, devoid of comforts beyond the essentials for living. Even Cuthbert's island conspired to ensure that his life was as ascetic as possible: he tried to grow wheat but the crop failed, leading him to resort to the humbler grain of barley. Herbert lived a minimal life on his island, no doubt fishing and gaining occasional supplies from a nearby community. On the shore of his lake, Friar's Crag is believed to mark the spot from where his fellow monks would row out to see him. Whether he planted any crops here is not recorded, the island today showing no signs of any cultivation. There are three early records of Herbert's life written a couple of decades after his death, all of which provide much the same scant information. The last of these three is Bede's *History*, where he writes that Herbert died after a long and painful illness.[26] There is a large, ruined circular building at the northern end of the island, which some identify with the site of the hermit's home. Other guides and the Ordnance Survey map describe a summerhouse on this island, but to me the round shape and the stone construction suggest the faint echo of an Irish 'beehive' structure of the sort seen further west. Certainly this construction technique did travel with the missionaries from Ireland, and there are examples still to be seen on a tiny, uninhabited island a little to the south of Mull, called Eileach an Naoimh, one of the many places sometimes referred to as 'holy island' mentioned at the start of this chapter. These beehive shelters have been linked to the famous navigator St Brendan but more likely date from the ninth century, one of many monastic outposts that claim a famous founder.

I'm no expert on religious architecture, but I do know that round things are often a sign of great age, and the circular footprint left behind by the mystery ruin on St Herbert's Isle looks nothing like the foundations of the summerhouse that was once built there. A nineteenth-century print shows a building with unmistakably square sides. Certainly Herbert's spiritual counsellor Cuthbert built a hut on Inner Farne out of uncut stone that was 'almost round in plan' and 'four or five poles from wall to wall'.[27] If 'pole' means the length of a typical walking staff, that feels very similar to the size and shape of the ruin where I prayed. I think it is very much older than is usually acknowledged.

I managed to reduce my own possessions for my night on the island to a single heavy load, which I carried in one go down from the road. Considering that this included a boat and oars, I was feeling reasonably in tune with the stripped down life of an ascetic, trying hard to forget about my car as I began this sojourn in the seventh century. I set off wearing a jumper and waterproof jacket, heeding every piece of hill-walking advice going, but when I arrived all my clothes had been soaked in the spray and splash of my crossing. I had nothing to wear even if I needed it, the boulders around my camp draped with these damp relics of my life on shore. For food I decided to cook from scratch rather than relying on the convenience of a meal in plastic pots, and busied myself for half an hour making a quintessentially Anglo-Saxon dinner of chicken curry.

None of this adds up to much more than the average camping holiday during a normal wet British summer, and I suspect that much of Herbert's life was reasonably comfortable. What I did start to notice, however, was the cold. As the sun lowered itself into the trees on the western shore, its last golden rays offered the final physical warmth to my nascent vigil, the temperature dropping fast as evening drew in. I sat gazing over the still waters of the lake as nature turned into a steely monochrome blue, my mind wandering at the growing solitude and peace, and I felt my first shiver. That night the temperature was 10 degrees. I busied myself about the camp to ward off the cold and then decided to find my way in the darkness to the ruined hermitage that lies hidden among trees at the northern end of the island, on a whim removing even my sandals. I had seen the structure earlier in the day, a fallen trunk lying across the circular enclosure, brambles growing up around the shattered remains of its thick stone wall. I had no possessions with me at all, not even a light to find my way as I stepped silently over the fallen masonry and sank to my knees in the centre. Resting my elbows on the fallen trunk, my bare knees and feet on the blanket of leaves, I stopped and felt the silence of the island throb through my ears. The fear of the darkness and isolation that I had long anticipated was nowhere near my beating heart. Nor did it feel strange to kneel naked in a holy place such as this; rather, I became acutely aware of the fact that Herbert too had a body on this island, felt the cold and hunger, rested on the damp earth, heard the birds and the leaves in the trees. The sensation of being connected to the natural world in this way grew louder until it suddenly overwhelmed me, like a wave of warmth and peace that seemed to pin me to the heart of this sanctuary, overflowing in every direction, to the lake water and the hills and the world beyond. It was the most intense feeling of pleasure I have known, a few seconds that I experienced twice more during my stay and once on a mountain in Wales. I have no idea what it was or how it happened, but I felt connected to the fabric of this beautiful place, identifying with something very much larger and more perfect than I could possibly hope to find or recreate in any form of human space or interaction. Such communion is not without precedent both ancient and modern. One recent writer who has undertaken a similar pilgrimage into the spiritual and physical landscapes of a Celtic island, albeit with a touch more clothing, is Alastair McIntosh. His wonderful new book *Poacher's Pilgrimage* describes a journey across Lewis and Harris, weaving in the theme of non-violence that so preoccupied my own thoughts as I contemplated our wounded planet.[28]

One comment in Bede's brief record of the final conversation between Herbert and Cuthbert stands out to me: 'Each in turn regaled the other with exhilarating draughts of heavenly life.'[29] I understand why Herbert had no fear of his own death. Afterwards I walked away glowing with warmth, and did not feel cold again for the next hour, until I sat outside my tent and began to let my mind wander back to matters mundane, possibly connected to cricket. I was beginning to realize that only doing nothing let the chill creep in, that both prayer and contemplation were work in themselves that would keep me warm. My head lowered and I prayed again, and felt the warmth and the peace hit me for a second time. Ironic though it might sound when considering such a simple life from the outside, I would say you need to keep busy as a hermit, mentally and physically, the work of prayer and daily life sufficient to fill and to clothe the day and night.

We haven't lost paradise, it is still there, but it is slipping away, it has always been slipping away. But it remains at hand. So that was revealed to me in the ruins of a shelter on a lonely island, which became the centre of a universe lit up with grace and peace. This was Herbert's seat rather than my own, but I did understand that he prayed for everything and everyone, that what was radiating out from his little enclave was love. The whole island felt so holy I did not wear my sandals again even as I packed and left, lest my heel rub against a rock and leave a stain of artificial rubber. To be entirely bare on an island such as Herbert's, bereft of any insulation against the cosmos as I was at birth, seemed not only appropriate but suitably self-effacing, nomadic, reverent even. If you can accept the paradox, I would go so far as to say that wilfully discarding all comforts and trappings of civilization to approach creation as an act of collective worship of our Creator is essentially an act of humility and even modesty.

6

In for the chill: sacred bathing

———◆———

I got up early and bathed in the pond; that was a
religious exercise, and one of the best things I did.
Henry David Thoreau, *Walden* (1854)[1]

Clothed in morning frost, my bare feet crunched over the grass of the
field as I made my way down to the riverbank. The pale gold of a January
sun brought colour but little warmth to the land and absolutely no comfort to my all-over goose bumps. The surface of the river flowed black
and sluggish as oil as it meandered through the empty water meadow, a
site set apart by nature, as good a place as any to serve the Lord in fear
and trembling. I had been coming to this blessed plot every month since
June, having decided during the halcyon days of summer that it would
be instructive to immerse my soul in a year of devotional bathing in this
wild stretch of the River Wey, a constant witness through the changing
of the seasons. This is the most raw of all rituals, Celtic or otherwise, so
primal that the basic requirements have not changed one iota since the
dawn of the human race. Even the muted colours were a palette of primary elements, the yellow winter grass stretching to the horizon under
an ice-blue sky, and almost lost between the two my tiny figure turning
slowly red in the stinging chill of the dawn air. This is Celtic nature ritual
at its most visceral, an engagement stripped to the barest of essentials,
without building, vestment, ornamentation or human artefact of any
description. It is the most unaltered of all engagements with the natural
world, a full-bodied embrace of the elements that is identical in every
regard to the saints who led the way into Britain's icy currents. Yet for all
its primal simplicity, any such bathing is curiously freighted with cultural
baggage.

In more ways than one this ritual is the most breathtaking of all Celtic
practices – wading into natural water at any season in the year in order
to ... well, do what exactly? This was one of the first questions that hit
me when I sat down and wrote a list of some of the expressions of faith

in the landscape to be found in the early church's engagement with the natural world. In all I found 50 descriptions of devotional bathing across the early literature of Christian Europe, of which a remarkable 39 took place in Britain and Ireland. What exactly was it about the streams, pools, springs, lakes and beaches that drove our ancestors to strip off and wade in? I decided I needed to piece this together carefully to see what lessons could be learned. One thing I can say at the outset, it was not the balmy warmth of the water.

The first devout bather in Christian history was a man called Evagrius Ponticus, a theologian monk who died in 399. It will come as no surprise to learn that he was yet another Egyptian prototype for what became a defining Celtic ritual. A man once given to waltzing around town in fine clothes and falling in love with a married woman, his life took something of a U-turn when he repented and went to live as a hermit in the desert. And it was there that Evagrius made the fateful decision to stand in a well one winter's night in order to quell the 'devil of lewdness'. The recorded details are sparse, revealing little more than the fact that his intention was to numb the flesh. Both versions of this holy man's life, in Greek and Coptic, also state that he was naked, although this word was removed when the Greek was translated into Latin in the nineteenth century.[2] The Coptic version adds that he prayed while in the water, and that is pretty much it. This was seemingly a prototype of the cold bath or shower in order to dampen down a monk's libido, an ascetic exercise that once again arises from the internal regulation of monastic discipline. Little wonder that the first modern scholar to write a serious study of Celtic bathing rituals, a French monk called Louis Gougaud writing in the 1920s, harked back to Evagrius and concluded that all these colourful stories of British and Irish saints were simply exercises in bodily mortification, dismissing most of them as 'improbable' without explaining why. It is an interpretation that historians have continued to follow ever since, monastic discipline as always the first and usually last explanation for pretty much anything the hermits did.[3]

One tiny scrap of evidence that has been overlooked in all these studies of devotional bathing is our own earliest recorded reference to it here in Britain. I am pretty sure that it first crops up in a very early Old Irish poem written a few years after St Columba's death in 597. This is a brief reference in a language so ancient it presents some difficulty even to the best translators, but the scene it conjures up is real enough. In the second stanza the poet appears to be celebrating one of the saint's most heroic spiritual feats:

> It was not on soft beds
> he undertook elaborate prayers,
> he crucified – it was not for crimes –
> his body on the green waves.[4]

A scrap of evidence, as I say, but one that offers an arresting image of a man pushing himself to extremes in his devotions. It seems to have taken place at night, given the reference to 'soft beds', which establishes a devotional matrix involving nocturnal prayers and immersion in the sea. And then there is this curious aside that it was 'not for crimes', which undermines any suggestion that Columba was motivated to correct any personal fault or failing, immediately moving us away from the narrow context that drove Evagrius into his libido-quenching well. I have read many writers who claim that Columba would stand in the sea with his arms out in a crucifix position for long hours of vigil, but I used to wonder what the evidence was for this. I think the reference to crucifixion in this early poem makes it fairly likely that he did indeed engage in such a ritual, although I have not seen anyone cite this poem as evidence.[5] We will leave Columba standing in the sea for now, but his cross-vigil posture before the swelling ocean ought to linger in the imagination as we find out what else became of sacred bathing in Britain's chilly waters.

To categorize Celtic bathing ritual as a means of cooling an unruly libido or punishing a wayward body does not seem a particularly satisfying explanation, partly because it doesn't explain why nearly 80 per cent of all references to it only take place in Britain and Ireland. This was an Egyptian invention by a well-known pioneer of desert spirituality, so it is reasonable to ask why the discipline only had intense resonance among Celtic Christians. It is an experience that is not wrapped up with matters of the libido one way or the other for me personally, and indeed all the open-water swimmers I know never mention this aspect, irrespective of what any of us wear or don't wear while doing it. But I do know that the outdoor devotional immersions I have recreated for this project deliver a very intense feeling of connection to the environment. This chapter is in some ways the centre of this book because of the amount of study I undertook, followed by such an intensive campaign to put it into practice, numbing first the brain and then the body with perhaps a hundred devout dips. The deeper I went the more sacramental the connection to the environment became, until I ended up coming across what I believe to be the root cause of a liturgical dispute between Roman and Celtic Christians. There is little to get people more worked up than involving the body in religious ritual: it is where differences are acutely expressed, where popular culture coincides with abstract theological argument. So it proved to be in early medieval Britain.

Many monks and some nuns were said to make dipping in their local river a daily habit, moving through barely perceptible changes as the seasons came and went, laudable determination undoubtedly but also joyous revelation. My own monthly visits to the River Wey in Surrey brought home to me just how far the cycle of nature turns during a year. In mid September the fields were a golden haze and the reeds buzzed with insects, while in October I slipped down the riverbank on brown wet leaves as the silence throbbed in my ears. In early March the trees looked as bare as I felt while stripping on a riverbank bereft of natural cover, stark and cold under a colourless sky. Six weeks later the banks were blooming with wildflowers and wildlife, birds joyfully flitting under the lime green of the budding trees. In June I winced my way past chest-high nettles, and in August sat for hours with my feet in the soothing stream. Nobody came past. It proved difficult to contemplate practising this discipline in other places, where there were people nearby, and I understand why the saints in times gone by went to extreme lengths to ensure their devotions were solitary. An Anglo-Saxon queen once sneaked down to the River Test at night, so curious was she to see the abbess of Romsey Abbey practise her nightly nude bathing regime in the depths of the winter. She ended up catching a virulent fever just by watching such chilly devotions, but the kindly St Ethelflaeda forgave her the intrusion and cured her with a touch. A sign in the abbey church today near the possible site of her grave refers obliquely to Ethelflaeda's 'ascetic devotional practices', although her late medieval *Life* positively wallows in the physicality of these hearty nocturnal vigils, going *nuda* as the author notes enthusiastically. Twice.

The mixture of disbelief, embarrassment and occasional disdain that historians and others have directed towards the arresting sight of our holiest leaders stripping off to embrace the chill has certainly helped draw a veil over such full-bodied antics. Yet as I worked my way through dozens of descriptions of bathing rituals it became clear to me that there are distinct patterns to be found, clear and meaningful liturgical shapes forming beneath the flowing surface of the texts and currents alike. And so I went down to the river to pray in a secluded water meadow in Surrey every month of the year to test the waters of my developing theories, and found a world apart from the rather dry academic understanding that a purely book-based study provided. It is always the body that disrupts the readings of these texts, always the physical experiences I had that caused me to look and look again at what was being described before bringing these ancient ways to life.

In Cuthbert's footsteps

In the borderlands of southern Scotland, about 20 miles north of the Celtic powerhouse that is Lindisfarne, St Cuthbert woke early one night and went down to the sea to pray. The monastery at Coldingham where he was staying is now little more than a few stones and bumps buried in the sturdy grass on the top of a steep hill, an unlikely place for anyone to establish a permanent settlement, exposed as it is to the full force of the North Sea's capricious moods. When I first visited, a storm was hurling vast waves into the base of these cliffs, making the ground shudder and the air ring. Yet in the midst of this harsh and rocky coastline Cuthbert was to perform a ritual bathing exercise that united the whole of creation around him in praise of the Creator, an immersion that revealed the innermost primal harmony of the cosmos.

We will begin by following Bede's account of this nocturnal vigil. The details he records are precise enough to reconstruct what the saint actually did in the water, something I managed to do on a return visit in rather calmer conditions. A steep path runs down from the site of the former monastery to a rocky inlet, now called Horsecastle Bay, where Cuthbert is believed to have performed his ritual. Arriving at the sea, he entered the water as far as his neck and stayed there, 'singing praises to the sound of the waves'. As the sun rose he emerged and knelt on the shore to pray, while two sea otters followed him from the waters and 'began to warm his feet with their breath and sought to dry him with their fur'. Clearly effective, or perhaps it was simply the thought that counted to him, the saint turned to give the pair a blessing for performing such 'ministrations', and they slipped back into their watery home. Cuthbert then returned to the monastery in time to join the community in singing the morning hymns. A monk who had secretly followed Cuthbert down to the shore out of curiosity was struck with fear after spying on such an intense scene, and fell on his knees before the holy man to confess and receive a pardon.[6]

Some of this ritual drama, the more observant readers will have noticed, would prove rather difficult to reproduce. The pair of obliging otters were notable by their absence when I emerged with my own chilly feet. But the part that takes place in the water is eminently easy to follow, and by doing so I think I have worked out how these details come together.

It was here on an earlier visit that something struck me about Bede's description, a single word that he never used again: *undisonis*, 'to the sound of the waves'. Singing psalms to the sound of the waves. As the water boomed against the rocks, I thought about how difficult it would be to focus on keeping afloat and filling the air with song.[7] Even sitting on the shore and going through a hymn in my head, it was all but impossible to concentrate, so loudly do the waves echo in this bay. It finally struck me some months later while sitting in a rather more comfortable church building back home that the remorseless beat of the sea fits perfectly with the natural rhythm of a psalm as it is traditionally sung. In Bede and Cuthbert's day the psalms were a near-constant soundtrack to the monks' lives. They were often sung using a technique known as 'antiphonal', two voices singing alternately, the end of each line punctuated with a pause and a response. And so it dawned on me that the Celtic saints might have found a remarkably creative way to work with rather than against this noisy environment: they spaced the lines of a psalm to the natural rhythm of the sea. The gap between breaking waves is roughly every ten seconds, which is the perfect amount of time to fit in the line of a psalm. Several of these biblical hymns even conclude each line with an 'Alleluia', the cadence of the sea breaking on the shore and subsiding with a hiss.

I managed to follow St Cuthbert into his echoing bay on my third visit. It is a half-hour walk from the seaside village of St Abbs along a coastal path of towering cliffs and broken headlands, and as I drew near it seemed I had all of creation to myself. The early summer sun shone on a sea breaking the most gentle waves, every element set fair for my attempt to reawaken this natural oratory. The very moment I arrived, however, an endless procession of walkers appeared from nowhere, the first of them an elderly man who silently followed me down to the water's edge and then stood staring out to sea for 15 minutes with his hands in his pockets while his dog sniffed morosely at piles of seaweed. Cuthbert reprimanded the monk who had intruded on his devotions at this little bay, unable to find the seclusion he had craved because of the 'fault' of a fellow human being. One sympathizes.

After an hour it finally seemed that the coast was clear, and I was ready to change into my hermit's uniform. Leaving 13 centuries of accumulated human progress crumpled in a pile on the shore, I moved swiftly towards the sea before stopping and remembering to take off the final thing that would render me truly naked and defenceless, my glasses. Without these I would have no chance of spotting anyone walking along the coast, giving me at most a guarantee of just five minutes of seclusion. It seemed a pity to rush when the waters of this bay have waited so long to receive another worshipper, but it is my personal hermit's motto not to be disturbed or to surprise others.

A fine scholar called Britton Brooks produced an excellent thesis about this very seashore vigil a couple of years before I completed mine. He reckons the hymn Cuthbert sang was Psalm 95, which would start the morning's worship in a monastery.[8] It begins with a call to worship God and moves to praise him as the creator of the mountains and seas in verses 4–5. I have to be honest and admit I did not learn this psalm before my immersion, in either English or Latin, but improvised with the famous hymn based on Psalm 23, 'The Lord's my Shepherd'. It is eminently suited to Cuthbert's rocky bay, a setting of grassy hills dotted with sheep, the pastures green and quiet waters of the song. It also had the distinct advantage that I already knew it. In similar manner I resorted to 'By the Rivers of Babylon' (Psalm 137) for my Surrey river expeditions. My siren voice across the rocks and gently rolling waves at Coldingham mysteriously failed to summon any otters from the water at the end of my devotions, something I will blame on their capricious nature rather than my hopeless singing ability. Assuming, that is, there are any otters left on this stretch of shore.

Even though we sang our psalms in different languages, I do think I managed to follow St Cuthbert very closely into the sea in other respects. This bay has a lot of uneven boulders on its floor, but on the right-hand side there is a vertical slab running down into the water, and by working my way alongside it I discovered a smooth rock floor at its base, where I had no difficulty keeping my balance until the waves lifted me gently from my neck upwards. The elements came together in an overpowering flood of peace as I embarked on this most primal of Celtic practices, the most unaltered ritual of all antiquity. Medieval, classical, biblical and pre-historic distinctions collapsed as I entered the mysteries of these brooding waters, the source of life and the site where creation is made and remade in so many human cycles of wisdom and experience. Out here where my breathing slows and the cold passes into being, there is only surrender to the eternal pulse of the waves, no way to speed back to the warmth of the shore, no way to manage time or tide. This is the rhythm of something much older and more enduring even than the oldest of liturgies; both Cuthbert and I are as nothing when aligned with the beat of the cosmos.

The elements may be unchanged since Cuthbert's day, but I certainly wasn't as I emerged from the sea, the glow still lingering with me even as I write this some months later. Whether this bay did once have sand, as Bede's account suggests, is hard to know. I did spot some lying on under-water rocks when I went swimming further out a little later on. But I did not pause to kneel on the shore in prayer as Cuthbert did, mindful of the busy coastal path. Entering the sea at night would help to ensure seclusion, and I think the rock slab as a hand-hold and the conveniently flat sea bed on the right-hand side make Cuthbert's nocturnal vigil seem entirely plausible.

Bede doesn't directly mention Cuthbert's state of dress as he bathed, although there is plenty of contextual evidence that he imagined the saint also went *nudus* into the waves. The later medieval church certainly assumed that he did. A fifteenth-century translation into Middle English verse added 'Up to the nek naked stode he', an interesting reversal of the trend towards censorship in post-medieval translations of so many saints' lives and historical texts.[9] Three centuries earlier a talented artist illuminated Bede's original text with an illustration of Cuthbert in the water, clearly arising from a culture in which depicting a saint's bare bottom would not cause the sort of anguish it might today.[10] Separately, Bede himself describes the bathing customs of his day, with a brief reference to the hot springs at Bath in the very first chapter of his *History*. In one of the few sociological observations contained in any early medieval text, he insists that bathing places are segregated by sex and age, which presumes communal nudity.[11] I rather suspect that Bede is simply the first in a long line of churchmen and moralists trying to encourage or reinforce an end to mixed-sex naked bathing at these hot springs. The wider historical evidence demonstrates that naked was how everyone bathed outdoors through nearly all of human history, including the early medieval period, sometimes segregated but sometimes not.[12]

The reason why this is important is nothing to do with my personal interest in skinny-dipping, but takes us to the heart of a profound clash of cultures, theologies and liturgies alike, and not just between our world and that of the hardy hermits of times gone by. As often mentioned, there was an earlier *Life* of St Cuthbert written by an anonymous monk on the Celtic island of Lindisfarne, and Bede copied it to form his own version of this vigil on the shore. Indeed, so faithfully does he follow the earlier text for this scene, scholars who have studied the texts in parallel are in agreement that he did not change any significant details.[13] Having followed the ritual into the waves, I could not disagree more strongly.

'That man of God, approaching the sea with mind made resolute, went into the waves up to his loincloth; and once he was soaked as far as his armpits by the tumultuous and stormy sea,' as the anonymous monk writes. In this first version of his seashore ritual, Cuthbert sings on the shore before entering the water, but the record goes silent as to his devotions when in the sea itself. Were you to observe someone engaging in rituals as described by this author and by Bede, the differences would all be as obvious as Cuthbert's disappearing loincloth. I have also followed the anonymous prescription for this ritual. Not only is it immediately obvious that the immersion is completely different, it has also been observed with particularly intimate detail by the earlier author. I have a strong feeling that he was describing something he personally experienced, the reference to underwear and anatomy suggesting first-hand knowledge. Armpits indeed. That was another of those curious details that stuck in my mind, particularly when I compiled a database of all the recorded bathing rituals of old. Saints are invariably described as wading into water up to their neck, shoulder or breast, or on one occasion to the loins.[14] But armpits are not really a yardstick on the body, because they are usually concealed, unless . . .

It was only by remembering Columba's 'crucifixion' in the waves of Iona that I suddenly realized why the anonymous monk of Lindisfarne mentioned armpits. He was surely imagining Cuthbert standing with his arms outstretched, which is the only way his armpits could be exposed to the waves. Mix that posture with the loincloth and a clear image of what I now consider to be the Ionan bathing ritual comes sharply into focus. This was a fully formed 'crucifixion' in the waves, a vigil that was developed by Columba and copied closely at Lindisfarne, which is one of his monastery's daughter foundations. These Celtic monks were wading out to stand waist-deep in the sea with their arms out in a cross-shape, in visible defiance of the waves: not just the symbolism but the embodiment itself of fortitude in the face of real physical challenge. When I copied this ritual it felt a very public expression of piety, a deliberate and visual witness to anyone watching from the shore that this is a confrontation between a man and the vicissitudes of nature. The Christian symbolism could not be more overt too. Yet none of that survives into Bede, not even any indication of physical hardship.

When you compare the two accounts of Cuthbert's nocturnal vigil all the other elements are the same: the beach, the night setting, the prayers afterwards, the spying monk, and even the friendly sea creatures drying his feet. But the descriptions of the immersion itself speak of two completely different activities and meanings. I tried to copy the anonymous account the day after I had decoded it, although I was standing in the least propitious environment possible for a nature ritual, using the wave machine in a public swimming pool in Guildford, a pair of shorts standing in for my loincloth. Even in this restricted environment I can confirm that this is once again an entirely plausible description of physical action. Waves that reach from the waist up to the armpits involve a swell of about

50 centimetres, which is not too rough to keep your balance – particularly if you use your arms outstretched to steady your weight. Anxious not to give the Guildford lifeguards an impression that I was signalling for help or attempting an impromptu piece of performance art, I spread my arms for just a few seconds as a wave broke over me. I have since performed this Ionan bathing ritual in the Atlantic, and outstretched arms were not merely a ritual embellishment but actually helped keep me from falling over, a detail that ties the anonymous account ever closer to bodily experience. Speaking as someone who has no embarrassment at all when it comes to nudity on the beach, I have to say that this is one bathing ritual that does require some form of dress. It feels like you are drawing attention to yourself; it is a deliberately provocative posture set against a neutral background of sea and sky. To focus your mind on prayer and contemplation of the mysteries of creation while mooning at anyone passing behind you is a tricky balancing act to pull off, no matter how devout your mind. It feels very much like a public act of defiance, but I am sure that was directed towards the elemental forces confronting the crucified bather rather than his or her monastic companions on the shore. The loincloth also indicates to me that this ritual was usually meant to be observed – one lesson I have learned above all from the hermit's symbiosis of nudity and solitude.

So it is notable that the writer who depicts the most sympathetic inter-action with the environment is Bede rather than the scribe of Lindisfarne, which runs somewhat counter to the notion that Celtic culture is the more nature-orientated. It is Bede's Cuthbert who fully embraces the elements, leaving his clothes and wading deep into the waters, immersed without inhibition in the environment, singing hymns of praise accompanied by the rhythm of the waves. Compared with the Ionan rite of standing silently, arms outstretched, partially dressed and in water waist deep, Bede offers much more of a full-bodied expression of ritualized joy and praise immersed in the natural world than an ascetic demonstration of bodily endurance. It is also, I will add in passing, a much more gender-neutral discipline too, the anonymity of the full-bodied immersion being suitable for both sexes in the way that standing in a loincloth with arms held aloft really isn't.

Interpretations of this enigmatic seashore vignette quite under-standably turn towards the friendly sea creatures, which Bede identifies as otters. Their act of kindness certainly unifies both accounts, bring-ing to a harmonious conclusion Cuthbert's immersion in the waters at Coldingham. It is an act that has a clear ritual shape to it, and scholars have not hesitated to identify the ministry of foot washing and drying that monks would perform on guests to their monastery. Indeed, in the previous chapter of both versions of Cuthbert's *Life* he has just offered the very same service to a stranger who came seeking shelter during a snow storm. The mystery visitor vanished when Cuthbert went to find him some food, leaving no footprints in the snow – an angel who came in from the cold and left behind three loaves of freshly baked bread. Recent scholars have therefore concluded that the story is designed to cement the notion of monastic discipline and service, nature rendering unto Cuthbert what he himself had dispensed to an angel.[15] This certainly moves the story on from the very narrow focus on bodily mortification that earlier writer Louis Gougaud discerned, a development to be welcomed.

If nothing else, this highlights the fact that Cuthbert's bathing ended up having a participatory effect on the environment, which is wholly absent from the Egyptian original. Evagrius' well is just a cistern, a functional means to an end that is entirely unchanged and passive in the short account of his bathing. When Cuthbert enters the sea, by way of contrast, creation is so moved by his touch it sends up two otters, reciprocating the saint's devout approach by responding in kind.

As we have seen, the provision of hospitality runs deep within the Christian tradition, deep within the ethics of the desert, where principles of human interdependence and rituals of welcome were matters of life and death. I agree with current thinking that this foot-washing incident is the culmination of the saint's bathing activity, but I have two different observations that move well beyond the confines of the monastic guest-house. The first observation is simple enough in the context of this book's developing theme, which is that Christian mission in Celtic Britain was designed to liberate the landscape from fear of the dark forces moving the elements and creatures. To that end I would place the otters as direct counterparts to their distant cousin in Loch Ness, creatures that emerged from the same watery universe in response to the presence of a holy man. What Columba began by exorcizing the demon from a murderous lake creature, Cuthbert took to its logical conclusion by welcoming the creatures of the deep into the orbit of Christian ritual, every bit as enthusiastic to benefit from the ministrations of a priest as his penitent ravens. These are elemental details in the same campaign to liberate the watery places of the north from the baneful forces that so preoccupied all the religious activity of early Britain. This is not to say that the story at Coldingham was simply written as a literary sequel to the monster in the Ness, but rather that both of them are products of an immense cultural transition in which the conversion of the people was one and the same thing as a conversion of their environment: confronted, exorcized, pardoned, redeemed and rehabilitated into divine service. This was surely aimed at converts both new and potential, very much the audience for Celtic nature rituals.

My second observation will be developed below. It relates to the extra-ordinary depths to which these missionaries dived within the well of Christian liturgy and theology to retrieve a sacrament so potent it has the power to reveal, indeed to remake, God's imprint in creation, which is baptism. Both of my observations connect Cuthbert's bathing to the concerns of his age. To understand that fully we need to read forwards in the text to see the direction where this bathing ritual led, rather than backwards to discover the monastic milieu from which it rather unsur-prisingly emerged.

Troubled waters up north

It was the sea that Cuthbert faced when he waded into the waves at Coldingham, the sea he was confronting and the sea he brought under the influence of Christian culture by the gravity of his ritual. What passes in a monastery guesthouse between stranger and monk is the starting point of a ministry and mission that faced the widest possible challenges and had the widest possible ambitions to meet them. In the chapter immediately after his dip with the otters, Cuthbert goes on another trip, this time to the land of the Picts, where Columba had previously been so preoccupied with natural water. Indeed, this next chapter sees Cuthbert descend for a second time to the seashore at dawn, performing what appears to be a regular prayer ritual. Cuthbert's party had been stranded on the shore by a storm, desperately short of provisions, but he finds that the sea has cast up some portions of dolphin meat, which the monks describe as tasting of honey. The day itself is Epiphany, which is the day of Christ's baptism, as the anonymous author points out. Once again the sea has been rendered not merely harmless by the presence of a holy man but actively supportive of him and his Christian mission. Reading further still, the next chapter sees Cuthbert heading west on a mission to people living in the area of the River Teviot, where he taught and then baptized many new converts. In yet another ritual interaction with the natural world, Cuthbert foretells that an eagle he sees flying overhead will bring their meal, and it subse-quently leaves a large fish that it has taken from the river, described in the chapter on birds. Cuthbert tells his companion to give some of the fish to the bird, not merely so it could participate in the meal but because he interprets the bird's behaviour in leaving the fish as 'fasting'. Time and again the natural waters of the north are demonstrating their benevolence towards a holy man, providing him with warm feet, food, and even taking part in Christian ritual. All of these stories were pushed ahead of Cuthbert as he moved across the land in his mission to convert: ripples in the fabric of creation itself that spoke of a new power at work.

As the Lindisfarne version of Cuthbert's bathing tells us, there was a hard edge to the campaign to confront the waters of northern Britain, especially when compared to the more full-bodied immersion of further south, something in the northern waters to fear and to tame. Cuthbert has been a wonderful guide so far, leading us deep into the heart of Celtic nature ritual, but it is time to leave him enjoying his meal of fish and look further and wider at the landscape into which he and his contemporaries were entering.

First let us start with one common assumption that is made when it comes to pre-Christian attitudes towards natural water, which is that Pagans were devoted to its celebration, and venerated it freely and enthusiastically as a life-giving source. The historian Anne Ross has helped to construct a rich and suggestive image of the pre-Christian landscape of Britain with her seminal book *Pagan Celtic Britain*. She writes without reservation about the existence of Celtic water cults to rival those found at natural springs in mainland Europe, but in doing so lets slip a curious weakness in her argument: 'In Britain positive archaeological evidence for temples situated at the sources of rivers is lacking, but something in the nature of those attested for Gaul, but in a less sophisticated style can no doubt be inferred.'[16] It is rather optimistic to think that anything can be 'inferred' about the religious beliefs and practices in such an obscure yet suggestive field of study. The water shrines in Gaul are best known for their collections of votive offerings of body parts, the aching limbs and troublesome organs of the sick placed in the hope of magically transmitting the water's healing properties to the owner of the original piece of anatomy. Eyes, hands and feet seemed to have given our French neighbours particular cause for concern. In his otherwise excellent translation of Columba's *Life*, the historian Richard Sharpe follows Ross's assumptions of a benign harmony attaching to water sources at the point of Christian conversion to conclude that 'Pagan well-worship was easily transmuted into Christian practice.'[17] I'm not sure it was quite as simple as that.

In reality, as Ross's assessment inadvertently reveals, the evidence for Celtic holy wells fades out rapidly the further north one travels across Britain, something that recent historians have started to acknowledge.

Ronald Hutton neatly dissects the gap between popular understanding and hard historical evidence on this point:

> despite the widespread modern talk of 'Celtic holy wells', there is not much sign of religious significance being attached to springs. The main exception is the most spectacular of these in Britain, the hot one at Bath . . . We know that this was sacred to the Iron Age British, because the Romans recorded the name of the goddess to whom they dedicated it, Sulis, but the quantity of objects which they actually deposited in it, or around it, still seems small compared with those in other kinds of water . . . there is much less sign of a cult of either springs or wells in pre-Roman Britain than elsewhere in the ancient world, including Greece and Rome.[18]

Push harder still at the evidence, into the beliefs that seem to accumulate around the watery places of the land, and what starts to emerge is not just an absence of positive cultic activity but the lurking presence of something altogether more sinister. Poisonous wells, deadly sea creatures and demonic storms can all be glimpsed in the early texts, keeping the Loch Ness monster well supplied with mischief-making companions. They also neatly illustrate Gildas' comment about the 'deadly' rivers that once troubled his Pagan ancestors. In one of many stories that illustrate this theme, St Columba visited a well that the local Pagan *magi*, or wizards, worshipped on account of its harmful properties.[19] Capable of causing leprosy, blindness and crippling, so the story runs, Columba's Pagan opponents were keen to see him touch the well in the hope of doing him harm. A seventh-century *Life* of St Patrick offers an interesting parallel, referring to a holy well which the Pagans honoured, offering gifts as to a god. As seen before, Ireland's landscape seems rather more benign than the harsher waters of Britain, since there is no suggestion that the Irish well had any baneful properties.[20] St Columba's dramatic response was to bless the well and then wash his hands and feet in it before taking a sip of the purified waters, which were subsequently known for their healing properties. Once again it is the landscape that is redeemed and converted to the Christian fold.

Liquid in general seemed to have a particular hold over the imagination of Columba's community, the saint even going so far as to exorcize a pail of milk that had a devil lurking in the bottom. Columba's companion Baithéne, whom we met wandering the sea in search of a hermit island, had another nautical mishap when he came close to being capsized by a great whale. Forewarned by his holy abbot, the monk was well equipped to deal with both the creature and the water itself: 'Baithéne without a tremor of fear raised his hands and blessed the sea and the whale.

Immediately, the great creature plunged under the waves and was not seen again.'[21]

The further north you go in early medieval Britain, the worse the demons and enchantments that linger around natural water, reaching their zenith in the lochs and springs of the Picts. Once thought of as exotic and unconnected to any other culture or race in Europe, the Picts are now far better understood to be just another part of the tribal mix of Celtic Britain, with language and customs showing marked similarities to their counterparts further south. But with one important difference: the Romans never made it this far north. What seems to be preserved as late as the seventh century in northern and eastern Scotland is a remarkably intact relic of Iron Age culture, scarcely touched by imperial influence. The Romans were keen on water cults, as their intense activity at Bath alone reminds us, which perhaps helped to calm the aquatic spirits to the south. But further north the old stories lingered long and deep in the landscape. One of many curious facts that modern science presents to us about the peoples of Iron Age Britain is that they hardly ate any fish, despite the natural abundance.[22] It would hardly be the first time in history that customs surrounding food and diet were affected by religious beliefs, if we infer that is the case here.

The most far-flung bathing site I have entered is the sacred lake of St Tredwell on Papa Westray, in the north of Orkney's archipelago. Documentary evidence about St Tredwell, or Triduana in her Latin form, is late and rather colourful, perhaps pointing to a hermit who lived here, blinding herself in order to avoid an unwanted match with an insistent king. Yet cult activity around the lake itself is real enough, causing much anguish to Presbyterian ministers as late as the seventeenth century for the crowds of pilgrims performing their devotions around its shores. I'm not sure what the kirk today would make of my family's own Orthodox–Anglican ecumenical pilgrimage to these holy waters, when I briefly stripped and bathed in St Tredwell's healing waters. It was late October and we were visiting the islands for the annual storytelling festival at Kirkwall Cathedral, taking a day off to enjoy our own revival of this ancient landscape tale. Even though it was grey and somewhat breezy, my brief encounter with these chilly waters was a memorable and wholesome way to connect with medieval ritual, and it occurred to me that this peaceful spot is one of the few ancient places in the north where Celtic legend makes no reference to monsters, being a site of healing rather than harm. If nothing else it draws attention to the torrid zone below Orkney and above mainland Europe where something lethal lurked in the waters that required missionaries to draw deep into the reserves of Christian ritual to shore up their claims of a single Creator God able to operate across all levels of creation.

Perhaps up in the other-worldly archipelago above Scotland's northern tip the fury of the demons had burned itself out under hardy Scandinavian influence, testament to Orkney's rich heritage of cultures and traditions that sets it apart from the main. As I waded into Tredwell's lake a goose flew out of the reeds behind me and the sun broke through the cloud in a stream of rays, at the precise moment that my wife Anna's camera phone decided to turn itself off. It has possibly saved you a front cover showing what looks like (but wasn't) the most airbrushed photo ever. Papa Westray is known for being connected to its neighbouring island by the world's shortest scheduled flight, which takes about two minutes, yet for all that some essence here remains elusive. Near and far, the island is something of a time capsule of unspoilt spiritual wilderness, a haven for nature lovers and souls in search of a cure.[23]

A ritual of reconciliation

Liberating the rivers, lakes and coast of Britain was a task of the utmost priority for Britain's northerly saints. It is remarkable how much attention Columba pays to the landscape during his travels to Pictland, particularly so given the fact that his main *Life* hardly ever mentions that he converted any of the people. The chapter preceding the story of the cursed well includes one of the few descriptions of actual baptism in mainland Scotland, a much more conventional application for holy water in Christian tradition. At first sight the powerful and effective rituals being conducted by missionary leaders seem an odd assortment of actions: exorcisms directed at the water, crucifixions on the waves, immersions surrounded by prayer and singing, and above all the bizarre spectacle of two otters coming and 'ministering' to Cuthbert after he had bathed in the sea by wiping and drying his feet. Somehow all these many activities were being deployed successfully to redeem the land and the waters for Christ, suggesting Christian ritual of the most profound symbolism and power attached to these meaningful actions, employed in a systematic way as a multi-pronged assault on the monsters of the deep. It is the sea otters to whom I owe the biggest debt of thanks for finally revealing just how systematic this campaign was. It was already clear to me that Cuthbert was on a mission of conversion as he moved into the land of the Picts, a mission of mass baptism, and it seems that extended to the environment as well as the people. The next few sections of this chapter wade into the depths that make up the early Christian view of creation and the Creator, before emerging back on to the shore with a fresh understanding of what devotional bathing really embodies.

As noted, the foot washing and drying is interpreted by modern scholars as a recapitulation of the monastic service of hospitality. And yet I remembered reading a comment that 'Celtic' baptismal liturgy of this period had one particularly unusual feature that was eventually phased out: part of the baptismal sacrament was a ritual washing and drying of the feet. When I started to look into this tiny clue, connections and patterns started to tumble out one after the other, and my collection of strange bathing rituals began to make sense in a far bigger framework than I had realized. It was rather like spotting a small bump in the ceiling and poking it with a screwdriver, only for the entire ceiling to collapse, along with several bathloads of water. We need to go quite deep into the theological plumbing of some primary Christian ritual to figure out the source of all this, but there are fundamental issues at stake and they do end up mapping directly on to the intense Celtic relationship with nature.

And so I turned to this baptismal text with its unusual foot-washing conclusion to the immersion, a precious early document known as the *Stowe Missal*. This missal definitely deserves the name 'Celtic' because it includes some Gaelic text, and dates from perhaps the eighth century. But I soon discovered that this is just one of many manuals for church liturgy in early medieval northern Europe that include this strange addition to the sacrament of baptism. It even has a technical name for it: the *pedilavium*, a ritual that is nowadays associated with Maundy Thursday in the church. Yet for a brief period in northern Europe it played a major role in concluding the ritual of baptism. Here was a liturgical shape that made particularly good sense in the context of Cuthbert's mission to baptize the people of northern Britain, first entering the sea and then concluding with a foot washing in order to demonstrate the full cosmological power of the Christian ritual of entry into the church.

Across northern Europe as a whole, the five surviving liturgical texts of this period and region, of which the *Stowe Missal* is one, consistently demonstrate that foot washing had a central place at the conclusion of the baptism, and not just in Celtic lands. Foot washing served many functions, revealing Christian truths such as hospitality, service and humility, but its most potent liturgical context in northern Europe was as part and parcel of the main ritual of initiation into the church. I needed to understand how that arose, and when I looked into the topic further I discovered it could be traced back to the work of just one prominent bishop in Late Antique Europe: St Ambrose of Milan. His theological fingerprints are all over the many surviving baptismal liturgies that include foot washing, because he wrote two treatises which set out directly his reasoning for including it.[24] It turned out that this foot-washing innovation was not a mere embellishment to the ceremony, and was far more than a polite way of ushering a new baptismal candidate into the warmth of the church. Rather Ambrose built extraordinarily powerful significance into this part of his baptismal service. The immersion in the font, he explained, was conducted in order to wash away your own personal sins, built up in time over the course of any ordinary life. But the foot washing was designed to cleanse something rather more significant and stubborn still: it was the only part of the liturgy that washed away your original sin. Claiming that this inherited sin had first entered Adam and Eve through the serpent's attack on the heel of humans (Genesis 3.15), an embodied reading of spiritual texts if ever there were one, Ambrose argued that only washing the feet could remove it. Furthermore, he went on to explain, this stain of original sin had been removed when Jesus performed his foot washing on the Apostles shortly before his arrest after the Last Supper (John 13.14–17). It was therefore an essential counterpart to the immersion baptism pioneered by John in the River Jordan.

Ambrose does have a point: nowhere in any of the Gospels or other New Testament literature does it even hint that the Apostles underwent any form of baptism, at least not of the kind dispensed by John the Baptist. A few decades before Ambrose added it to the baptismal liturgy, one church father had made the connection between these two applications of baptism: 'our Saviour washed the feet of his disciples on Passover night, which is the mystery of baptism. For you know, Beloved, that the Saviour gave the true baptism on this night.'[25] It was Ambrose who found a plausible explanation for why the New Testament contained twin ritual washings. For Augustine, who was himself baptized by Ambrose, this foot-washing ritual was quite literally a step too far away from the font.[26] He was worried that Ambrose had destabilized the centre of gravity away from the font in baptismal liturgy. Given what I have discovered about Celtic baptismal practice through my own immersion in this topic, I have a feeling that Augustine might well be right.

Ambrose had separated the primary cause (original sin) from the mundane consequences (personal sins), offering a dual nature to sin, and two different if closely connected rituals for dealing with them. Augustine believed this opened up a dangerous chasm in theological argument, particularly as it threatened the enormous amount of store he placed on the overriding significance of original sin to determine every aspect of an individual's spiritual destiny, including their own personal sins. Ambrose himself acknowledged that his ritual of foot washing was not practised in Rome, hinting that this was already a point of disagreement in his day.[27] After Ambrose died in 397, Augustine was as diplomatic as he could be in trying to undo this one specific innovation of his former mentor.

The anonymous monk of Lindisfarne seemed to be recording a decidedly partial form of ritual immersion when he described Cuthbert's night by the sea, bathing only his legs and then following up with a ceremonial foot drying. It was more than a little curious that the Roman-facing Bede had chosen to change these seemingly mundane details to push Cuthbert all the way into the sea, the disappearance of the loincloth a clear indication of the intention to go fully into the water. Nudity was a liturgical requirement for entering the font in the early church, something that causes considerable angst to one or two modern scholars but a detail that is supported by unambiguous evidence.[28] It is clearly not necessary for a foot-washing ritual, however. With this in the back of my mind, I felt I had just enough to suggest that there were vague shapes of the Ambrosian baptismal liturgy visible in this example of a Celtic bathing ritual, an interesting but not exactly conclusive connection.

The creature of water

While reading these early liturgical texts I also spotted that there was an interesting precedent for the other great Celtic wilderness rituals that so shaped the stories of the north – exorcism directed at natural bodies of water – because the font itself underwent an exorcism before being used to baptize. The ritual that the northern saints were directing at spirits in the lakes, rivers and sea turns out to be another part of formal baptismal liturgy that was being greatly extended, repurposed as a means of redeeming the landscape itself. The language of the ritual lent itself to such cosmological reach, referring to the contents of the font as the 'creature of water', and acknowledging its capacity to act as a habitat for evil spirits. This exorcism would also be accompanied by anointing the font by pouring consecrated oil on it, a detail that appears in all five of the surviving northern European liturgies, the family of texts mentioned above.[29] This seems to be a direct precedent for the celebrated ritual Germanus had performed on the North Sea in 429, pouring oil to quell a storm whipped up by demons. If anything justifies my rather in-depth examination of the fundamentals of baptism here, it is the notion that a bishop from Gaul somehow managed to turn the North Sea into one vast baptismal font. The island of Britain was permanently changed as a result.

And so it seems that exorcism directed at water and foot washing are two signatures of formal baptismal practice of the period that had been repurposed and extended into the most evocative Celtic wilderness rituals, conceived in the widest cosmological scale possible. When I was writing all this up, I began to wonder whether it would be possible to trace back the history of this curious exorcism of the baptismal waters, partly out of simple curiosity but partly because it did not seem to fit any of the biblical descriptions of John's baptisms in the Jordan. Someone must have invented it, and it did not take me long before I tracked down the person responsible: Ambrose of Milan.

'For as soon as the priest enters,' Ambrose wrote of his procedure for preparing a font, 'he makes an exorcism over the creature of water, afterwards he offers an invocation and a prayer, that the font may be consecrated.'[30] Ambrose's decision to direct exorcism towards what might be considered an inanimate object, water, is a remarkable liturgical turn when considered in its historical context. As described in the previous chapter, it was the general rule in the early European church that exorcism was directed towards people. There were blessings of baptismal water before Ambrose, but nowhere have I found any precedent for this remarkable innovation of a font exorcism.

At this point very curious indeed as to what else Ambrose had written about the baptismal liturgy, I sat down to read his works on baptismal theology and practice carefully, and it took about two minutes before I spotted a third idiosyncratic dimension that might by now seem rather familiar. Woven through all his imagery of the font and the experience of immersion there is one word that stands out above all others: he describes entering the water in terms of a crucifixion. And not just a metaphorical one either, since Ambrose says the priest should even physically dip a cross in the font water as part of the preparations. Furthermore, he goes on to alter the three main credal statements of faith in the Trinity, the fundamental building blocks of the Christian religion, with a unique addition to the second statement: 'Do you believe in God the Father almighty . . . Do you believe in our Lord Jesus Christ *and in his cross* . . . Do you believe also in the Holy Spirit?'[31]

Having worked out independently that Celtic water rituals were notable for three strange and seemingly unconnected ritual patterns – exorcism of natural water, crucifixion imagery, and foot washing – I was therefore more than a little surprised to discover that these are precisely the three innovations that Ambrose had introduced into his baptismal liturgy in Milan many hundreds of miles to the south. All three of them also disappeared from baptismal practice over the course of the following centuries. At the point when Celtic Christian missionaries were starting to find their way through the landscapes of Britain, it was Ambrosian liturgy that dominated north of the Alps, and I think I have identified fragments of it all over the rituals that the missionaries pushed out before them to cleanse and rehabilitate the landscape.[32]

The only component missing in fitting these two together is how and why Ambrosian theology found its way across the English Channel at a sensitive point in the genesis of Celtic Christianity. There are so many parallels it seems impossible to dismiss them all as coincidence. And there is no reason to in any case. Just because Augustine's single-minded focus on the font and on original sin came to dominate European Christianity later on, it is a mistake to look back and see everything through the filter of his very sharply delineated theology. In fact it would be more surprising if Ambrosian liturgy had not found its way to Britain in the early fifth century, since for a short period of history all of northern European church ritual was far more influenced by Ambrose of Milan than it was by his counterpart in Rome. This happens to be the same period when Celtic practices were first starting to emerge, a coincidence that merits more than a second glance. Augustine was still alive at the time the first shoots of Celtic Christianity were emerging in sub-Roman Britain, with the mission of St Ninian to the Picts around the year 400 and the early church's struggles following the collapse of imperial rule. It was into this volatile, transitional milieu that Germanus arrived in 429, which is coincidentally the year that Augustine died.

As far as I can tell, it was this mission of Germanus that appears to have encouraged the first impulses of Celtic Christian culture towards the natural world. It was he who cast oil on the demon-infested waves surrounding Britain, and as we have already seen in the chapter on sacred trees, he harnessed the spiritual power of the British landscape to provide a platform for delicate negotiations. It would be no surprise to find that this bishop of Auxerre had come prepared with a missionary strategy to shore up the British church, and no surprise either to find suggestions that he was steeped in Ambrosian theology and church practice. He visited Milan personally, and the latest translation of his *Life* suggests in a footnote that he went to that city in June 428, a mere nine months before his departure for Britain.[33] We do not know much more than that, but it does draw attention to the fact that the British mission would have required considerable planning, and not just from a logistical point of view. The Pelagian heresy in Britain was a serious threat to Roman Christianity, and as evidence from patristic writers further south abundantly indicates had a substantial intellectual pedigree. Germanus had to go equipped theologically and liturgically to deal with the challenges, and it bears repeating here that a large component of the Pelagian heresy was a denial of original sin.

As has already been demonstrated, Celtic nature rituals rested on the notion that there had once been a 'first creation', a state of harmony in the cosmos that was shattered at the moment of the Fall, the original sin of Adam and Eve. It seems no coincidence therefore that the Celtic Christians also adopted an unusually intense focus on the foot-washing aspect of baptism and devotional bathing: this was the one part of the liturgy that was designed around the notion of original sin. Ambrose argued that foot washing had been instituted by Jesus Christ himself as a means of washing away the fault inherited from Adam and Eve, which is as robust a defence of the concept as you are likely to find. Whether or not Celtic Christians were deliberately using foot washing as another tool in their attack on Pelagianism is difficult to say, given the lack of direct evidence. It certainly adds to the impression that Celtic theology was not in any way Pelagian, and that it might have developed some of its quirkier traits as a way of countering the heresy. Either way, it is not hard to see evidence of a missionary strategy in the creative use of Ambrosian liturgy and the demonstrations of spiritual power over the natural world, even if the specific target of this mission remains a little hazy. Pagans and Pelagians alike would both be challenged in a campaign based on undoing the environmental damage of original sin. In all honesty we can only guess at the target of this missionary campaign, because we are only hearing the mainstream church's response to a voice or voices that have not been documented in their own words. If I had to hazard my own guess, I would say that the response was designed to encompass both: spectacular nature interventions and promises of benevolence to gain attention from the common folk, and a more abstracted theological argument about original sin to deal with any lingering Pelagian sympathies.

A cosmological bath

As a few drops of room temperature water splash over the head of a baby undergoing baptism in our local church, it is a little difficult to gain a sense of the terms in which this ritual was originally framed and conceived by the first Christians to perform it. Today the comfort and speed of the liturgy is a concise and gentle way to introduce a young baby into the family of the faithful, with little if any hint of the realignment of the cosmos quietly taking place in the background.

The vast significance of this ritual hangs in large part on one of the biggest riddles that confronted the early church: why did Jesus undergo baptism? The Son of God was born without sin, and yet he willingly submitted to a ritual of repentance and cleansing conducted by a human being, John the Baptist. Or at least he did if you read Mark's Gospel, the first account to be written. By the time you get to Matthew's and Luke's versions, Christians had spotted the problem with this, and both accounts add in details that John tried to put Jesus off, saying he was unworthy to perform the ritual. If you read the last version, John's Gospel, it rather artfully avoids mentioning Jesus' baptism at all. Early church writers were soon to explain that the descent of Jesus into the River Jordan was not actually performed for his benefit or purification, but rather for our benefit, to sanctify the element of water for our own baptisms. Correspondences were found between Christ's original role in the making of creation, when the spirit hovered over the waters of primal chaos, and Jesus' descent into this creation as a fully embodied part of it. Needless to say they did not miss the fact that a bird appeared to fly over the water both times, coming to rest on Christ at this recapitulation of the original creation. The baptism of Jesus was a cosmological event, purifying the physical element, the Creator entering fully into his creation and sanctifying it with incarnated grace, undoing the debilitating effects that human sin had wreaked upon the cosmos. The entry of Christ into the Jordan was nothing less than the inauguration of a new creation.[34]

All of this might sound rather far removed from an individual baptismal event, but this was precisely the language in which the ritual was framed, and Celtic Christians lit up their understanding of the significance of the moment with a kaleidoscope of biblical events. The *Stowe Missal* describes the priest invoking all manner of aquatic mysteries over the newly exorcized 'creature of water' in the font: the waters of chaos at creation, the Flood, the rivers flowing out of Eden, and Jesus turning water into wine, undergoing baptism, and pouring water and blood from his side at his crucifixion. It is only surprising that this most Celtic of all early baptismal liturgies fails to dwell on the imagery of rebirth despite its focus on a new creation, a point to be resumed below. Related texts from mainland Europe such as the *Bobbio Missal*, which is identical in many regards, adds this line: 'there may come forth from the unspotted womb of the divine font a heavenly offspring.'[35] Across the early church generally the notion of rebirth was seen not merely as a nice metaphor or parable but a physically embodied reality. One of the first early church fathers to produce major writings on baptism, St John Chrysostom, rejects the idea that the baptism is merely a place for the remission of sins; rather it is a bodily recreation, akin to the making of Adam out of earth. This is not a rinsing or a washing but a regeneration.[36] Chrysostom and others were also entirely clear that this rebirth had to be signified bodily and physically enacted, developing a brief mystagogy around the requirement for nudity in the font. Cyril of Jerusalem seemed positively delighted at the innocence of it: 'O wonderous thing! ye were naked in the sight of all, and were not ashamed.'[37] Nudity was mentioned as a strict baptismal requirement in some of the earliest surviving descriptions, the *Apostolic Tradition* of 215 further stipulating that all jewellery and hair fastenings had to be removed along with clothes: 'Let no-one take any alien object down into the water.'[38]

The water in the font was recognized as the waters of creation and of scriptural history, harking back not just to the baptism of Christ but also to the making of the cosmos at the dawn of history, and specifically the making of the first man, Adam. The human body was not an object in this sacrament but a subject; it did not simply have things done to it, but it took part, had meaning and purpose, agency, sensation and experience.

None of this is likely to find any parallels in modern Christianity, and even scholars have been working to draw a veil over such early baptismal proceedings. It might seem a bit of a niche preoccupation, but for reasons that will become clear this modern discomfort over baptismal practice might well echo a discomfort during the Celtic era too. One short article is quoted repeatedly by academic texts now, in an attempt to claim that 'naked' in all these baptismal rituals meant wearing some form of light clothing. I am certain this is incorrect. The writer Laurie Guy does at least reveal what seems to be his main motivation for such an ambitious rewriting of history, since he is incredulous that a male priest would baptize a naked female candidate, and also perhaps more tellingly attempts to downplay the possible role of women deacons administering the sacrament of baptism. The notion that the baptismal ritual needed to be altered from verbal prescriptions in order to accommodate a gendered division between men and women is, to put it mildly, absurd. Yet in Guy's argument there is a chasm, a fault line running so deep through creation that even God's purpose is unable to bridge it, and is required to work around human sensibility and cultural preferences. But this article is little more than a victory for wishful thinking over the unambiguous historical records, collapsing under the most cursory scrutiny. He claims that the 'best pointer' to the matter of baptismal clothing is that John Chrysostom refers to the candidates wearing a single robe at their exorcism, which takes place just before their immersion.[39] And indeed I am sure they did, since standing around in a room with no clothes on to be exorcized would have little symbolic resonance. Looking at another of the treatises that Chrysostom wrote about baptism, a more detailed one in fact, we can find out very easily what happened to this single item of clothing immediately after the exorcism concluded: 'After stripping you of your robe, the priest himself leads you down into the flowing waters. But why naked? He reminds you of your former nakedness, when you were in Paradise and you were not ashamed.'[40] It is unarguable that the candidates were baptized wearing nothing. Guy's article stands and will be quoted for all time in academic texts, creation and the historical record alike diminished and divided by the sensibilities and prejudices of modern-day shame and inhibition, but it is flawed beyond measure.

Nakedness is one of very few universal elements of the human condition, one of the visceral materials used to reconstruct this book's immersion in Celtic practice. Like hunger, sleep and cold it is part of the raw daily life of the hermit, and deliberately so. These practices have been erased from the landscape as the stuff of devotions, and now it seems they are being erased from the page too, for reasons that are hardly commendable or inspiring.

Baptism was a physically enacted rebirth, and it required the candidate to wear their original birthday suit accordingly. I believe that this is at the heart of the difference between Celtic and Roman baptism, and that it shapes the two very different bathing rituals that I have recreated from the Celtic era.

Foot or font

All of this serves to further highlight the fact that Ambrose's theology and practice of baptism were innovative in their focus on crucifixion and curious avoidance of any womb or rebirth imagery, and indeed without reference to remaking the condition of Adam found so often elsewhere. The Roman church never adopted Ambrose's foot washing in a baptismal context, as he says himself, and his very narrow interpretation of font immersion as a form of crucifixion gradually fell out of favour too. Yet in the early decades of Celtic Christianity it seems that Ambrose's language and ritual specifications had been firmly planted in the religious culture. When Roman missionaries arrived in 597 with a plan to regularize the churches in Britain, they came up against a major deviation in baptismal procedure, and it is my view that this was in large part caused by the enduring legacy of Ambrosian custom. The idea that a theological dispute between Ambrose and Augustine should be discovered two centuries later eddying in the far-flung waters of northern Europe might sound a little unlikely, but cultural expressions of faith run deep and long through human history.

There is just one very short description of this baptismal dispute between the Roman mission, led by St Augustine of Canterbury, and Celtic Christians. Augustine says he is happy to accept all other peculiarities of British custom, but draws three red lines. This is what Bede records:

> If you are willing to submit to me in three points, we will gladly tolerate all else that you do, even though it is contrary to our customs. The three points are: to keep Easter at the proper time; to complete the sacrament of baptism, whereby we are born again to God, according to the rites of the holy Roman and apostolic Church; and to preach the word of the Lord to the English people in fellowship with us.[41]

All attempts to figure out the precise nature of this baptismal dispute have focused on the word 'complete', and the consensus among scholars is that it relates to the omission of consecration at the end, the confirmation of the candidates by a bishop.[42] But the evidence for this seems very weak, not least because Bede could simply have said so directly. The early *Life of St Samson* indicates twice that bishops did actually perform this confirmation in Britain, while the pope himself had only recently issued a concession to the church in Sardinia, allowing deacons to perform the confirmation rather than bishops.[43] And I have never found any text of this period that uses the word 'complete' to describe the conclusion of the baptismal service with a confirmation: Samson's *Life* uses the word *adimplere*, fulfil, while numerous other examples use the word *perfectio*.[44]

I think there is another term in Bede's little summary that stands out just as much: 'born again'. For one thing it seems rather superfluous to add in the fact that baptism means being born again, since Jesus himself draws attention to it (John 3.3–5). It was also a point that was universally acknowledged by all the early writers who discussed the theological implications of baptism, cited as early as the second century by the Christian writer Justin the Martyr.[45] Cyprian, Ephrem the Syrian and Augustine of Hippo all spoke of the font as a womb for the candidate to be reborn, baptism universally described in terms of a second birth – with one exception: Ambrose. Despite the fact that he wrote two of the longest surviving treatises on baptism in the early church, at no point does he describe the font as a womb, and nor does he even allude to this notion. Rather, for him the font is a tomb and above all else a place of crucifixion: 'Consider where you are baptised. What source can there be for baptism, save the cross of Christ, the death of Christ?'[46]

I could fill this book with ever more detailed and – I'll be honest about this – more tedious points of evidence about the deviation in Celtic baptismal practice. I am pretty convinced that the problem was an over-reliance on the foot-washing part of the ritual as developed by Ambrose, which allowed the various British converts to avoid a full immersion in a font. I'll give just one final piece of evidence that Bede's comment alludes to Celtic reluctance to go for a full-bodied soaking, which is the same word 'complete' that other scholars have seized upon. Having read more than enough early baptismal texts to keep me entertained for a lifetime, I could find nowhere that uses this word in the context of confirmation, as mentioned. But I did find the word used once in a liturgical text arising from Roman custom, a document known as the *Gelasian Sacramentary*. This was written during the years that Bede himself was active, and other scholars have noted that it appears to reflect Bede's understanding of church ritual in other contexts.[47] Here is what it says about baptism:

> You must believe that the resurrection, which in Christ became a fact, must be *completed* in us all, that what started in the Head shall follow in the whole body. Moreover, the very sacrament of baptism which you are to receive expresses the form of this hope.[48]

Here we have the word 'complete' used in conjunction with the phrase *toto corpore*, 'the whole body'.

All the evidence I can find, from every angle, suggests that the native Britons of various tribes had a peculiar set of inhibitions about natural water. The tales of monsters, poisons, storms and infestations of demons would be enough to give any reasonable person pause for thought before wading into the murky depths of the Celtic landscape. The bathing rituals I have put together seem to suggest precisely the same thing: a half-hearted Celtic dip compared to the full-bodied Roman plunge. Far from being a place of healing and rebirth, we see water as a place of danger and physical hardship, crucifixion, endurance and a very limited form of immersion in the Celtic texts.[49] For Bede and others of the Roman party, baptism meant stripping off and wading with full-bodied enthusiasm into the water. It would be entirely understandable that Bede was reluctant to mention it, his discretion about nude bathing already evident in his description of the preferred arrangements at Bath. Apart from that, it would also be rather difficult to reject out of hand the practice of foot-washing, given that it had biblical authority and an honoured place in the baptismal theology of Ambrose. Bede's reluctance to say all this clearly might well arise from the fact that baptism meant stripping off and entering the font without reservation or inhibition, possibly in mixed company. Certainly this book has shown on numerous occasions and in many contexts that there is a powerful instinct to hide the stark reality of the naked body, particularly in a religious context. There is a reason why I have compiled all this evidence when attempting to go back to the physical reality of a spiritual connection to nature: it demonstrates an aversion to the human body so deep seated it is almost undetectable, accepted uncritically even in modern scholarship. To put it another way, Bede would not have been the first or the last person to be shy about acknowledging let alone demanding baptismal nudity for a full-bodied immersion.

I will finish this point by leaving Bede to one side and turning to one of his contemporaries, the fiery bishop, St Wilfrid. Originally a Celtic Christian himself, he switched to Roman practice and became one of the fiercest critics of his former traditions. He even took the lead at the set-piece confrontation known as the Synod of Whitby in 664, which sought to stamp out the wayward practices promoted by the monastery of Iona concerning the date of Easter and other ecclesiastical matters. Wilfrid, the most vehemently anti-Celtic campaigner of his day, also used to take time out from his attacks on non-Roman practice by going in for a ritual form of bathing. His hagiographer Eddius Stephanus leaves us in no doubt as to the symbolism of this nightly bath: 'He kept his body, as he testified before the faithful, pure from his mother's womb, and unspotted, for he made it his custom to wash it during the night hours, winter and summer alike, with blessed and holy water.'[50] Wilfrid's bathing is starkly described as a rebirth, Stephanus taking great care to emphasize this point with an arresting and bodily allusion, eliding Wilfrid's post-immersion state with the innocence of a newborn baby. He even goes so far as to invoke the bishop's own birth mother and her womb to explain the purpose of this very Roman devotion. One thing I will say about this arresting and rather detailed description of devotional bathing is that it is impossible to imagine any crucifixion posture taking place in such an intense evocation of rebirth. There was certainly no loincloth involved. Women are frustratingly absent from the written historical record of this period, but this wholly positive reference to motherhood is one of those chinks of light that shines through the gaps and gives considerable pause for thought.

Turning blue

If the terrors lurking in Britain's waterways were even half as bad as the scene described by early Christian missionary reports, then one can sympathize with the people for any reluctance to wade in and celebrate the regenerative power of water. But that is not to say the Picts and their neighbours were inhibited about stripping off generally. Indeed, one of the curious and consistent criticisms levelled at them was over their lack of shame about nudity. Gildas, the British monk, described the Picts as 'readier to cover their villainous faces with hair than their private parts and neighbouring regions with clothes'.[51] This is probably the nearest you will get to a sixth-century joke. But there was nothing funny about the nudity of British tribes when the Roman legionaries first encountered their opponents charging at them wearing little more than a light coating of blue woad. Numerous references to the British, and particularly Pictish, practice of going into battle naked have been compiled by modern scholars, which also tie in with the frequent depiction of naked warriors on monumental carved stones, some produced by Romans but some also produced by the Picts themselves, indicating that it was not mere propaganda. It is hard to believe that running into battle in your birthday suit offers any genuine tactical advantage, although if it does perhaps modern warfare will rediscover it. All of which tends to suggest that the northern Britons believed that the skin itself had some sort of magical properties, perhaps linked in some way to the bodily decorations that give them their name: *pictus* means 'painted'.

In summary we know virtually nothing from the written record about the beliefs and ritual practices of the ancient Britons. But we do know about this frequently observed habit of decorating their skin and also wearing nothing or as little as possible, customs that are almost certainly linked. The colouring on the skin was culturally a form of clothing, every bit as meaningful as any other dress code. Nakedness and body decoration were two sides of the same coin, suggesting that the skin was considered sacred or spiritually significant because of the decorations on it. With that in mind, it seems fair to speculate that this skin decoration was another reason why the people were reluctant to immerse themselves fully in water. A fear of the environment is also a fear for the body. Northern inhibitions about water are both extreme and recorded consistently in all the literature of the Celtic period and before. My conclusion at the end of this study, with rather a lot more in the background, is that bodily fear of the waters of Britain was sufficiently strong to cause a deviation in the ritual of baptism. Leaning heavily on Ambrose rather than Augustine, the ritual of foot washing was a perfect solution for those who would not submerge themselves.

A personal rebirth

Such wonderful tales were woven into the watery places of our landscape. And, as I have discovered, there are such adventures to be had today in reawakening all the many primal rituals and stark bodily sensations to embrace the Celtic elements in their full spiritual glory. Ancient holy wells abound right across Britain, their unceasing flow through the centuries a testament alone to the enduring power of nature lore and affection for the munificence of the land. In the spa town of Buxton in Derbyshire, the natural spring has been venerated as a sacred source since before the Romans came. The Celtic tribe called this naturally warm spring Arnemetia. Then the Romans came and called it Aquae Arnemetia, the waters of Arnemetia. The Christians followed and changed the name Arnemetia to Anne, and the spring became known as St Ann's Well, the mother of the Virgin Mary. Then the shrine was closed down at the Reformation and the spring in Buxton became a health spa. Then spas went out of fashion once we started going to the seaside, and so the water was bottled. And now it is a famous brand, owned by a multinational organization very different from the medieval church, the company Nestlé. The rows of Buxton mineral water bottles on a supermarket shelf might seem a long way from the tribal devotions that once found focus here, yet some things remain even so. We might not call this water 'holy' any more, but spring water is still sold and purchased in vast quantities in Britain, seen as somehow a healthy option, sufficiently so to justify its plastic bottle. Strange as it may sound, the word 'healthy' and the word 'holy' come from the same source in our language, the Saxon word *halig*. Holy, healthy, hale, and even the word 'whole', as in wholesome, all find their origins clustered together, perhaps nowhere better expressed than in these lingering traces of attachment to the most ancient of spiritual elements.

And so I finish with my own devotional bathing experiences, the most recent of which took place the week before I sat down to write this book. It was the newest venue and yet in some ways the oldest of them all. Standing naked in an echoing stone building, immersed up to my waist in a chilly cistern, the flow of a natural spring pounded in my ears as I blinked hard in the candlelit gloom and looked again at the statue before me. In what must be the most Neo-Pagan of all places in Britain, Glastonbury, there is a healing-well centre called the White Spring. It is positively flowing over with all manner of exotic and colourful artefacts and folk expressions of cultic attachment to the goddess of the well. Run by a local trust, it is just a few steps from the sedate and rather drier setting of the Chalice Well.[52]

I first read about the White Spring in *The Guardian*, which noted disdainfully a sign that gave permission for people to bathe naked, and I visited it three days later. Walking into the cavernous hall, it appeared to have only a few tourists wandering around in the darkness, looking somewhat bemused at the tunnels of woven branches that were placed in two of the corners as some sort of ritual bower. I glanced over a collection of votive offerings in front of a statue of the lady of the spring: feathers, twigs, many crystals and a surprising number of prayer beads. Elsewhere is a shrine to St Brigit, the Celtic Christian leader of Ireland who is often claimed to be a thinly disguised pagan goddess, although opinion is divided on the matter.[53] The high ceiling echoed with what sounded like whale music being played as the water thundered unseen into an upper chamber in the far left-hand corner. From there it cascaded down in a series of smaller plunge baths before flowing into the main pool, a large circular basin about four metres across that sits in the centre of this echoing stone building. And then on the other side of the room a young woman walked purposefully towards the tiered chambers, naked as the day she was born, and climbed her way up to the top pool. The ambling tourists seemed scarcely to notice.

Within a couple of minutes others had joined her, including me, and I stepped into the large circular pool trying to remember the fragments of rituals, postures and meanings that flitted through my mind, scrambling to put together some semblance of shape to my devotions. The noise and the tranquillity, the emptiness of the pool and the gathering of visitors in the room seemed a cheerfully curious mix but a world apart from the wilderness silence of my valleys, springs and Celtic shores. It struck me then how very medieval this seemed, a place where inhibitions about both belief and the body were left at the door, a popular and folk expression of piety. Within a minute I found no difficulty in losing myself in the rituals learned over a decade studying ancient devotions at holy wells: the Lord's Prayer, a psalm hymned silently in my head. At the still active Christian bathing site at Holywell in north Wales the custom is to wade (wearing a swimming costume) around the edge of the pool three times while reciting a 'decade' of the rosary, a series of ten prayers that I would imagine consists of ten Hail Marys in a row, perhaps starting with the Lord's Prayer.

Nobody seemed that bothered by the presence of half a dozen naked bathers in the gloom, the families continuing to meander slowly around this mildly diverting scene. In the cascade of pools to my left there were now four young women engaged in some sort of purposeful ritual, one of them reciting before a statue what sounded to me like a Buddhist chant. Beside them an elderly man sat, long white beard tied half-way down in a knot, looking a picture of contentment as the water splashed over his legs, blissfully unaware of any of the comings and goings around him. There was and is no structure to this unmediated space, no religious instruction that shaped any part of its use. It didn't feel intrinsically Pagan or Christian to me, or indeed Buddhist; it was almost a blank currency that lent itself to any number of interpretations and experiences, the raw material from which a faith can be and was being forged. Eventually the chanting women moved en masse into one of the dark side chapels with its bower of branches, pausing neither to dry nor dress, and I went to explore the cascade pools. The top was deep enough to perform what I have learned from my Orthodox other half is a devout immersion ritual often conducted in a hole cut in the Russian ice at Epiphany. Submerging myself three times in the pool beside the thundering flow of water from the spring, pouring from an outflow near the high roof, I emerged to cross myself and stepped down to the lower pool in front of the statue that had seen the Buddhist chanting. As my eyes focused in the gloom I was astonished to make out the features of a traditional Black Madonna, carefully carved and surrounded with flickering tea lights. Remembering the devotions of Holywell I lost myself in a decade of Hail Marys.

At the exit the custodian of the day stopped me to comment that I had seemed particularly in tune with the place, and we paused to exchange thoughts on the holy bodies within. She was Danish and when I told her of my own German roots she conspired with some wry but affectionate comments about English inhibition. There had been little in evidence that afternoon, I pointed out. As for the Black Madonna, she said it had been brought to Glastonbury by a group of women pilgrims from Brazil, who had originally set out with the intention of leaving it on the summit of the Tor. After visiting this spring at the foot of their intended hill they had fallen entirely for its subterranean charms and unanimously decided that the well should be her shrine. And so I found it – this was medieval devotion that at times for me reached heights and touched depths that I have previously only ever found when alone.

As I stepped back into the midsummer heatwave of the street a man wearing only a T-shirt was noisily directing a builder's van out of a tight driveway, while a woman sat topless on the pavement, her eyes closed as she soaked up the sunshine, perhaps one of the devoted bathers I saw earlier. A cheerfully gap-toothed visitor was talking noisily to some tourists at the entrance, the words 'Benefits Cheat' emblazoned on his stained shirt. A police car drove slowly past this scene, the officer looking on with an air of detached bemusement.

The church as an organization has never gone for this sort of unruly cavalcade of bodies and nature, but the holy wells it has redeemed for Christ were always liable to such untidy outpourings of folkish energy.[54] To me it was reminiscent of medieval piety at its most popular, more Geoffrey Chaucer than Thomas Aquinas but no worse for that, and no less holy either. A day's walk from Glastonbury are the ancient sacred waters of Bath, where Bede had suggested that segregated bathing rules should be observed. And nor was he the last churchman to weigh in on the subject either. A similar appeal to the people of Bath can be glimpsed throughout the following millennium, a succession of increasingly exasperated attempts to persuade men and women either to bathe separately or to pop on some form of bathing attire. In 1449, Bishop Thomas Beckington decreed that all bathers above the age of puberty should be 'decorously clad', complaining that locals not only entered the water naked themselves but even forcibly undressed anyone who attempted to use the baths with clothes on. William Turner, in a treatise of 1562, pleaded for the introduction of segregated bathing. A thousand years after Bede somewhat optimistically delineated the locals' bathing habits, John Wood the Elder in the eighteenth century felt moved to fulminate: 'The Baths were like so many Bear Gardens, and Modesty was entirely shut out of them; people of both sexes bathing by day and night naked.'[55]

Mother nature

A world apart from the noise of Glastonbury, tucked in the corner of a field along a river valley in north Wales, lie the shattered remains of one of the strangest well chapels in the country. Hedged around by brambles and ivy, this enclave of timeless spirituality speaks of rituals and devotions all but forgotten, the powers of a holy well harnessed, tamed, channelled into a complex so wrapped around its veneration it once had an indoor bridge, carrying visitors over the flowing stream as they entered the building. A couple of miles from the town of Nant-y-Patrick, this water shrine is known as Ffynnon Fair, the lost remains of a fifteenth-century bathing complex still powered by the same unfailing source that once brought medieval pilgrims to bathe here. A stone well chamber was built to capture the water at its source, a sort of star-shaped pool with seven points that is reminiscent of the still busy bathing site of Holywell, ten miles to the east, which in turn is based on the 'seven-sided' healing pool that Jesus visited at Bethesda. Many early manuscripts of the Bible explain that these waters would be disturbed on occasion, and still others interpret this to be the action of a visiting angel. Others omit such landscape lore. Your version of the Bible could therefore be missing John 5.3b–4, what might be called the 'angelic verses', further testament if any were needed to the power of nature spirituality to disturb the personal prejudices of some believers. Needless to say, Jerome follows up his censorship of the sacred trees of the Old Testament, referred to in Chapter 3 of this book, by cutting these verses about the holy well from his translation of John's Gospel into Latin.

No angel was needed to encourage me to strip and enter this well, which contains about a metre of the clearest spring water. As I lowered myself into its timeless flow I did pause to wonder when the last such unaltered devotions had taken place as I felt for a firm foothold. It was impossible to tell where water ended and the softest of silt began as my feet sank slowly down into unseen depths, eventually coming to rest on an uneven floor of fallen masonry. I emerged with my birthday suit renewed, as St Wilfrid had once boasted, reborn in the womb of living waters so old they can only really be calibrated by the geological formations that first moved them into being, flowing here for millennia as humans and our rituals come and go. This Ffynnon Fair is a Welsh-language well dedicated to St Mary, a twin in some ways to the Black Madonna of Glastonbury, the Mary who made everything new. It was her womb that first broke the chain of transmitted sin, bearing Jesus Christ, the second Adam. If that is the function of a font, to give birth to a neophyte washed clean of hereditary sin, then water can be a vessel every bit as holy as the Blessed Virgin herself. As a starting point for a Christian theology of 'mother nature', early baptismal and bathing ritual in natural water looks fertile indeed.

7

The serpent's lair: harrowing caves

———◆◆◆———

The breath of that dragon, fuming in hot battle, first
came forth from the cave. The earth resounded.
Beowulf, Anglo-Saxon epic poem (c. 700–1000)

At the top end of the Kintyre peninsula in Scotland a single-track road meanders its way along the shores of Loch Caolisport before coming to a dead end at the settlement of Ellary. Signs on the final gate warn that the track from here to the ruins of Castle Sween is unpassable to any vehicle, a hinterland of unspoilt glens and beaches enjoyed by the deer and red squirrels alone. The collection of neatly maintained holiday cottages at the end of this winding journey offers a surprisingly snug and domesticated sight in the middle of such Celtic wilderness. A mile back from Ellary, my intended home for the night promised more or less the exact opposite. A dark chasm in a cliff face known as St Columba's Cave has been the site of veneration since the Middle Ages, and looks scarcely touched since. It lies only a minute's walk from the road, but feels like entering a place abandoned by a world that has moved far onwards, the shattered wall of a medieval chapel looming out of the dense vegetation around its entrance. Britain has many ancient hermit's caves, and for reasons that escape me I decided this ought to be the site of my attempted revival of a vocation that has lain dormant for half a millennium. I had not reckoned on the fact that this place is still animated with powers beyond the realm of human understanding. As I pushed my way through the ferns and tall grasses, an unseen legion of demons awoke and gathered in a silent cloud behind me.

Nobody knows for sure whether Columba himself came here. Early records of his travels make no mention of any cave-dwelling incidents, and he frequently travelled with a large entourage, as much an ambassador for his faith and homeland as he was a pioneering missionary to the people of the Highlands and islands. His life took place entirely inside the sixth century, one of the least documented periods in British and Irish history, and he died in 597 on his monastery island of Iona. But he certainly travelled a lot too, and the cave would easily provide shelter for a lonely vigil or for a dozen or more monks had he passed this way. It is about the size of a large room or indeed a small chapel building, the damp walls slanting diagonally to create a natural arch many metres above head height. I was about to find out what sort of comfort and shelter this cave would have given to anyone who had tried to live here before me.

I heaved my rucksack on to the ground at the cave's black entrance, wondering which area would be most likely to provide a modicum of sleep, when the demons came in for the attack. Midges, by now more of a storm than a cloud, had sensed my passing through the bush and descended on me in a vortex of itching and pinpricks of pain. Later that month I read that 2018 had been a vintage year for midges, and I don't think that was entirely down to my generosity. As my only consolation, none of these biting monsters followed me when I retreated deep into the cave, where the dark rock walls barely reflected any daylight. I was dimly aware of a second, smaller chamber that led from a low opening at the back, and wondered whether anything else lurked unseen in the blackness that was closing in from all sides. You can probably guess which aspect of my naked hermit's night vigil was starting to look doubtful.

Pulling tight the hood of my jacket, I stacked my possessions at the mouth of the cave and set off for a brisk walk along the shore, remembering that humans move faster than midges. I stopped at the head of a deep inlet to take a dip in the chilly loch waters, losing the biting swarm that gathered in the 30 seconds it took me to strip by diving towards the sun-dappled rocks on the bottom, and out into the freedom of the open sea. An island lay just offshore and I wondered whether I could row out to it in my inflatable boat and make that my authentic hermit home instead of the bleak and midge-infested lair behind me in the woods. But then I fell to reflecting on the many hermits' caves I had visited in Britain, 16 so far plus one I couldn't reach because an angry man was cutting down trees on a narrow track and would not let me pass. What hermits did in all these caves was a matter of hard-fought Christian devotion to a higher calling, and I knew that I had no choice but to immerse myself in whatever darkness came my way.

There are many of these atmospheric natural holy sites around Britain should you wish to explore the underworld of early Christian nature rituals, most of them simply open to the elements in the wild as they have always been. But they come with a spiritual as well as a physical warning: it is not all angels and doves when pushing into the wilderness. Many of the hermits' lives talk of caves full of monsters and devils, and the British stories once again chime with those from the East. The first man to found a monastery, St Antony of Egypt, was beaten so badly by demons after descending to live in a subterranean tomb that his friends began to recite a funeral service over his battered body. The following chapter of his life describes another night attack by wild spectres, taking the shape of snakes and lions, wolves, scorpions, leopards and bears.[1] The sixth-century pioneer St Benedict, a Western counterpart to Antony who greatly developed a monastic rule in Europe, went to live in a remote cave in Italy for three years. One day he was distracted in his prayer by a blackbird, which he dismissed with the sign of the cross, then had a vision of a woman he once knew well. Stripping naked, he threw himself into a patch of brambles and nettles and rolled around until all desire had been eviscerated.[2]

So clearly not all the flora and fauna of the hermits' witness in the wilderness have provided acquiescent service to the holy minded. I was at least confident that the red squirrels and deer of this wild shore would heed my desire for solitude, even if the midges were proving thoroughly disrespectful. We have encountered many animals on my journey, the Celtic stories laying down a pattern for a generally harmonious relationship with fellow creatures that certainly reflects my preferred narrative. On caves, however, the evidence is rather more mixed. Which brings us to one of the most striking subterranean stories of all in the early Christian record, that of St Samson of Dol, who entered the lair of a monstrous serpent. He merits a special place in the hearts of all those who love the Welsh and Cornish saints, and indeed for anyone interested in early medieval history generally, because his *Life* is just about the only early record we have for a missionary active on the western side of Britain. So many great names are famed and celebrated as icons of Celtic Christianity in this region, but the textual records were written many centuries later, indeed mostly after the Norman Conquest, when writers had a very good reason for celebrating local heroes over continental ones. But St Samson stands out as the best attested of his generation, his hagiography giving us a rare insight into the ritual preoccupations of a missionary who tackled the challenges of the western landscapes. He ended up dying around the year 565, an old man in the town of Dol in Brittany, where his *Life* was compiled by one of the community. It is clearly based on early material, and could have been set down any time from the early seventh to the early ninth century. If you are interested in Welsh or Cornish saints, this is where your story begins, and thankfully it is a rich and rewarding one, and Celtic to the core with its intense focus on natural features.

Of all the landmarks he visited, it is caves that feature most prominently in Samson's many travels. In fact three of them make an appearance, two in Britain and one in France beside the River Seine. Perhaps there is something of a clue in the fact that he goes to live in the two British caves, but merely evicts a snake from the French one, an indication that they were particularly charged places on this side of the English Channel. The first of Samson's caves is located in a forest near the River Severn, and although his *Life* says it became a site of pilgrimage it has unfortunately left no long-term footprint in the landscape, no place name that identifies it today. Here the saint prayed for a spring of water to bubble up miraculously, which was still flowing by the time the *Life* was written. His fellow monks formed a small monastery in the nearby castle, and would bring him bread each day.

The second cave is where it starts to get truly interesting. I have seen the entrance to it myself, a dark and rather uninviting crevice at the foot of a cliff beside the River Fowey in Cornwall. Up the hill in the village of Golant is a church that still bears a dedication to this heroic saint, the site of an early monastery that St Samson founded once he had sorted out a rather serious problem inside the cave. Samson had already been making waves among the local people by ordering them to destroy a stone idol and resurrecting a boy who died in a horse-riding accident. Realizing that Samson was clearly a man to reckon with, the local chief told him about a giant serpent that lived in this cave and had all but destroyed two villages. Taking the resurrected boy with him, Samson entered its dank lair and through his charisma alone put the fear of God into the snake, which tried to bite its own tail. Grabbing his linen girdle, Samson made a sort of makeshift leash to capture the writhing serpent, which he dragged outside and killed by dashing it against the rocks. So not quite as harmonious as other Celtic animal interactions, and also not that hard to read this story for its allegorical content: the destruction of a standing stone idol and the clearing of the cave together talk of Pagan mythology being overwritten by a new Christian narrative.

The cave itself is easy enough to locate today, but is once again inaccessible to ordinary folk, not because of any serpent but rather a railway line, a seldom-used track that carries wagons full of china clay from Lostwithiel to Fowey. When I visited, a sign warned that a trespasser might be fined £1,000 or killed by the train, a rather modern variant of the sort of spiritual dangers that Samson himself faced. For the second time in his *Life*, the saint moved into this cave while his fellow monks established a monastery nearby, and he again produced another spring of water through his prayers. It would be interesting to know if this cave's holy water source remains active: the author of his *Life* claims once again that it was still flowing in his day. On two occasions, therefore, Samson chose to live in a cave as a hermit even though he had a monastic community a short walk away, which suggests that considerable significance was attached to his ability to inhabit these dark and gloomy places. By way of contrast, the story of Samson's third cave, which is beside the River Seine, has no suggestion that the saint felt the need to move in. He again used his clothing to leash a wild serpent that had been terrorizing the local people, ordering it to cross the river and live under a rock for the rest of its days, but he confined his cave-dwelling exploits to Britain alone.[3]

I kept mulling over the dangers both modern and ancient that attached to the story of St Samson and his forbidding cave as I walked slowly along the edge of Loch Caolisport, wondering briefly if sleeping in the car nearby would give me at least a partial insight into the spirit of St Columba's Cave. But I knew in my heart there was no getting round the fact that the witness of Samson made plain the need to face down our worst fears. The Celtic saints did not inhabit these caves despite the fact that they were terrifying and inhospitable places, but because of it: the worse the cave, the more this witness was necessary. It seems fair to conclude that Samson's mission to the landscape in Britain once again had that peculiar Celtic impulse to demonstrate the power of God to exorcize and redeem all corners of the land and sea, to turn a lethal subterranean space into a place for the living. We will return to this theme later in this chapter: the cave as a place where the grip of death is loosened, where fears are met and conquered. As the light began to fade I turned back towards my home for the night, feeling curiously nostalgic about the time a chainsaw operator blocked my path.

A night in the cave

Once your eyes adjust to the gloom, there are some reassuringly solid monuments to the liberation of St Columba's Cave from malevolent spirits.[4] An altar has been constructed of stone towards the back, set on a natural rock ledge against what is clearly the east side. Those who know about church orientation will recognize the evidence of an authentic devotional layout, since altars are usually placed at the eastern end of a structure. So deeply engrained is this practice it even gives us the word 'orientate', to align something towards the East, towards the Orient. On the altar lay a collection of offerings covered in mould: coins in abundance, crosses made of twigs, dried flowers, burnt-out candleholders and a year-old entrance ticket to a transport museum in Hampshire. I turned it over wondering if someone had left a prayer that I could offer up on their behalf, but was disappointed to find that nothing had been written. You need things to keep you busy as a hermit.

At the back of this seemingly consecrated cave lies the secondary fissure in the rock I had dimly noticed, a crack that leads on to another low chamber, a feature that had haunted my imaginings more than any other. I wondered what beast might live beyond its lair-like entrance, and remembered there was no phone signal anywhere in this area to check the sleeping arrangements of adders. The week before I began this trip I had a dream of demons advancing on me from the darkness of the earth, menacing figures dressed in what seemed to be black catsuits, clearly intent on harm as they padded towards me with arms held high and hands open like a claw. One had leapt from the roof of the cave to land in front of me, hissing with hatred, and I awoke in a cold sweat. I did not want to sleep in a remote cave.

In the dying vestiges of daylight that found its way to the rear of my cavern, I shrugged at the memory of my dreams and remembered once again I had no choice but to get on with things. Crawling my way into this second chamber with a torch, I was determined to shed as much light on this cave as I could by rational means, charting the unfathomable void of my fears. The second chamber finished abruptly in a series of vertical rock formations, the narrow cracks at the rear too small for any serious form of predator. The only monsters that swarmed around my chosen cave were smaller than St Samson's snake, and rather harder to tame.

Place name evidence from further south, in Anglo-Saxon England, suggests there was an association between fissures, hollows and pits in the ground and a colourful array of medieval creatures, including elves, goblins and monsters.[5] If anywhere gave me a chance of spotting such exotic fauna my cave would be it, but none turned up that night – even when a pot of stew was bubbling enticingly over a flame. Later that evening I had just served up my dinner when a fat drop of water fell from the ceiling right into the middle of my plate. All night long the drips fell at regular intervals. Half asleep, they sounded like footsteps. The ground outside was dry, but in the dank gloom of the cave I could see that there was rather more inconvenience to this shelter than was apparent when I was sitting at home planning my trip. I considered putting up a tent inside the cave in order to get some sleep without interruption from the drips falling out of the darkness, but thought that might damage the floor. A hermit could not have slept inside this place without a secondary form of shelter above, or something to lie on, because the ground and walls were covered in black and dark green moulds. At many of the caves I visited, including this one, it was wetter inside than out, and colder too. In theory they might seem like a highly convenient natural dwelling place, but in reality the comforts of caves are few and far between. Shelter from wind and heavy rain would be the only advertisement I could offer for one of these rocky dwelling places.

In the end I compromised and put up my tent at the mouth of the cave. I did spend an hour inside the dark chamber at prayer that evening, after tidying away all my things into a tent firmly zipped up against the midges. It proved no difficulty to lose myself in the silence before the altar, the primary work of the hermit yet again bringing a sense of order and purpose to this otherwise inexplicable gloom. As my eyes slowly adjusted to the subterranean twilight it was just possible to make out a cross carved into the rock above the altar before me. This was once considered the only essential possession for a hermit, and I felt a pang of gratitude for the person who had painted a white outline around it, a little kindness going a long way in such straitened circumstances. It was my last thought before disappearing into my tent and sleeping the night through without dreams.

Peak District pioneers

Cave-dwelling hermits lurk on the margins of early Christianity across the whole of Christendom, self-made outcasts from comfort and community in pursuit of a life stripped of all worldly distractions, of all inessential items. The naked hermit of my book title is a case in point, taking refuge in a cave on the slopes of Mount Sinai and casting off all trappings of human company. But there are many British examples who seem to have followed the vocation with just as much enthusiasm, if usually more clothing, a cluster of intriguing caves in and around the Peak District in particular providing a reminder of this long-abandoned life. Should you wish to experience first hand the setting for such gloomy spirituality there are several sites in the Peaks that preserve these rudimentary dwelling places more or less untouched. The most lonely of all that I have seen is a cave cut into an undercliff shaded by ancient yew trees on Stanton Moor, about a mile to the west of the village of Birchover. It still has a battered, fourteenth-century carving of the crucifixion chiselled into the living rock at one end, the hermit's one vital piece of furniture. To this day the unnamed cave remains isolated, apart from a prehistoric stone circle known as the Nine Ladies a few hundred metres away, the juxtaposition alone hinting at a matrix of landscape rituals and narratives we can only guess at.

The precise role that cave hermits played in the conversion of the various British tribes and their landscape can otherwise only be glimpsed through the limited written records. But it became clear to me that this was not a discipline to be undertaken lightly, and was testimony by itself to the fact that early Christians took their calling seriously. The evidence from St Samson suggests that these sites were contested, places where the light of the saints came to vanquish the darkness that had shadowed the hearts of their converts, and to evict any unfortunate vertebrates that happened to be in the way. As this chapter will go on to explain, caves might also have had a role to play in changing people's attitude towards death. Quite a lot of religious heritage, in other words, is to be found by burrowing deep beneath the Celtic landscape.

In choosing my first cave to sleep in, I was initially tempted to explore one of those that cluster around Derbyshire. It is fairly obvious why the Peak District is so well supplied with holy caverns when compared to somewhere like, say, East Anglia, the crags and cliffs offering a considerably more promising terrain for excavation than the sandy, flat soils of Norfolk and Suffolk. The earliest hermit I managed to find in records from this part of central England is linked to a truly spectacular site known as the Anchor Church, a remote spot near the village of Ingleby. Its name alone is redolent of ancient desert spirituality: 'anchor' refers not to a ship but to an 'anchorite', based on the Greek word *anachōreō*, meaning to withdraw. An anchorite is therefore another word for a hermit, perhaps referring in this instance to a man who leaves almost no trace in the historical record beyond his name: St Hardulph. A twelfth-century text mentions him a few times in passing, a hermit associated with the nearby village of Breedon on the Hill, where an ancient church is dedicated to him. On the other hand, it might not. Some historians believe the St Hardulph in question was not some half-dressed hermit living in obscurity on the margins of society but rather King Eardwulf who ruled Northumbria for 12 years. 'Not to be confused with . . .', as the saying goes.

One thing we can say through all of this baffling and obscure collection of historical records is that the Anchor Church itself is most definitely a solid artefact of early landscape spirituality. It is serenely sited above a backwater tributary connected to the Trent, a riverside cliff face 100 metres in length, carved over many centuries with a series of intriguing chambers, all of which stand open should you wish to explore. The central cave is clearly the one that merits the name church, its design graced with arched windows, vaulted ceilings and even some roughly shaped pillars, a veritable troglodyte cathedral compared to many of Britain's other dank fissures with a holy legend attached. It is certainly one of the most agreeable of the natural dwelling places I have encountered on my long journeys into the wilderness, perhaps rivalled only by St Ninian's Cave in Scotland, which I visit at the end of this chapter. I did not, however, opt to spend a night at the Anchor Church, since it would require lengthy negotiation with a landowner and might well be mistaken as the act of someone driven by desperation. Whether homeless people do ever use this cave is hard to say, but on my second visit there were empty beer cans about the place, relics of a night perhaps less full of contemplation about divine mysteries than a hermit might undertake, although such matters are relative.

Further small dwellings, chambers and caves have been cut into the soft sandstone on either side of the central 'church', perhaps suggesting that more than one anchorite came to live here. When you put two hermits together you don't have a paradox but rather the ingredients for something altogether more substantial: a monastery. The word 'monk' is based on another Greek word meaning 'alone'. A hermit or anchorite might well also be a monk or a nun if he or she has formalized a calling by taking some sort of vow, and the first monasteries began as essentially a community of hermits, opening up two different forms for this most dedicated of callings. It is impossible to date the caves of the Anchor Church back to early medieval times, since they have been so extensively reworked over the centuries, but the historical record just about gets us there. The aforementioned text that refers to a hermit living near Breedon was written in the twelfth century, the *Life of St Modwenna*, an Irish nun who is said to have died at the remarkable age of 130. This rather colourful collection of tales includes the interesting detail that Hardulph's cave was above a river, and indicates that he would have lived sometime in the seventh century. We can get no closer than that to his life and the purpose of his solitary existence.

Another hermit's cave nine miles to the north-east of here was also carved enthusiastically with a sort of crude ecclesiastical design in mind. This single-room chamber now sits on a hillside above the ruins of Dale Abbey, boasting a row of evenly spaced yet entirely mismatching windows and doors. This chamber was never a natural cave, but excavated into a sandstone rock face by a rather determined baker from the city of Derby, inspired to abandon his ovens following a vision of the Blessed Virgin in 1130. The biography of this baker Cornelius offers a suitably scant description of the hermit's daily life, which strikes roughly the sort of downbeat note I would give this vocation:

> He found that the place was a marsh, exceedingly dreadful, and far distant from every habitation of man. And turning himself to the southeast of the place, under the side of the mountain, he cut out for himself in the rock a very small dwelling and an altar turned to the south, which had been preserved to this day, and there, by day and night, he served God in hunger and thirst and cold and nakedness.[6]

Britain's climate is perhaps rather frosty when it comes to the matter of such bodily extremes, particularly the last one. The most widely quoted translation of his Latin life replaces the word 'nakedness' with 'contemplation', another alteration to the historical record that seeks to protect us from any glimpse of bare flesh among our Christian ancestors. Such recoil from the embodied reality of a hermit's calling helps to explain why the ascetic life generally is so veiled in obscurity, but averting our gaze denies us sight of Christianity's full and authentic cultural heritage.

One or two academic writers have mused about the need for a hermit to bother with clothing at all, and come to the conclusion that nakedness does indeed seem to be one of the hallmarks of a solitary life. Karel Innemée's study also proposes an intriguing connection between athletes in biblical times who stripped to compete and Christian ascetics facing their own physical challenges.[7] Several New Testament epistles used such sporting metaphors approvingly, including an extended comparison between athletic events and the Christian life in 1 Corinthians 9.24–27. Hebrews 12.1 talks about the need to 'take off' everything that hinders us in order to run our designated race, a verb used elsewhere in the New Testament to mean undressing. These Jewish epistle writers spoke with disdain about many aspects of Greek and Roman culture, yet were entirely happy when it came to the very bodily imagery of classical athletics. Despite the lack of midges, or snakes for that matter, the caves of Cornelius and St Hardulph felt too public to serve as any sort of modern-day stadium in which I could follow the sport of these finely honed spiritual athletes, even with clothes firmly on.

The four difficulties that Cornelius faced are all connected to physical suffering, to the bodily hardships that living alone in a cave entails: hunger, thirst, cold and nakedness. Finding time for contemplation, the word substituted to hide Cornelius' nakedness, would not be much of a challenge for any hermit, given that this life involves spending 24 hours a day in solitude with nothing much to do. Even I managed hours of contemplation during all of my overnight stays in the wilderness, not that my experiences bear much comparison with true hermits. Where they once ran the spiritual equivalent of a marathon, my efforts have been more of an egg-and-spoon race run by a middle-aged dad at a school sports day. It is taking part that counts, as they say.

If truth be told, I cannot describe the life of a hermit, of anyone who goes into the wilderness driven by a simple love of nature, as any sort of competitive act. It is an absolute, a constant, a fixed experience of universal, even cosmological, significance. There are no winners or losers, there are no better or worse ways of doing it. What I can confirm is that any long-term stay in these dank caverns would have been every bit as hard and physically uncomfortable as medieval writers claim.

Burial and crypts

When I talk, as I often do, of very long narratives etched and embedded in the landscape, no site comes to mind more readily than a small and remote cave in southern Britain, known by the unexciting name of Goat's Hole Cave. Despite its rather modest size and obscure location it is in fact the oldest known site of ritual activity in the whole of Western Europe, a remote sea cliff that is one of the most thought-provoking yet absolutely unadorned places I have ever visited. I spent a morning there entirely alone, and would imagine I was the only person who visited that week, if not that month, so isolated and difficult to find is this sacred spot. It lies on the south coast of the Gower peninsula in south Wales, the path down to it unmarked, and for the last 15 metres across a slanting rock face with little in the way of foot or hand holds. It was here in 1823 that another spiritually minded explorer came to visit, and unearthed an extraordinary ritual burial, one so ancient it involves the skull of a woolly mammoth. The fragments of this burial are not merely very old, they date as far back as thirty-three thousand years.

At the heart of this cave's mystery lies a skeleton, whose body was laid to rest with meticulous attention to detail and a complex array of grave deposits, including shells, necklaces and a variety of ivory rods and rings. Initial confusion about the significance of this extraordinary find is best summed up by the fact that this skeleton, whose body had been covered in red ochre for burial, is known as the Red Lady of Paviland. More recent tests have since established that this red lady was in fact a young man. The ceremonial significance of the red ochre is unknowable, but the grave clearly had symbolic meaning. The skeleton itself is now kept at Oxford

An aquatic pilgrimage: swimming along the river Wey to sit in solitude beside the ruins of Newark Priory, in Surrey

Windows on the soul: the mismatched openings in the rockface above Dale Abbey in Derbyshire embellish the rustic charms of this hermitage, first occupied by the baker Cornelius in 1130

Columba's Cave, Argyll, proved somewhat short of creature comforts during an overnight stay, although the midges of the forest were happy to greet a modern-day hermit

The battered crucifix carved into the rock of the hermit cave near Stanton in Peak, Derbyshire, offers something of a mirror for the ascetic devotions performed by its inhabitant

Light work: St Fillan's Cave in Pittenweem, Fife, has a modern altar to mark the place where a Celtic hermit spent long hours studying Scripture, illuminated by a miraculously glowing left arm

A veritable troglodyte cathedral, the Anchor Church near Ingleby in Derbyshire has been carved into the sandstone above a stretch of the river Trent, a lonely spot even today

Where angels tread: like many prominent landmarks in south-west Britain, Glastonbury Tor has a church dedicated to the archangel St Michael, its ruinous state a reminder of the mix of passions that holy places attract

Perched on a moorland crag outside the village of Roche, Cornwall, this enigmatic ruin is one of many high places dedicated to St Michael, the site of a hermit's cell whose origins are obscure

Heavenly shades: wading into the sea at dawn by St Ninian's Cave, Galloway, marked a fitting if somewhat bracing end to a night experiencing the vivid extremes of hermit life

University, while grave goods from here can be seen in Swansea Museum and the National Museum in Cardiff. The discovery and interpretation of this ritual burial place is in itself a revealing exercise in getting to the heart of the nature and purpose of the cave's holy status. The man who first properly excavated the caves, William Buckland, was both a geologist and a clergyman who believed in the strict Creationist teaching that the earth is no more than six thousand years old. To fit this world view, he simply declared that the burial was that of a Roman-era witch, neatly explaining away the mysterious collection of carvings and charm-like objects buried with 'her'. A slightly more sensitive and informed attitude towards the human story would recognize that this burial demonstrates an unmistakable early belief that something significant needed to be marked at the point of death, that the body needed to be somehow equipped or adorned for an ongoing journey. If the people who buried this man had believed that the individual story ceased at death, then the corpse would have been disposed of without ceremony or possessions.

Although it is entirely off the scale when it comes to interrogating the Celtic conversion period studied in this book, the Red Lady of Paviland does at least act as a reminder of the fundamental question that all religions have been trying to answer since the dawn of time: what happens to us when we die? Around this perennial concern there were narratives that the missionaries would have needed to address in their own day. What of the fate of our ancestors, their potential converts asked, and what of their burial places? What do you even mean when you talk about death and resurrection in the same breath? The presence of a resurrected boy entering St Samson's cave is enough by itself to touch on mortality and its resolution, perhaps something the writer felt moved to include subconsciously. Whatever the pre-Christian hopes and fears about the afterlife, if any, we can be certain that the Christian religion offered a new perspective on it, and addressed its legacy in the landscape.

There is just enough evidence that early Christians sought to engage with pre-Christian burial traditions by disrupting or more accurately adopting and gradually adapting traditional landscape memorials and cemeteries. This is an area for specialist archaeologists rather than a Celtic journeyman, but the few examples scholars have highlighted offer a thought-provoking juxtaposition of church and barrow. Sarah Semple's study of Christian activity at such ancient sites suggests there are signs of a gradual transition and assimilation rather than an abrupt change in burial ritual. Her study of the fluid and shifting patterns of ritual seen at Avebury, from late Roman settlement to the gradually evolving post-Roman and early Christian activity, makes a compelling case for very long-held attachments to the landscape that help communities cohere and work through periods of transition collectively.[8] Stone circles, dolmens and standing stones almost never appear in early medieval Christian writings, but they must have been hard to avoid on a practical, everyday level. Avebury is famous for its vast configurations of monoliths, an entire village sitting inside its earthworks. Early Christian missionaries were sometimes keen to associate their early churches and burial sites with Roman remains, no doubt happy to take some reflected glory from these grand imperial structures. Examples can be seen at the former Roman forts of Burgh Castle in Norfolk and Holyhead in Anglesey. Although early Christian writings very rarely mention the great monolith complexes of Britain, they were and are dominant in the landscape.

The beliefs and technology of the henge builders had of course been entirely forgotten for thousands of years by the time Christian missionaries arrived. Yet the practice of using monumental stones remains another enduring pattern of communal activity. It is just possible to discern that certain landmark rocks and stones were adopted and used in some way to serve a cult of ancestors. The standing stone carved with an idol that St Samson ordered to be smashed was used by the Pagan folk to conduct a public performance. His hagiographer, a monk in Gaul perhaps more used to classical descriptions of Paganism than British rituals, compared the performance to the Bacchanalia, the drunken festival dances of ancient Rome. But the tribal chief in question was reluctant to give up his idol, saying that it was used to 'celebrate the mysteries of their ancestors in a play'.[9]

It is just possible – but only just – to speculate whether Paganism had a sense of the spiritual so deeply embedded in the physical world that the inanimate world of rocks, caves, mountains, hills and even rivers signified death, as Gildas' formula for pre-Christian cult activity records, whereas the animate world signified life. Certainly the glimpses we have seen of the role of trees and groves in pre-Christian negotiation suggest to me that they might have been places to preserve the living. I think that both Paganism and Christianity, in its early days at least, shared rich traditions in which spiritual energy tended to find physical expression, in the idea that materials have an inherent sense of the sacred about them. Although the missionary Boniface chopped down a sacred oak tree in Germany to overthrow a Pagan cult, there is a suggestion that he did at least respect the significance of the timber, as if the wood itself were some sort of battery carrying a spiritual charge, because he used it to build a church. The

Penitential of Theodore, written around the year 700, stipulates that wood from a demolished church must only be reused in another church or religious community's building. If no suitable reclamation can be found, the wood must be burned rather than given over to lay purposes.[10]

Whatever the complex beliefs that are hinted at in so many intriguing ways, it was clear from going underground during my own brief experiences of cave dwelling that it felt very much like a descent into an otherworld, where the abundant life forms of the surface rapidly fade to nothing. From ferns to moss, then mould to bare rock, the dwindling of light and life are acutely felt when you stop to dwell here. As Samson's story touches on, there are tantalizing suggestions of subterranean stories and associations with places of death. And it was here beneath the surface that Christians had something rather dramatic to demonstrate about the power of their faith over the grave itself. In one of the most striking innovations of the conversion period, some of our earliest church builders decided to bring a cave-like ritual space into the heart of their new religious buildings: the church crypt. Some very early examples of these survive to this day, caverns dug into the bedrock of churches that date from the first decades of English Christianity. Their dark, narrow corridors and collections of bones lit by candle must have been absolutely shocking to the local people, a place not just to enter in some ghoulish adventure but to worship, pray and seek healing.

Perhaps there is some precedent for this in one of St Guthlac's many slightly disturbing practices in the Fens. He chose to live in what sounds like a long-barrow burial chamber, a tumulus on an island with a stone structure inside. His *Life* identifies it as a 'cistern' but then refers to the possibility of treasures buried in it, not quite going so far as to identify it as a grave but the inference is clear.[11] Put together, all the scraps of evidence indicate that the early hermits sought out places that had negative spiritual associations in order to purge and adopt them, a process of landscape exorcism that spills across all chapters of this book. There is an association between prehistoric burial sites and early Christian activity, a desire to disrupt notions of death and the afterlife with a new narrative and sense of hope. And this is where the crypt makes its entry into the ritual toolbox of the missionary church: effectively man-made caves built into rock at the heart of missionary churches, where new converts would have been surprised and probably slightly appalled to find themselves being ushered into what is effectively a grave. So much of this book talks of the missionaries pushing out into the landscape, but there is no colonization without counter-colonization; the cave made its way from the margins of the landscape into the heart of their churches in equal and opposite reaction.

Three old examples of crypts are found in northern Britain, and today offer some of the most interesting, atmospheric and authentic experiences of unchanged early medieval devotion. They are in essence an artificial cave and tomb combined, subterranean homes for the dead that contained the bones of saints. But their purpose was built around a very deliberate Christian theology. Unlike the actual caves with their rather forbidding narratives, these vaults were specifically designed not to be frightening, dangerous or haunted but rather the opposite, to serve as places of devotion and prayer, of love and indeed of healing. I have a feeling that the early crypts of Britain were a way of presenting the shock of the new religion to the common folk, transgressing the most visceral assumptions about the dead and their tombs. Certainly early Saxon burial practices centred on inhumation, burying people or their cremated remains in the ground, and it seems as good a way as any to shake up people's thinking to offer the living a means to go down into the earth to meet the departed. The desire to erase the borders between the living and the dead needs no long explanation here in connection with a religion that emphasizes the immortality of the soul and the resurrection of the life to come.

I once visited the famous Caves monastery in Kiev, which is built over a labyrinth of narrow chambers and passageways, and shuffled along in semi-darkness with many Orthodox pilgrims. It is above all a place for the living and the dead to meet and communicate. At one point I heard someone sobbing and noticed a woman bent over the glass case containing the body of a saint, lost in the fervent supplication of a soul suffering some personal tragedy. A dead human body in this Christian tradition is not an object for disgust or superstition, but rather love for the achievements of the great ones who have gone before, and hope that the soul and its language of prayer will continue. It might not be a devotion to everyone's liking, but of course it put me in mind of the Catacombs in Rome. To their fellow citizens, early Christians were entirely ghoulish for their juxtaposition of worship and burial places, here again disrupting the very strong taboos and superstitions about disposing of the dead. Roman cemeteries had to be outside the walls of the city, away from places of human habitation and religious practice.[12]

The Catacombs in Rome were still being used in the seventh century, when many of the early Christian missionaries mentioned in this book were able to visit and marvel for themselves at these extraordinarily evocative places. The bishop St Wilfrid, who began life as a Celtic churchman and ended it as a fierce opponent of anything he considered non-Roman, was so impressed by the Catacombs he saw on his journeys to meet the pope that we have him to thank for two of the three early English versions. You can still visit them today at Hexham in Northumberland and Ripon in North Yorkshire, buildings where you can immerse yourself in an unaltered early Saxon place of worship. A third crypt at Repton in Derbyshire also dates from Wilfrid's time, around the year 700, and might have originally been a baptistery, another symbolic way to use the underground as a place of transition.

The crypt at Ripon is a particularly disorientating space, sitting as it does beneath a lofty and much later medieval cathedral. Here the labyrinthine layout is one of the oldest intact complexes of rooms in the country, an early Saxon crypt more or less as Wilfrid himself designed it, a theatre set every bit as choreographed as the liturgical space above. Carved into the rock, this man-made cave is not merely a northern version of the Catacombs but also an evocation of the tomb where Christ's body was laid for three days. It is a place where people can come to experience for themselves the spiritual significance of underground worship, although it is currently lacking one detail that was central to its original function. It was once used to house an exotic collection of relics that Wilfrid had gathered in Rome, the bones of martyrs whose prayers would be sought for healing and renewal by pilgrims in search of solace. None of Britain's ancient crypts currently have relics in them, but as a way of embodying the notion of the continuity of the soul, there is little else that so fully embodies the implications of Christian theology. The cave-like stone crypts of the early British Christians sent a shocking message to the converts that the old divisions had been broken down by a resurrected God. Caves and crypts are a place not just to confront our fears but to confound them, to remember them as a place of hope and resurrection even in such forbidding surroundings, a dimension to my journey that might have passed me by were it not for Samson and his snake. Finding hope to illuminate a cave's tomb-like chill became something of a theme on my subterranean explorations.

A light shines in the darkness

The lives of cave-dwelling hermits were not all spent in gloomy struggle with demons and the cold, and nor indeed was my brush with their world entirely given over to cursing at the blackness and the midges. I would, however, have benefited from one saint's miraculous means of dispelling the literal darkness from his cave, a left arm that would miraculously glow at night. The home of this particular hermit can still be seen today, tucked into a side street in the Scottish seaside village of Pittenweem. A number of saints have been mentioned in connection with this intriguing natural formation, such is its appeal, but the one most closely associated is St Fillan. It was here that the saint laboured in solitude, using his unique gift of a glowing arm to pursue his study of the Scriptures with unceasing diligence. An altar now sits in the cave, which is in the care of the local Episcopal church with the support of other ecumenically minded devotees. It is one of the few caves that sees active church maintenance and regular liturgical use, and feels irradiated with a peculiar spirituality, a more inviting spot to linger and reflect than many of the other hermit caves I have visited. A spring of crystal clear water wells up in a natural limestone basin in a chamber to the left of the altar.

St Fillan originally came from County Wexford in Ireland, a man who led a full life in serving the Lord and who boasts impeccable Celtic credentials, at least for those who think the word 'Celtic' means 'not English'. Robert the Bruce credited his victory at the battle of Bannockburn in 1314 to the presence of the saint's arm relic, wielded in a spiritual sense alongside more conventional weaponry. We can presume it was the arm that once glowed, but sadly that relic is now lost. Today visitors pay to borrow a key from a local cafe, and can illuminate the saint's former cavern with the aid of a light switch. The cave was once pressed into service as a prison for witches, and subsequently used as a rubbish dump, before the church managed to regain ownership and revive its devotional functions in 1935. As far as I am aware nobody has attempted to spend the night here in honour of Pittenweem's shining witness to the power of Celtic legend, but it looks as comfortable as any other hermit's cave, and is the only one connected to the national grid.

There are several other examples of this spiritual light firing up the lives of the early British saints, burning bright in the darkness for a servant of the Lord to read his prayers in the night. Not all are recorded in the later and rather imaginative medieval records either. St Columba's hagiographer Adomnán tells of the time this holy abbot locked himself in his house on Iona for three days and nights of intense fasting and prayer. 'But from the house rays of brilliant light could be seen at night, escaping through the chinks of the doors and through the keyholes,' another manifestation of this spiritual fire that Adomnán interprets as a sign of the Holy Spirit.[13] The purpose of this penetrating brilliance is made plain: Columba emerges from his vigil saying that the most dark and difficult passages of the holy Scriptures had become as clear as day to him. Perhaps this serves as a model for St Fillan's nightly studies. Another saint who also wore this divine glow was St Ethelflaeda, whose fingertips lit up at night to enable her to read the Scriptures at her abbey in Romsey, Hampshire. As described in the previous chapter, she is noted for her practice of ascetic immersion in a river, something that her northern counterpart St Fillan also performed in a stretch of the River Fillan near Crianlarich in Stirling: two saints of fire and water.

Adomnán has no hesitation in describing this light as the presence of the Holy Spirit, but because we will encounter it again in this book, a few thoughts about the fire that illuminated so many of our Celtic ancestors will not go amiss. In the next chapter, about sacred mountains, another form of rock-based landscape feature, there are also dazzling lights to be found, the brilliant glow of the burning bush before Moses on Mount Sinai being one of them. It is a light that appears repeatedly in the Bible from the birth of creation onwards, and sheds a lingering after-glow on the saints of Britain and Ireland during the years of mission and conversion.

The most obvious Christian model for a body that glows is Jesus at the Transfiguration, when his face is illuminated like the sun, as Matthew's account has it, and his clothes glow a white more brilliant than any wash could achieve. The more you start to look at this strange phenomenon, the more examples of it you will find. Take for instance the famous ascent of Elijah into heaven described in 2 Kings, when a whirlwind of fire carries him up into the skies, and the aforementioned burning bush on Sinai that puzzled Moses, a fire that did not consume the plant itself. Both of these two Old Testament prophets appear beside Jesus at his Transfiguration, all of them touched by this same strange fire that does not burn.

The phenomenon continues into the chapters of the New Testament after Jesus has ascended into heaven. Many Christian writers have seen it at work in the conversion of Saul: 'As Saul neared Damascus on his journey, suddenly a light from heaven flashed around him. He fell to the ground and heard a voice saying to him, "Saul, Saul, why do you perse-cute me?"' (Acts 9.3–4). Yet another well-known example is at Pentecost, when the apostles were touched by tongues of fire separating out from one divine source. From the first light that illuminated the chaos as God called creation into being, this notion of a heavenly fire runs long and deep through Judaeo-Christian history and appears to have blessed quite a few of our saints during their solitude. I did see some strange flashing lights in the sky during my own stay in a hermit's cave on the west coast of

Scotland, as I will recount, but suspect there are any number of modern causes now for such phenomena.

All the way through our religious history there are repeated references to this strange and unearthly light, the fire that doesn't burn, the lightning that doesn't kill, the brightness that blinds the sinner, and the glow that illuminates a hermit's private study. What is this light exactly? Those who know anything about theologians might not be surprised to hear that discussion on the topic became so heated at one point in the Middle Ages it nearly split the Eastern Church in two. Known as the Hesychast controversy, debate raged in fourteenth-century Constantinople about the precise nature of this curious fire that appears so often in encounters with the divine, a phenomenon that has been described as the 'uncreated light', so much does it transcend the nature of the rest of physical creation.

At the time of the debate, some Christians were claiming that a very devout person would be able to experience God directly. A holy man or woman could, if they prayed deeply enough and contemplated for long enough, have a face-to-face encounter with the majesty of God, which would be made manifest to them in this wondrous uncreated light. Others were aghast at such a suggestion: how can the physical eyes of a sinning, mortal and material person possibly see the essence of God? These are questions of some significance in defining the limitations of human understanding in the face of the divine.

In the end it took a first-rate theologian and archbishop called St Gregory Palamas to work out a plausible explanation for this recurring phenomenon. His proposal also has the benefit of being reasonably simple, which is no bad thing for a theological proposition. His answer was this: what is revealed in this light is not God directly, but rather the energy of God in action. If St Gregory is correct, humans can in fact see God revealed in the world by virtue of his actions. The whole of creation is ultimately powered by this wondrous power, this light that dazzles, this fire that burns but does not consume. The miracle of the Transfiguration shows us that it is truly God who is in Jesus Christ, that Jesus too shines directly with the energy of God, makes God known to us, visible to us, connected to us.

So the dispute was settled, as all too often in church history, by a robust theological debate followed by a civil war, which ended in 1347 with victory going to the party of Gregory Palamas. I visited his shrine in Thessaloniki with my family a few years ago to pay homage to this redoubtable thinker. Sadly some theologians to this day exploit the lingering traces of the controversy to widen the split between Eastern and

Western Churches, as if any help were needed on that, but the witness of the saints and of St Gregory in particular is to reflect on a light that can illuminate every part of the cosmos. It is also a light that flickers at us through the scant records of what is sometimes known as the Dark Ages, the early medieval period of British history when Celtic Christianity flourished. The term 'Dark Ages' is out of favour with scholars of the period these days, and I've been reprimanded for using it in an academic context even when doing so to acknowledge its limitations. Perhaps the Age of the Saints would be a better alternative, if no more palatable to academia, reflecting the fact that only the glow cast by these saints and their written *Lives* illuminates this period.

Demons

I have visited over a dozen hermit's caves in Britain, and spent the night in two of them, and can safely say that the experiences today are just as memorable and as diverse as the stories of old would have it. My night at St Columba's Cave may not have been the most uplifting of experiences, which was precisely the point of it – to understand just how far the Celtic saints went to confront the collective fears of their communities, to put their bodies on the line in a demonstration of the universal reach of our Creator God. Nowhere so viscerally embodies the cycle of descent and burial, the ignition of the divine spark, the exorcism of the shadow of death and the rising triumphant to face a new day. Or, at least in my case, gratefully to get into my car and head off to a cafe. But if my experiences at this cave were a lesson in hardship and gloom, my next night in a cave offered more or less the exact opposite, a vision of creation gilded by the grace-filled presence of the divine.

I will talk about my final revelation at St Ninian's Cave in the last chapter, because it was so intense, drawing together all the elements of this book in a flash of insight. But as a place to stop and dwell, this cave's setting and the feelings it evoked were ones of light and of peace, a world apart from St Columba's Cave 100 miles to the north on the same coast. The cave itself is situated at the far end of a stony bay, a mile's walk down a wooded gulley and a scramble along the boulders and pebbles of the shore. By this point of my journey I was able to travel considerably lighter, having found ways to make do with fewer and fewer items for an overnight stay. Water was the bulkiest and heaviest of my needs, and it was surprising how much of it a single evening and night required, even when used sparingly. St Samson's ability to produce a fresh spring in his caves is a convincingly appropriate skill for a long-term hermit. St Ninian's Cave has no water supply, but does sit a few metres above the high tide line, offering an infinite opportunity to bathe. The cave itself has no deep chamber or winding passageway but rather appears as an indentation pressed into monolithic slabs of rock, quite dark at the far end but not enclosed in the tomb-like manner of so many similar places. The saint named here is one of our greatest, and the history of devotion at this site as early and as authentic as it is possible to find.

St Ninian could even be considered the forerunner of the Celtic missionaries, so early are his dates. It was he who perhaps first crossed the borders of the Roman Empire carrying the gospel, bringing its light into places untouched by imperial history and its civilizing influences. Sometime just before the year 400, as Britain approached its final decade under Roman control, this pioneering leader asked the guards on Hadrian's Wall to open one of the heavy gates and let him slip quietly into the uncharted terrain that was to become the Celtic Christian heartland. Bede recounts the journey of this apostle to the Southern Picts in a brief chapter, barely hinting at the extraordinary meeting of cultures and beliefs that flowed from such a historic moment. Ninian's monastic base was ultimately established at Whithorn in Galloway, its central building so striking to the local Pictish tribes it became known as the *Candida Casa*, the White House. His cave lies just three miles to the south-east, and is said to be his place of retreat from the demands of establishing Scotland's first monastery. Some historians today are unconvinced that Ninian was a Briton of such early provenance as Bede describes, preferring instead to identify him as an Irish bishop called Finnian of Moville, who died nearly 200 years later around 589. Yet for all his achievements St Finnian did not found this monastery, because it was already well established by the time he arrived. Writing later in the fifth century, St Patrick refers to the 'apostate Picts', which means they had once been converted to Christianity and then lapsed. Some remarkable pioneer was in Pictland centuries before Finnian got there, active around the time that Bede indicates, and Ninian is the name that history hands down to us. We might as well use it.

There are also very early Christian monuments to be found, not just at the Whithorn site of the *Candida Casa* but even in this very cave where I was to dream of Celtic things. These stone crosses are on display in the visitor centre in Whithorn, and have been dated from the sixth century onwards, indicating a place of very considerable and enduring Christian devotion and pilgrimage. A few crosses are also engraved into the rock at the entrance to the cave, of uncertain date and difficult to spot unless you look carefully around waist height along on the left-hand cliff, some distance back from the mouth of the actual cave near an information panel. I placed my bags against this rock face and turned to survey my hermitage for the night. On a grassy knoll someone had placed a cross made of washed-up branches and a length of fishing rope, and I went up there to kneel and look out across this wild scene.

It was from this natural lookout point that I spotted my intruder. Far down the shore, at the point where the footpath met the back of the beach, a tall, slender man dressed in tight black clothes, with his sleeves rolled up to his elbows, stalked rapidly out of the gulley and down towards the sea, before stopping abruptly and turning to gaze towards the cave. I could sense his eyes searching the end of the beach where I knelt, certain I was invisible behind long tufts of grass, a quarter of a mile away. Then with long strides he marched back up the beach and disappeared. I waited perhaps an hour afterwards to ensure he had gone before taking off my own hindrances to a night of absolutely naked solitude in the wild, feeling all over the breeze of the distant sea and losing myself in the timeless breaking of the waves to pray. The cold did not trouble me as I contemplated this beautiful scene, the far headland lit up in gold for a final hour of sunshine. Later I sat beside my stove and saw on the ground before me two items of litter at the mouth of this holy cave, a cigarette butt and an empty packet of chewing gum. As I put them in my half-empty rucksack I could not help but think of these two as the most superfluous of all the resources we consume, taken for pleasure without any nutritional value whatsoever, no discernible benefit to anyone or anything. I consume as much pointless rubbish as the next person, but I do at least try to take my litter home with me.

As dusk drew on I stood before the cave and felt two brilliant flashes of light behind me, as if someone was firing a camera with a flash. I turned and scoured the boulders and shore but there was nobody near. As it happened I had my own camera running at the time, capturing the darkening scene, and just before I turned there are indeed two changes to the light, the camera suddenly stopping between frames as if reacting to some surge in brightness. There was no lighthouse that I could see when darkness fell, although the flashes occurred again a little later. Perhaps it was some military exercise or ship's flare, I have no idea, but I did fall to musing on the stories of hermits and their lights. I remember in particular one Russian monk living alone on an island in the White Sea who told me he was visited by angels during his six months of the year cut off by snow, which he described as moving lights. I have no reason to doubt him, and my own flashes of brightness seem artificial to me in comparison. But my thoughts did return to the dark stranger I saw far down the shore, and I suddenly remembered my nightmares before I began this journey, a vision of demons: the figure in a tight black catsuit stalking me, intruding on my solitude, breaking the silence. And I realized the only demons that populate our landscape today are us, the people who have covered it with the chaos of our desires and our appetites unchecked. If there is any indigenous species that has gone extinct in Britain, it is the demons who lurked in the landscape, harried first by missionaries and absolutely out-competed by human activity ever since. I went to sleep that night no longer afraid, and no longer frightened to confront any sort of darkness head on. We have proved far more destructive than any of the spirits that haunted the Celtic landscape of old, more damaging and dangerous even than the monsters who left St Antony for dead, deep under the ground.

8

Misty peaks

———▶◆◀———

*Mountains are not stadiums where I satisfy my ambition to
achieve, they are the cathedrals where I practise my religion.*
Anatoli Boukreev, Russian mountaineer (1958–97)

Split asunder

The lair of fiery dragons, haunt of demons locked in titanic combat with
saints, and a magnet for divine lightning and visitations from archangels:
life on a sacred mountain is rarely dull. Celtic peaks were the arena for cosmological battles that shook the ground below, giant rocks hurled down
by superhuman beings in a conflict between dark and light that raged
through the myths, legends and lives of our greatest saints. It was here
that I was to find some of the most dramatic and terrifying tales, enough
to make anyone think twice before even venturing into the foothills of
early medieval lore. How to gird oneself before entering this primal struggle: a Bible, a vial of holy water or consecrated oil, perhaps a crucifix to
brandish in front of me at the fearsome shapes looming out of the swirling
mist? As I pulled into the little car park at the foot of Skirrid, the mystical
holy mountain of the Brecon Beacons, a gentle drizzle began to fall on the
muted green fields. I was equipped only with what I could find close at
hand, an energy bar from the local petrol station and a waterproof jacket
from the boot. I turned my windscreen wipers off and within a minute
the top of this long ridge had smeared into the grey of the skies. I wondered about drinking my coffee as I began my walk, then decided to stay
in the warmth of the car for a little longer before beginning my assault on
the summit, all 340 metres above me.

If truth be told there are few holy mountains in Britain or Ireland that
present much of a challenge today, spiritually or physically. The stories
of old cast a colourful narrative over our high places, and there are some
authentic fragments contained within them that give us an idea of the
spirits that once wreathed their peaks. Skirrid better deserves its name

in Welsh: Ysgyryd Fawr, 'the great split', a reference to a highly charged origin story that ties this mountain to Jesus Christ himself. 'According to legend', say the guidebooks, the mountain is said to have split asunder at the moment of Christ's death on the cross, an aftershock of the earthquake that tore through Jerusalem, recorded in Matthew 27. It sounded a promisingly ancient legend when I first heard it, enough to motivate me to seek out and explore the intriguing split peak for myself. If I could introduce one law I would probably ban history books and guidebooks from referring to legends without giving some idea where they first arose. In Skirrid's case this seems to be a local story first recorded in 1909, placing it far beyond any sort of Celtic devotion.[1] And yet . . .

At the far end of this distinctive ridge lie the ruins of a medieval chapel, a windswept relic of a time when Christians did in fact seek out the high places of our lands and built places to gather and pray, churches with no parish but the bare flanks of bracken, no congregation but the birds and the sheep. Something had moved the good people of Abergavenny and around to build a stone chapel in this windy spot, to mark this place as somehow spiritual and special. The cleft in the summit is certainly striking enough, in reality the remnant of a landslip that took place in the last Ice Age, which you can admire close up as the track meanders through the fractured rock. As I made my way further along this mountain track to find the chapel, a dense mist descended and the path narrowed to a slippery ridge. I was wondering about turning back when I stumbled across a symbol I recognize well from my travels, a sign I have learned to decode as a marker of ancient and wondrous things: the National Trust logo. Fixed to a stone trig point, this also marks the site of the former chapel, a few pieces of stone sticking out of the grassy summit the only visible reminder of a pilgrim destination now fallen into disuse. The chapel is said to have remained active until long after the Reformation, a venue for clandestine meetings of Roman Catholics. So often I have come across places where the landscape has provided natural seclusion and shelter for religious outcasts in Britain, places to worship beyond the disapproving eyes of whichever national denomination happened to be abusing its power at the time. One local Member of Parliament wrote with contempt of meetings, sermons and services delivered by these 'Papists' at this mountaintop chapel as late as the 1680s.[2] This author, John Arnold of Monmouthshire, became increasingly deranged in his anti-Papist campaigns, organizing the arrest and execution of a clandestine Roman Catholic priest elsewhere in south Wales, now recognized by the church as St David Lewis for his martyrdom. I can no longer count the times I have been grateful to find a landscape spirituality that rises above religion's cruelties.

So none of this sounds particularly uplifting or even that relevant to the notion of hilltop cults, but it does illuminate one aspect of holy places that deserves particular prominence in a book dedicated to the subject, because it forms an essential part of the story of nearly every sacred site in Britain, Celtic ones included. It has occurred to me time and again on my travels, not least while hunched over the ruins of this chapel on Ysgyryd Fawr, something that gets to the heart of the identity of holy places: they are where bad things happen as much as good.

So many ancient places of pilgrimage and local devotion lie in ruins today: across Britain I have visited literally hundreds of ransacked monasteries, shattered chapel fragments, desecrated shrines, toppled well houses and defaced artworks of every kind. It might seem counter-intuitive but I have seen more than enough to know that holy places are not just beautiful places where good people come and sit to pray quietly, often embellished today with a pleasant tea room and gift shop. Rather, they bear witness to just as much anger and destruction as they do to love and devotion, they are places with a history of death, of mourning, of desecration. They are places in the landscape where the most extreme of human emotions have found focus over very long periods of time. The damage and destruction is by no means simply the result of our Reformation and Dissolution, but run longer and deeper still than that, all the way to their very origins. Take for example the first site of pilgrimage in all Britain: the shrine of St Alban, well known deep in the Romano-British period of history, a time when the common folk were Celtic to their core. This was a place where an innocent man was executed, along with a soldier who refused to wield the axe against him, a place whose very founding moment speaks of the worst of human instinct and action, a place where the divine met the harsh reality of the world and its values. As my journey shows time and again, the founding instinct at many holy places in the wilderness was to seek out a landmark that was bristling with pre-Christian stories of demons and dark suggestions of other spiritual and physical dangers, to exorcize them and to inhabit them. Missionaries sought out sites with a negative spiritual charge and worked hard to make that positive, from the demons on Inner Farne to the snakes on Iona, from the depths of so many lakes, rivers and the sea to the heights of our mountaintops.

My personal awakening to this accretion of the sacred and the profane at holy sites took place far from Britain, indeed far from pretty much anywhere, on the remote monastery island of Solovki in Russia's extreme north. Its beautiful forests and lakes are warmed for a short summer by the pale, sub-Arctic sunlight, and locked in white for six months of the year by the deep freeze that gives its name to the surrounding waters, the White Sea. This was and is the most holy site in Russian Orthodox monasticism, founded by two monks in the fifteenth century, islands already marked out as holy by pre-Christian tribes, set apart by nature for the most intense spiritual life imaginable. At the start of the twentieth century it was not long before the newly installed Communist government turned its gaze to these holy islands, seeking the most vicious of desecrations by converting it into the first of Russia's many gulags. Mass graves of its victims are still being uncovered today, martyrs and saints of the persecuted church among them. This is not a history to forget or excuse: the order for establishing this prototype gulag was signed by Lenin himself. Yet signs of hope will grow here, like the daffodils and other spring plants I saw flowering in July, despite or perhaps because of the darkness that has been. I met my wife Anna in the shadow of these monastery walls, and the cycles of spiritual and earthly life continue to turn through the generations.

The power of holy places to draw out the strongest of human emotions was something the poet Ifor ap Glyn articulated so well to me as we knelt by the shrine of St Melangell, a hermit of the Welsh mountains whose pastoral care for many years extended no further than the hares of her valley. As we looked sympathetically over the pile of prayer requests, it was obvious that holy places are magnets for praise and thanksgiving but also for petitions and supplications, where people bring their heartbreaks, their desperate cries for help – in earlier times a place of resort for those with a sick child in their arms. They are places of burial and loss, yet sources of the most profound solace, where the lines between life and death are blurred as a saint is called upon to intercede from their eternal home in the heavenly kingdom: a place of burial that somehow symbolizes immortality. To this extent I have come to the conclusion, to cut a long story short, that holy places are a miniature version of the cross.

Or since we are looking in this chapter at holy mountains I might as well square the circle and refer to these sites by an entirely appropriate name: Golgotha, the 'place of the skull' outside Jerusalem where Jesus was executed. This has long been considered a hill, the apex of which is the Rock of Calvary, now housed inside the Church of the Holy Sepulchre. This might seem a long train of thought bearing us far from the damage at the top of Ysgyryd Fawr, but remember the origin legend of its split peak, fractured at the moment of Christ's crucifixion on Golgotha. A fault line runs through all of human history: the power and desire to control and destroy what is good and beautiful. It is a story that illuminates much about the human condition, and it also connects our most sacred sites together.

Holy places are the most human of narratives fossilized into the landscape, places where emotions are memorialized in stone. Even today in a society supposedly moving on from religion, you can still end up on the front page of a national newspaper for urinating – if you happen to do so on a war memorial. There are still places imbued with enormous communal significance, charged with memories and certainly able to be desecrated. A letter that Pope Gregory the Great wrote to celebrate the conversion of the Anglo-Saxons in 598 talks of people who had previously worshipped trees and stones. The chapter in this book on trees suggests a shape that tree veneration might have taken, and on stones it is not hard to imagine some of the ways we invest spiritual meaning in such durable landmarks. I suspect it might have something to do with ancestor worship, a contested topic during the conversion of Britain, which is examined in the previous chapter on caves.

The top of this misty mountain in Wales was something of a lightning rod not just for the heavens to vent their fury, or rain down their light drizzle at least, but for humans of the seventeenth century as they sought to overthrow the traces of an enemy belief system. As my exploration of mountaintop cults in the Celtic era will show, this cycle of devotion and destruction is a pattern that stretches back further still, across millennia rather than centuries. What goes around comes around, a revolution of holy places that has seen more than one generation usurp the ancient devotions. Why mountains and hills attract such intense spiritual interaction is no doubt testament in part to their richness and symbolism, features that seem to be universal across so many cultures and regions of the world, that Celtic Christians inherited and adapted for their own purposes. These are places set apart by nature rather than human artifice, in some ways bearing a spiritual history comparable to sacred islands, with their tradition of devotional activity stretching back well into pre-history, into the time before written records.

Some of our mountain lore is therefore obscured by the passing of time. I for one would dearly love to know what devotions were considered appropriate for this high place, even those conducted in the seventeenth century by the Catholic faithful. It is not my era and I would not hazard a guess, other than to report that the chapel was supposedly visited on the day when its patron saint was celebrated: the Archangel Michael, the feast of Michaelmas on 29 September. This dedication does not reveal much by itself, but is at least one clue that helps to unlock the secrets of Celtic beliefs about the high places.

Fiery the angels fell

The many sacred 'mountains' I have climbed cluster in the south and west of Britain, perhaps in itself something of a clue as to the regional spread of cults around our high places. I spent the night on the summit of one such mountain in Pembrokeshire to draw deeply on this rarefied atmosphere, a place where a Celtic saint would converse with angels. I was enchanted by my experience in unexpected ways, as I will explain. Even on a shorter visit to these summits it is possible to pick up a sense of what made them holy, and many of them are familiar landmarks, iconic even of the British landscape. The opening shot of the London Olympics in 2012 was modelled on the most striking of these, Glastonbury Tor, although it had an oak tree rather than the tower of a ruined church at the top. This tower has stood alone and abandoned since the last abbot of Glastonbury Abbey was dragged up here and hanged alongside two of his brethren, another reminder if it were needed of the extreme uses to which holy places are put. The tower still bears the name of its former church: St Michael. Further to the south-west still, in Cornwall, is another famous hilltop building at Marazion, named after the dedication of the chapel that lies in the heart of its castle: St Michael's Mount. Inland, the haunted ruins of a hermit's chapel perch above the rocky Cornish moorland, far less busy with visitors, but just as striking and still preserving something of the solitude that drew its solitary inhabitant. Perhaps by now you might not be entirely surprised to hear of its dedication: St Michael's chapel, which lies beside a village called Roche.

So it doesn't take long to realize that all of these hilltop chapels and churches are dedicated to the Archangel Michael. There are a few other mountains with a sacred history and a different dedication, but these are among the most recognizable. At first glance, therefore, these are places that would appear to have a positive association and origin story, places where people have gone to receive a message from God via one of his winged emissaries. Perhaps one can imagine the angels and archangels fluttering down from heaven in the manner of a butterfly, alighting on the highest point of land before imparting news of hope and joy to the startled people. St Michael's Mount is said to have been made holy in the year 495 in such a manner, when the Archangel appeared to a group of fishermen to warn them of imminent danger. The first definite reference to the Mount as a religious site comes in 1044, when Edward the Confessor ceded it to its counterpart in France, the abbey of Mont Saint-Michel. Although it later became a castle, a small church remains at the heart of this complex. In reality the founding legend is another of those late stories, and is almost certainly a copy of the better-attested account of the founding of Mont Saint-Michel in 708, when a local bishop received a visitation from St Michael and was instructed to found a monastery on the French side of the Channel.

Despite the poor early record keeping of the legends of our holy mountains, I would be reluctant to write off all tales of angelic encounters as later inventions based on this French model, partly because there are so many examples and partly because the French legend clearly resonated with the stories of other peaks. In addition to the ones listed here, there are other hilltop dedications to the archangel, such as the pretty chapel of St Michael perched above Torquay. Mountains are places where people go in order to receive visions and encounters with the divine, as biblical evidence alone testifies repeatedly. So, on one level, this association with angels is part of a broader phenomenon. My study here summarizes a certain amount of previous research by other writers into this high-altitude expression of spirituality, particularly when it comes to St Michael's role as guardian of the peaks. This rich material is worth rehearsing before we start to look afresh at what early evidence does survive about the cult of high places, because I think it is possible to tie some of these fanciful and colourful narratives together with my theories of Celtic mission and the natural world.

As you may have read in guidebooks and history books, there is thought to be one very good reason why St Michael is a suitable patron for peaks, which is found in the very last book of the Bible. Revelation 12 describes the heavenly war in which Michael fought the dragon and cast him down, along with his followers. 'Fiery the angels fell,' as William Blake nearly said, the serpent described in the first book of the Bible identified with Satan in the last, as he is hurled down to work his mischief on earth. The devil is usurped from on high by God's messenger, a tale that sets the pattern for the cult of St Michael during the conversion period. It is commonly claimed that in the early landscapes of Britain high places were viewed as sacred to the Pagan gods, which meant that the Christians coming along would overthrow the old order by placing a chapel dedicated to the one who vanquishes the supposedly demonic cult, casting down the infrastructure of Pagan religions on the peaks. It is a dramatic idea, one that lights up the early medieval landscape with an epic, cosmological battle between good and evil that appeals to the storytelling instinct in us. The early twentieth-century historian of Anglo-Saxon England Frank Stenton was convinced that the Old English term *hearg*, meaning a temple or shrine, was commonly used in place names connected to hills, thereby immortalizing the existence of a Pagan place of worship atop such locations as Harrow-on-the-Hill in north London and Harrow Hill near Patching in West Sussex.[3]

Yet it must be said this chapter has almost no mention of Bede or Anglo-Saxon writers, which makes me think that there wasn't a close association between high places and Anglo-Saxon Paganism as Stenton has assumed. I have read a lot of texts, and there just isn't much there. I did find one very interesting set-piece description of landscape exorcism contained in Bede's *History*, which even gives a ritual formula for clearing an area of land of negative spiritual associations. This refers to the actions of a Celtic bishop, albeit one who was ethnically Anglo-Saxon. There are no mountains to be seen at the site in question, or even rocky crags. It relates to the establishment of a monastery at Lastingham, now in North Yorkshire, by St Cedd. Bede's description of the site seems curiously overstated in emphasizing just how dreadful this place had been when the saintly bishop turned up, and how hard the missionary needed to work to reclaim it for Christ, describing it as 'more suitable for the dens of robbers and haunts of wild beasts than for human habitation'. Walking around the pretty village today, it is difficult to imagine what was once so dreadful about it, and indeed Bede is suspiciously vague on this point. There are no significant landscape features or any archaeological evidence of pre-Christian activity. Yet it became the scene for one of the most clearly defined rituals of landscape purification in the historical record. This is one I have not performed myself, I should add, but the ritual process for founding a Celtic monastery is clear enough should you have need of it:

> The man of God wished first of all to purify the site of the monastery from the taint of earlier crimes by prayer and fasting, and make it acceptable to God before laying the foundations. He therefore asked the king's permission to remain there throughout the approaching season of Lent, and during this time he fasted until evening every day except Sunday according to custom. Even then, he took no food but a morsel of bread, an egg, and a little watered milk. He explained that it was the custom of those who had trained him in the rule of regular discipline to dedicate the site of any monastery to God with prayer and fasting.[4]

Bishop Cedd had managed 30 days of this Lent when the king sent an urgent summons to him, and he handed over the reins to a fellow priest. Although lacking in any notable landscape feature before its rehabilitation for Christian use, Lastingham subsequently gained one of the most atmospheric of Christian sites afterwards, one that probably still contains the relics of St Cedd. But there is no evidence of any *hearg* or other pre-Christian cultic site, even though it sounds as if Bede was positively itching to tell us there was one.

I rather suspect that the willingness to see Pagan shrines on hilltops is a narrative that owes more to the Old Testament than to any written or archaeological evidence. The two books of Kings are full of references to idols and cults located on the 'high places', which the Jewish leaders seek to overthrow.[5] Biblical precedent does not automatically mean that a story is suspect, not least because Christians would often seek to emulate what they read in Scripture, but there is always a danger that it might be applied retrospectively by either the original writer or later historians. Peaks were part of the managed transition of the landscape from pre-Christian to Christian significance, but that does not mean they had temples on them. The best early evidence I have found for a Pagan cult of high places in Britain is that of St Samson and the idol carved on a stone, described in the previous chapter on caves, in a context far removed from Anglo-Saxons with their *heargs* further to the east. One detail highly relevant in this context is the fact that the stone idol is described as 'resting on the summit of a certain hill'. Indeed, St Samson's hagiographer claims to have climbed this very hill himself and traced his finger over a cross that the saint carved on a standing stone using an iron implement. Perhaps more significantly still, all of this took place in Cornwall.[6] We have so few early records of the early saints of western Britain, the evidence from St Samson's life is precious indeed, a clear-cut case where the actions of St Michael resonate loudly, where a Pagan high place of worship was indeed usurped by a Christian monument. Something similar could have happened further east, but there is not enough evidence to claim that it did.

The most dramatic tale of a mountainous place of pre-Christian resort being overcome by a Christian missionary is the epic landscape at Maentwrog in Gwynedd, north Wales. The local church's founder, St Twrog, is said to have seized a boulder from a nearby mountain and hurled it down to crush a Pagan altar in the valley below. A monolith worn smooth over the passing centuries lies by the church door to this day, perhaps a pre-Christian standing stone around which this colourful story appeared. Supposed finger prints of the saintly giant can be seen on its edge, too far spread apart to fit my own or anyone else's hands. Even at this site so suggestive of the overthrow of Paganism, the site of the temple lies near the bottom of the valley rather than any summit. Local historians have long noticed that the village sits at a crossing point in the River Dwyryd, a factor of greater practical significance than the mountain, of which there is no shortage in this part of Wales. The textual traces of this epic battle are also relatively late, appearing from the twelfth century onwards and more fully narrated in the even later *Bonedd y Saint* genealogical records.

Despite the somewhat elusive nature of mountaintop Pagan shrines, particularly in eastern Britain, I do think there is very good evidence for angels congregating at peaks in the landscape, and not always in conjunction with demons. The lowest sacred hill in Celtic lore is also one of the most spiritually charged. The Hill of Angels on Iona is found a few hundred metres inland from the beach on the western side of this monastic island, little more than a low mound covered in grass. In the saint's *Life* written by Adomnán around the year 700, Columba is described as climbing this hillock and conversing with angels. A monk of his community follows him and spies Columba

> on a knoll among the fields, praying with his arms spread out towards heaven and his eyes gazing upwards . . . For holy angels, the citizens of the heavenly kingdom, were flying down with amazing speed, dressed in white robes, and began to gather around the holy man as he prayed.[7]

These angels disappear quickly when they realize they are being observed. This story gives some credence to the poetic idea of angels fluttering down to alight on a high point of land, and in this instance sound somewhat like a flock of white birds. This hill is not simply an incidental detail but rather a place charged with ongoing spiritual power, since it appears in a landscape-blessing ceremony that takes place after the saint's death during a long period of drought.[8] The monks carry Columba's white tunic and books around the ploughed fields then take them up the Hill of Angels and read from the books, at which point the rain starts to fall. The Irish association between birds and angels has been considered in more detail in Chapter 4. More interesting still is the story that Columba climbed up here to pronounce his power over the snakes of Iona, rendering them harmless to the Christian community, a story described in Chapter 5. Once again the demons and angels of Celtic lore seem much more like indigenous creatures than any human cult site or activity.

I had once thought that all holy places were marked by darkness as well as light, but there are a few I have read about and then encountered in person where the witness does appear to be simply holy and peaceful from start to finish. In Chapter 5 I describe the intense beauty and calm that descended on St Herbert's Isle as night fell around me, the most notable corruption in that beautiful place being the fragments of discarded plastic I kept spotting in the soil and shingle. Iona too has borne witness to the horrors that accrete around the sacred; the site of a massacre of 68 monks by the Vikings is still known as Martyrs' Bay.

As a Celtic devotion, therefore, one action I am unable to reproduce in my modern journey through the ancient ways is the destruction of any shrines on Britain's high places. Nor indeed would I want to. All the Pagans I know are lovely, leaning heavily towards environmental activism and other entirely benign interventions in the natural world. There is a very small, barely connected Neo-Pagan movement, sometimes described as one of many versions of Heathenism, which promotes a hard national-ist rhetoric based on tribal mythology, but as I understand it this is mostly found in Eastern European countries. I've never met any proponent of this variant of Heathenism, and even if I did I cannot imagine ever want-ing to destroy anyone's shrine or temple.

Arguably the greatest theological aversion that Paganism has faced since the conversion of Europe came from one of the newest Christian denominations. George Fox and the Religious Society of Friends were so determined to avoid any lingering trace of Pagan culture they even attempted to rename the days of the week, which famously include sev-eral names of the ancient gods: Thor's day for Thursday, Saturn's day for Saturday and so on. Funnily enough the replacement scheme of 'first day', 'second day' and so on somehow failed to capture people's imagination and was quietly dropped. Perhaps this initial Quaker hostility towards Paganism stems from the fact that of all renditions of Christianity it is in some respects the least sacramental, the least willing to accept the idea that the spirit can enter water, bread and wine to become the elements of baptism and Eucharist. Yet I know Quakers who believe that the spirit is found everywhere rather than in a few specific sacramental rituals, that all life is to be counted sacred and holy. And I can never forget one of my own joyful holy encounters in the British landscape some years ago as I walked up Pendle Hill in Lancashire to gaze over the patchwork of fields and roads and reflect on the view that a certain seventeenth-century walker named George Fox experienced up here too, recorded in his autobiography under the year 1652:

As we travelled, we came near a very great hill, called Pendle Hill, and I was moved of the Lord to go up to the top of it; which I did with difficulty, it was so very steep and high. When I was come to the top, I saw the sea bordering upon Lancashire. From the top of this hill the Lord let me see in what places he had a great people to be gathered.[9]

Some modern accounts of this ascent claim that George Fox saw God at the summit, but his was a vision rather of human souls waiting to be harvested, no doubt inspired by the patchwork of fields that stretch to the horizon. He might not have liked the notion that any place can be intrinsically holy, or at least more holy than others, hence his preference for meeting houses over dedicated church buildings. Yet it is hard to imagine having such an archetypal vision of souls anywhere other than a high place, where so many Scriptures, histories, hagiographies, traditions and folk tales talk of divine revelations. Fox hurried back down to the local inn and 'declared the truth' to the innkeeper, who must have been delighted as he busied about his work of the evening. We will meet the Quakers again in this chapter, and it is pleasing to share common ground with a denomination not known for its reverence of holy places. Far from casting down any cultic associations on Britain's peaks, even Fox has added to these colourful traditions. He also drank from a little spring that flows from the side of this massive hill, which remains to this day a quiet place to sit and contemplate the tapestry woven across our landscape by so many renditions of Christian and pre-Christian belief.

Haunt of demons

So were there Pagan temples looming over the Christian missionaries as they first arrived and attempted to persuade Britain's tribes to abandon their former ways? My own feeling is that the evidence for actual Pagan buildings and structures is not really strong enough, even in western Britain. Rather it seems that the model we have seen operating at many other holy landscapes in Britain, particularly natural bodies of water, seems more plausible. These were places where Pagan narratives were deeply embedded in local lore – stories rather than physical buildings. Like the monster-filled water courses of northern Britain, these mountains and hilltops were spiritually dangerous places that the Pagans avoided, no-go areas that exercised the missionaries because they bore witness to a divided cosmos dotted with exclusion zones. They certainly represented an immediate challenge to anyone promoting the idea of a single Creator God able to operate across all levels of his divine creation. As it is one of the very few written records of pre-Christian belief, it is worth repeating here the comments by the Celtic monk St Gildas about his ancestors. I will also include the sentence that precedes it:

> I shall not enumerate the devilish monstrosities of my land, numerous almost as those that plagued Egypt, some of which we can see today, stark as ever, inside or outside city walls: outlines still ugly, faces still grim. I shall not set out in detail those mountains or hills or rivers, once so deadly, now so useful for human needs, on which in those days a divine honour was once heaped by a blind people.[10]

Gildas is specific about the way in which both hills and mountains were once thought of as 'deadly' or 'destructive' but had been rehabilitated through Christian ritual. As said previously, it might seem counter-intuitive to suggest that Pagans had any negative attitudes towards the natural world, but that is to filter the past through our own preconceptions. I include the first sentence of this passage here because it directly compares the cult of idols, 'devilish monstrosities' and their grim faces with the anxieties that once adhered to high places and natural water, wrapping up the entirety into a matrix of spiritual beliefs. Cultic objects made by hand are associated with places of human habitation rather than hills or mountains in the wider landscape. Perhaps Gildas lived in a different part of Britain from Samson and the Cornish hilltop idols, because they were almost certainly contemporaries, both dying sometime around 565–570.

Another interesting point that occurred to me on my travels was the extent to which Britain seems to be divided on the legacy of these landscape stories. As mentioned, the mountains and hills dedicated to St Michael cluster in the south-west of Britain. Tales of monsters lurking in the deep, and missionary action to exorcize and redeem their watery habitats, are found most prominently in northern England and Scotland. When it comes to the notion that dark spirits lurk around high places, it is also possible to detect an echo of the stories from south-west Britain in the Irish evidence. The best fit is found in the *Life* of that island's most prominent saint, although unfortunately it is a rather late version, dating from the ninth century. Known as the *Tripartite Life of St Patrick*, this text was designed to be read in three stages over the patron saint's three-day festival and includes sections in vernacular Old Irish in addition to Latin. In a passage describing Patrick's Lenten fast on top of a mountain, it is easy to spot the themes we have already met on our travels across the high places of Britain:

Now at the end of those forty days and forty nights the mountain was filled with black birds, so that he knew not heaven or earth. He sang maledictive psalms at them. They did not leave him because of this. Then his anger grew against them. He struck his bell at them, so that the men of Ireland heard its sound, and he flung it at them, so that its gap broke out of it, and that [bell] is 'Brigit's Gapling' . . . No demon came to the land of Erin after that for seven years and seven months and seven days and seven nights. Then the angel went to console Patrick, and . . . brought white birds around the mountain, and they used to sing sweet melodies for him.[11]

The mountain in question is known as Croagh Patrick in County Mayo, western Ireland, which continues to attract mass pilgrimage. I had wondered when I first read this story whether there was any mileage to be found in the notion of the Celtic handbell as a ritual agent in the landscape, ringing out a vortex of holy sound that would clear the surrounding area of demons. My research on that topic proved to be as ineffectual as Patrick's own bell as a means of engaging with devils, and indeed he ends up in this story simply picking it up in exasperation and hurling it at them. Such are the frustrations of trying to pin down early medieval demons. The reason why I thought this might be significant is because a similar tale appears in the *Life* of another early Irish missionary, St Gall, who travelled to mainland Europe with one of the greatest ambassadors for Celtic Christianity to the Continent, St Columbanus. The missionary party established a monastery on the shores of Lake Constance, to the great dismay of the local demons. One night St Gall was out fishing on the lake when he hear voices from on high:

> Once upon a time in the silence of the night, as Gall was casting his nets into the lake, he heard a demon calling with loud voice from the summit of the nearest mountain to some fellow of his who seemed to inhabit the water. He who was thus called answered (as it were out of the lake) that he was there. 'Rise and come to my aid,' said the other, 'that we may cast out these strangers who have come from afar, for they have driven me from my temple and shattered my images.'[12]

Uniquely in all the literature of the early medieval period there is a situation here where demons in the water and on the mountains are present at the same time, conspiring against Christian missionaries with ruinous intent. Set this against the record in Gildas that rivers and mountains were considered deadly in pre-Christian belief and we have as perfect a match as can be found. For good measure we might as well note the presence of the idols too, another dimension of the complex of Pagan culture that Gildas recorded. It is just a pity that Lake Constance is in modern-day Switzerland, and the missionaries were Irish rather than British. But there does seem to be a strong Celtic character to this scene even so. Like their country's patron saint, the monks opt for the same combination of bell and psalms that St Patrick employed, this time to rather better effect. St Gall rows quickly to shore and informs his abbot of the baneful voices from the landscape:

> When Columbanus heard it, he went to the church and striking the bell, summoned the brethren together. But 'ere they had finished chanting the psalms, they heard the awful voices of the demons passing from crest to crest of the mountains, in mingled tones of despair and fear as though they were taking their departure.

To the Celtic cultures at least, it can be said that peaks were prominent places, not just physically and topographically, but culturally and spiritually too. If you do happen to encounter demons on any peak, it is at least reasonably clear what you would need to do: sing a psalm at them. This is not a devotion specific to high places, needless to say, since we have heard saints singing these songs beside and in the sea in previous chapters. Incidentally, the reference to 'maledictive' psalms might sound rather counter-intuitive, but it refers to verses that cry out for victory over enemies. The early spiritual writer Adomnán helpfully includes a list of these at the end of one of his texts.[13] Psalm 68 (67 in the Vulgate Bible) is a particularly interesting example, its opening lines also used by the English St Guthlac to dispel demons that haunted his wilderness hermitage: '[Guthlac] sang the first verse of the sixty-seventh psalm as if prophetically, "Let God arise", etc.: when they had heard this, at the same moment, quicker than words, all the hosts of demons vanished like smoke from his presence.'[14] This is one discipline I have never felt the need to recreate on a mountain or hill, the monsters that leave their mark on our landscape being all too human today. The sound of psalms rang out across the Celtic landscape in numerous contexts, a soundtrack to the everyday working life of the missionaries as they busied themselves about the task of redeeming creation.

The Sermon on the Mount

I once gave a talk on holy places, pilgrimage and shrines to a gathering of priests, as benign an audience as one could hope for, and was met by a question at the end that surprised me with its implied hostility to my topic: had I ever heard of the Reformation? I had, as it happened. Those who think we have reformed our way out of any meaningful relationship with the natural world and its spiritual significance might care to consider some of the many biblical interactions with the land – indeed the Holy Land – that resonate deep within the Gospels. The Old Testament is full of incidents connected to mountains, and not just the conflicts with Pagan temples and cults described above. Mount Horeb is where Moses sees the burning bush, at which point he is instructed to remove his sandals because of the nature of the place itself: 'Do not come any closer,' God said. 'Take off your sandals, for the place where you are standing is holy ground' (Exodus 3.5). Horeb is almost certainly an alternative name for Mount Sinai, and is where Moses returns to speak again to the Lord and receive the Ten Commandments. Exodus (chapters 19 onwards) recounts numerous other details about this holy site: the mountain becomes sacred land that the people cannot touch; it shakes and is covered in smoke and fire, and a mist descends on it. After receiving the Ten Commandments, Moses spends 40 days on its wilderness flanks, and has an altar and 12 pillars set up at its base. It is not difficult to spot the ways in which Jesus entered into a similarly full-bodied embrace of the same landscape features. At the beginning of his ministry he too went into the wilderness for 40 days during his temptation, and ended on a high place overlooking all the kingdoms of the world. The best biblical model for a Christian theology of holy places, however, is perhaps the Transfiguration, when Jesus climbs a mountain with three disciples in order to pray. That detail alone is enough to justify extending one's devotional activity into the hills and mountains. A cloud descends, interpreted as a representation of the Holy Spirit, and Jesus' face and clothes shine as bright as the sun, that mystical fire that burned but did not consume the burning bush, the uncreated light that was explored in the previous chapter on caves. The dazed apostles were aware of the depths of this transformation, sensing that it extended to the place itself. 'It is good for us to be here,' says St Peter, and suggests setting up tents so they can stay longer. Christ's mission involved an active engagement with the desert landscape that surrounded him, and the early Christians were soon seeking out these landmarks to honour the memory of what had passed. The third-century Christian scholar Origen was the first to identify the geographical site of the Transfiguration as Mount Tabor. I imagine few Christians today have climbed a mountain or hill in order to pray, yet our country is full of hilltop chapels and churches, most of which are now evocative and peaceful ruins given over to contemplation and reflection on all manner of things spiritual and religious. Reformation or not, the Bible's numerous mountain stories haven't changed.

There is one further journey that Jesus takes to a high place for the instruction of his people: the Sermon on the Mount, which contains so many of the fundamentals of Christian teaching, including the Lord's Prayer. The current high place in many churches, the pulpit, is not actually modelled on this lofty preaching place, but early British Christians did make ingenious use of the landscape to help them project the gospel in the outdoors. As noted earlier in this chapter, there is a distinct lack of mountaintop chapels and churches in northern Britain, and also a distinct lack of stories telling of demons lurking on their peaks. But there are some crags with a Christian history that are just as salutary. Perhaps in anticipation of the passionate sermons that were to come in Scottish churches, the rocky crags I have encountered on my journey in northern latitudes have a history as preaching platforms, as pulpits provided by nature for the instruction of the soul. On the Isle of Skye, a couple of miles from the bridge at the village of Ashaig, there is a river with one long rocky bank higher than the other on which St Maelrubha is said to have stood and preached during his mission to the west coast of Scotland. The crag is known by its Gaelic name of Creag an leabhair, meaning 'the rock of the book', in honour of this apostle to Skye. He could certainly pick a spot. His monastic home at Applecross on the mainland opposite the island remains one of the most beautiful and memorable of all the holy places I have visited, set at the head of a gently shelving bay. When I visited St Maelrubha's preaching platform on Skye, the sound of the river and the sea made quite a noise, suggesting a man unafraid to declare the gospel in stentorian tones. Some 120 miles to the south of here another holy rock can be seen on the Holy Island that nestles alongside Arran, which we visited in Chapter 5. St Molaise's Table is said by some to be his preaching platform, although this site is also known as his place of quiet retreat from the cares of tending his flock.

Further south I explored a similar crag in North Yorkshire, a flat rocky platform several metres above the River Wharfe, where St Wilfrid preached to the people of Burnsall before baptizing them in the swirling waters below. There is certainly a deep pool directly below the crag, as a young couple demonstrated by leaping from this overhanging rock into its black waters, a sport known with good reason as tombstoning. Showman though he was, I find it hard to believe Wilfrid sent his many converts hurtling towards their salvation from on high after winning them round to the faith. There is a perfectly easy path down to the river a few steps further along, which the holy bishop would no doubt have preferred. One final rocky crag in northern England evokes another powerful preacher of Christian history who has appeared already on this high-altitude tour of Britain. George Fox delivered a sermon from Firbank Fell on Sunday 13 June 1652 to around a thousand people, those same souls awaiting their harvest that he espied from the top of Pendle Hill a few weeks previously. He could certainly deliver a substantial sermon: a plaque on this rock today records the length of this message as three hours.

I would imagine all religions and every denomination within them have something meaningful to say about mountains. There is a universality to the message of these peaks, that nature and God alike are greater than all of us, that we are bit players dwarfed by the boundless cosmos. Even the darkness is present alongside the light, Jesus himself standing on a summit with the devil. At Pendle Hill this story continues – a place notorious for the trial and execution of eight women and two men for witchcraft in 1612.

We make use of the landscape as we see fit, exploited to serve a purpose for any number and manner of human activities and beliefs. The Celtic Christian vision glimpsed from the high mountains to the low valleys on my journey is at heart an orientation towards the natural world based on respect for its Creator, a sense that we need to align our uses with the care of a loving God who 'breathes in all things, makes all things live, surpasses all things, supports all things', to borrow the words of St Patrick again. Both divine and demonic purpose alike are revealed in human deeds and interactions. It was a rock on which Jesus founded his very church, yet it was also a rock that killed one of its earliest members, the martyr St Stephen, stoned to death. We have natural resources at our disposal to use and abuse as we see fit, building blocks for our own creations.

Into the light: Carningli

And so to conclude with my efforts to emulate the ways of Scripture and saint alike by ascending a mountain in search of my own perspectives on the divine. St Brynach was to be my guide for a night of dazzling revelation beneath a cloudless sky, a sixth-century monk who founded a monastery at Nevern, two miles to the north-east of my chosen summit in western Pembrokeshire. Welsh history is populated by some of the greatest Celtic heroes and wonder-workers, but all too often their *Lives* are written many centuries after the golden Age of the Saints had long passed.

In St Brynach's case a twelfth-century work of considerable imagination represents our best glimpse of the man himself. He was instructed in a vision to found his monastery when he encountered a white sow with her piglets, and set about establishing a life of strict devotion at Nevern, bathing in the coldest water he could find and fasting until his body was quite wasted. 'Thus he led a life so pleasing to God, that as he deserved, he frequently enjoyed the sign and discourse of angels; and the mountain on which they met, at the foot of which a church was built, was called the Mountain of Angels.'[15] The name Carningli is almost certainly a corruption of Carn Engylion, the crag of angels.

The naked hermit of Mount Sinai, who lends this book its title, was himself living on the side of a mountain for his solitary life of prayer, a mountain whose presence looms over this journey through the biblical symbolism of high places. It was he who provided the formula that only by putting off all trappings of human company and community can one hope to meet with angels. So with that in mind I decided to climb this Welsh sacred mountain naked, once I had put a discreet amount of distance between myself and the empty lane where my car was parked. Arms and back laden with provisions for my single night's vigil, I paused for a final time to remove even my sandals and began to tackle the green flank that rose before me, its slope becoming ever more steep as the summit neared. For the last third of the climb the low sun dazzled my eyes as it grazed the side of the hill, my feet in shadows so deep I was finding it ever harder to pick my way through the gorse and patches of sharp stone. My progress slowed with each step, and I stubbed, winced and finally hobbled my way to the top, an ascent accompanied by utterances rather less devout than angels like to hear.

Another legend that I cannot date to a time before the existence of the internet claims that anyone spending the night on Carningli will either go crazy or take up writing poetry, a warning that I came across only after finishing my stay on its summit. I had at least prepared for as many eventualities as I could, carrying with me both a tent and a bivouac bag, uncertain if I would find any flat ground on which to camp. An ancient hillfort, with traces of huts and enclosures, nestles into the side of the rocky crags that make up Carningli's peaks, remnants of some long-forgotten population of mad poets or Iron Age hill farmers. It was behind one of these ancient rocky ramparts that I found a perfect spot to pitch my tent and dream of visions past. Beyond the wall lay miles of empty moorland, bounded by a far distant line of houses and roads stretching around the coastline, the Ynys Dinas headland rising out of a sea so calm it reflected the tall black cliffs in the waters below. Beyond that was the magnificent sweep of Cardigan Bay, a promise of Ireland unseen in the haze of the setting sun.

Throwing my burdens gladly to the ground, I picked up my camera and scrambled higher, heading for the tallest of the many crags, when a bright blue flash caught my eye. Moving towards it through the clumps of bracken, I could see a flap of material gently rising in the breeze, and realized it was an abandoned pair of Lycra jogging bottoms streaked with brown, held down by a large stone. Perhaps they had been placed on a boulder in the forlorn hope someone would come and reclaim them. That will never happen because these artificial fibres ended up in a rubbish bin the following day, along with an abandoned sandwich wrapper. As I drew near this discarded garment, a large butterfly launched itself into the air from the patch of blue and rose up to join a gathering of its companions I had not previously spotted, flitting their way through the golden light of the setting sun. I sat entranced for a moment out of time in the stillness of the empty moor and began to piece together the bare elements of Celtic lore. Later that evening a blue-black crow came and perched on a crag near me, crying its hoarse cry over the empty land. I didn't have a bell or psalm to hurl at this creature, nor the inclination to do so either, since I was very happy to share my place in the sun with the age-old companion of the hermit. The only harmful creatures who frequent this mountain now are the ones who cover it in rubbish. Any other darkness has been entirely eclipsed by our own shadows, the demons driven to redundancy and extinction.

Contemplating the raw elements that filled my horizon, I began to see St Brynach's night revealed through the eyes of a medieval hagiographer. These butterflies would become clouds of little angels flitting over the heather, and the crow a shape-shifting demon sent by the enemy of all good people to distract me. The bright sun miraculously cleared the sky of every cloud and there in the middle was a small figure praying and giving thanks to his maker. This was his story, and so it became the story of our land, and on that one still evening it became mine.

After watching the sun lower itself into the horizon, I suddenly re-membered the needs of my own wasted body and fell to harvesting the bilberries that grew in abundance around my makeshift home, then hur-ried to get my camp set and food cooked before it got entirely dark. If any demon or angel had chanced upon me I would merely have asked them to give me a hand finding a spot where I could drive the tent pegs in, so focused was I on making it through the night successfully. Later that evening I sat down to rest on one of the flat boulders, perhaps placed there three thousand years ago, and sank into the mountainside. The sun had warmed the stone, and the moss and lichen made the softest seat I have ever sat on, my bare bottom on the bare rock and bare plants, my feet on the naked soil, and felt for a moment out of time that creation was being remade. That was the closest I came to experiencing heaven on earth, and it involved absolutely nothing. Really nothing, not a single item of artifice or invention made such an experience possible, but rather their absence. We are formed from the earth and we can feel that still; we can feel that the closeness of our original paradise remains within touching distance.

9

Lessons from the Celtic shore

*In the third chamber was an eagle with wings and feathers
of air; he caused the inside of the cave to be infinite.*
William Blake, *The Marriage of Heaven and Hell* (1790)

'Liminal' is a word that has not featured in these pages so far, though it usually appears liberally in books on Celtic Christianity, in an attempt to define and pin down what is so special about this spiritual culture. In some ways it is the perfect word to encapsulate the Celtic experience: it sounds like it carries theological weight, offers what appears to be a re-assuringly technical definition, but doesn't actually mean anything very specific. It comes from the Latin word *limen*, meaning a threshold, and is often applied to the holy places of the Celtic landscape. I'm not entirely sure what a liminal space is supposed to feel like in the real world, what thoughts, feelings and images it is supposed to conjure up. In Celtic lore there is nowhere more 'liminal' than the shoreline, the boundary between sea and land, but what exactly is 'liminal' about spending time on a beach? When people use a term that sounds as scientific as a medical diagnosis, it would be helpful to know exactly what it is supposed to signify. You will often find liminal used interchangeably with the notion of 'thin places', described in Chapter 3. Once again I don't dismiss either term out of hand, but these phrases work very hard to cover some of the gaps in our understanding of Celtic Christianity. And once again, I would say these are terms that are applied as easily to humans as to the places themselves.

My journey certainly feels more about being pushed to the edge than crossing boundaries, going to the furthest point possible away from the city and into the wilderness, shedding comforts and company from one direction and embracing the creatures and the cold in the other. But in fairness to those who use the term, the instinct that drove Celtic Christians to these liminal places was also about crossing boundaries, pushing a new faith into old places, missionary in origin and purpose. In this context liminality does seem an appropriate concept to apply to a period of transition for both the people and their landscapes, on the cusp of a truly radical change. And I did eventually gain a very strange and specific sense of being caught in the middle of a threshold when I spent enough time at these marginal places.

It occurred to me one night under the stars that the condition of being naked is for nearly everyone a 'liminal' state. It is most closely associated with changing, going from dirty to clean in the shower, from home to the outside world, from cold to warm, from day to night and sleep to awake, from sedentary to active in the gymnasium and from dry to wet in the swimming pool. It is for most people a temporary state, an in-between condition that is necessarily brief. It is the embodiment of change itself, and as such it perfectly encapsulates a moment of transformation, a condition for rebirth that makes particularly good sense in the context of baptism, something that early church writers and liturgies freely and abundantly celebrated.[1] Living naked as a hermit, therefore, is like hitting a pause button on life, freezing a moment between states, suspending animation, and dwelling inside that gap. Perhaps inhibition to the un-adorned human body has something to do with this condition of crossing boundaries, the supposed interim nature of it, like being interrupted in the most intrusive way possible. As a means of taking time out, of absenting yourself from routine human affairs, it does work well to press pause as a naked hermit and explore the depths to be found in that in-between state. It became to me a place where time seems to stop running normally, where a single moment collapses into the history of a place, where experience is unmediated, indeed where truth is naked, as the phrase has it.

The malleable and elusive nature of language means anyone can lie with absolute impunity, but an incarnated faith can offer something that stands against that. A liar can claim they killed nobody, but the body pins the lie to the floor, just as it pins words and ideas to physical reality. Extremes of every sort will ignore or deny evidence and experience: the scientific, the factual, the hard, cold, sharp reality violated by any ideology that runs away with itself. Science itself makes such solid connections to the physical world through experimentation and testing, and all manner of intellectual endeavours could do well to follow suit: religion, politics, ethics and ideologies are all susceptible to detachment from embodied reality, perhaps now more than ever. Public discourse seems frighteningly removed from observable fact at the time I am concluding this book, bodily denigration being just one part of a wider denial of our physical imprint on the world. Pretty much all prejudice is based on denial and rejection of the human body in some form or other: skin colour, sexual difference, genetic inheritance, notions about appropriate food and dress. Truth is not a string of words in isolation, but rather the word made flesh.

Sacramental life

And so to end this journey to the heart of what makes Britain's Celtic faith unique, I have reasons to refrain from offering too many definitive conclusions. Apart from anything else, it is difficult to understand fully the spiritual impulse towards nature because I believe we are effectively hearing only one side of a conversation. If the evidence compiled in my research is even half right, there was a missionary purpose to these epic battles with the elements, animals and spirits that moved across the British and Irish islands. It owes an enormous debt to the pre-Christian beliefs that had been etched into the landscape and embedded in the culture and daily routines of the ordinary folk. Celtic landscape lore was the product of a dialogue between missionaries and their potential converts, and the common language they managed to find was articulated in terms of landmarks and birds, spirits, storms and caves, mountains, trees and the restless sea. Liturgies spoken in Latin, moralizing about marriage laws and appeals to act in a merciful and gentle manner fell on largely deaf ears. I think it would be unfair to call this ultimately successful Christian approach using nature interactions cynical or appropriative, given the enormous sensitivity it displayed towards the delicate matrix of landscapes both mental and physical. And rather than stitching together a patchwork of hastily rewritten scraps of ancient stories, it drew very deeply indeed on the innermost core of Christian ritual and teaching. Some of this material was so raw it had scarcely been processed by later church teaching, and was particularly untouched by Augustine's theological refinement. So it was missionary but also liturgical, completely transcending the modern divisions between High and Low churches, between evangelical and sacramental spiritual expressions. In so many senses of the phrase, Celtic spirituality managed to combine the best of both worlds.

It emerged at a time when the faith could be adaptive and nimble, unencumbered by much hierarchy or infrastructure. It was required to engage passionately and consistently with some pretty formidable and stubborn opposition. The very fact that it was missionary in purpose perhaps makes it inevitable that it was also transient, transitional as it served as a bridge from one set of stories to a new and eventually much more formal religion. But that is not to dismiss it as a mere shadow on the hills or a morning mist at the dawn of Christianity, because it did leave some enduring marks on the landscape. It could also be repurposed today as the church once again enters a time of widespread scepticism. Apart from anything else, our modern condition is yet again burdened with a sense that something seriously dangerous is looming over us from the natural world. And once again this spiritual impulse would have to prove its worth by demonstrating some practical benefits, some physical evidence that a different orientation towards the natural world will improve both us and our environment. To borrow a phrase first offered by Gildas, a modern Celtic missionary theology would need to be useful.

The missionaries had worked out a way to engage with the shifting and elusive shapes that played in the minds of their potential converts, sharpening a theological argument that is remarkably robust and consistent. It was not a tactical, opportunistic response, but strategic, the same verses of the Bible appearing in completely different and unrelated texts (and there aren't that many of these) when it came to preaching to the common folk, a sympathetic reading of Genesis 1.28 at the heart. I think Germanus' mission to Britain in 429 brought just such a strategic vision of harmony in creation, which had been specifically designed to outflank any narratives that spoke ill of the natural world, narratives that saw only antagonism between us and nature, a sense that the elements seemed set against us: harsh, capricious or at best indifferent to human interest. Complaining about the British weather remains something of a national pastime even today. However, it is the climate that causes concern at an even deeper level, and the message from the Celtic missionaries seems more urgent with every passing year: a sacramental approach to nature enhances life for us as much as for our environment.

To put it another way, every single interaction that you have with the natural world would be beneficial in a 360-degree radius, good for us and good for it. It is a thought that lingers long after my Celtic nature rituals, standing in absolutely stark, primal simplicity in front of creation and wondering what we should make of it, a view from the starting point of the human condition. Ancient sacramental simplicity ripples through the centuries when contemplating our lakes, rivers and seas; the baptismal ritual as it is first recorded insists that no foreign object be taken into the water. Never mind the many plastic bottles lining our shores, big and obvious signs of degradation, the water itself is now saturated with an invisible soup of microfibres from clothing and textiles. Apart from the absence of fabrics whenever I go swimming, I am as bad an environmental offender as the next person, but I will give one example from my own natural enclave that emerged during the research for this book. Late one night while reading through some obscure Celtic text, I heard a scratching at the front door. When I opened it there was the triangular face and black, beady eyes of a little hedgehog, sniffing about hopefully for a bit of sustenance. The next day my daughter picked out a hedgehog house in the local garden centre and we carried it home between us. I also started to read online about how to encourage these little creatures, and discovered to my horror that the one thing you should not do is put down slug pellets. We have slugs and snails all around the front of our house and I had been as guilty as original sin itself by sprinkling little blue granules of poison all around the boundary. So I stopped. Some months later we were in the garden and decided to clear away the disused hedgehog house that was sitting under a bush, but when I picked up a corner I could see it was completely full of dried moss, leaves and twigs, and let it drop immediately. Since then I have seen the hedgehogs many times, some small, some large, and consider every single encounter a blessing and a lesson.

I wrote most of this book in the same suburban garden over the heatwave summer of 2018, increasingly aware of the many other animals that inhabit it: birds, butterflies, squirrels, frogs, hedgehogs and foxes in the evening, and any number of insects crawling across my screen, stray characters that I brushed gently into the grass. We poison slugs, we concrete over lawns, and my daughter's church school even replaced its entire area of grass with a plastic turf substitute around this same time. This is not a sacramental approach to the natural world, but rather the opposite, another remorseless step away from that first creation which we lost. It is curiously easy to forget that all this was resanctified amid the animals of a stable and the waters of the Jordan in my religious tradition, and there are others that weave divine purpose into the landscape in their own creative ways.

Inhibition comes through in the Bible itself, spiritual interaction with nature proving contentious from the start. Scripture is repeatedly compromised at precisely these points: the sacred trees of Mamre and Shechem, Matthew's omission of bodily worship, the nefarious raven *not* returning to the Ark, and the angels stirring a holy pool in Jerusalem. The very fact that Jesus underwent baptism fades out from Gospel to Gospel. That people were so keen to edit these awkward points makes them more curious and significant to me, not less. Where religion touches the interface between humans and the natural world seems to cause the greatest amount of scriptural anxiety, setting the tone for religion to follow. But crucially the Celtic missionaries were far-sighted enough to see the benefit of verses that had disturbed their imperial counterparts to the south, perfectly happy to see angels and other spiritual forces stirring the waters around Britain.

This Celtic vision of nature as a paradise waiting to be redeemed is not exactly environmentalism; it almost stands one step before that, a wider view if that were possible, cosmological in its scope. It is entirely fertile ground in which to plant an environmental theology, a modern one, and it was built on entirely conventional early church writings. It was also broad enough to cross tribal boundaries and inspire both Celtic and Roman-facing writers in Britain. The natural world is too large an arena for religious activity and culture to be constrained to any single ethnic identity. A faith that truly appreciates the cosmological scale of its reach will inevitably be inclusive of all other creatures, irrespective not only of tribal divisions but also the divisions between every other aspect of creation, including animate and inanimate creatures. A theology that embraces the full cosmological reach of a Creator God incarnated and operating within his creation is one that will reconcile people to place.

The golden cave

I am going to end this book by describing what I saw on my last night in a hermit's cave, as the sun set on the west coast of Scotland and the hour of evening prayer drew me to kneel. St Ninian's Cave is one of the oldest natural sites of worship in all Britain: carved stone crosses were deposited here as early as the sixth century in honour of the saint who used this remote shore for his own peaceful contemplation. It is not a deep chamber of a cave, no gloomy cavern where spirits or snakes once lurked, but more of an indentation in the yellow and grey rock, a short chasm that quickly narrows to a dead end. When I knelt before it at the entrance I was not tired, and I was not expecting or hoping for anything much to come my way, so what follows next did not feel like a trick of the mind. I had spent the previous week on an ever-deepening journey into the landscape rituals of the Celtic heartland: St Herbert's Isle in the Lake District, bathing at Coldingham and Old Melrose in the Scottish Borders, St Columba's Cave on the Kintyre peninsula. Earlier that evening I had been feeding the swallows that live in the roof of Ninian's Cave, and had been down to the water to perform a short immersion, both activities marking my sacramental approach to this coastal enclave. So I knelt in the shingle and shut my eyes. What came to me in the next few moments is quite hard to explain but I will end my journey with it. The sequence was rather like a series of dawning realizations, those moments when something occurs to you suddenly, unbidden by any chain of reasoning or calculation.

So as I knelt in honest simplicity, the walls of this cave lurched unexpectedly in front of my mind's eye, flattening out and rising up in front of me as a single wall of gold, with two winged figures on either side of where the deeper cave had been. It all looked of a piece, the statues a part of the growing slab of golden cliff face that had fused itself together. The best way I can describe it is similar to a stone screen in a cathedral, a narrow stretch of blank wall with pillars soaring up on either side, where the angels were fixed. I could also see myself in front of this gilded cave, not just kneeling but entirely bent forward, face to the ground. My first surprise was that I was still naked, which was immediately answered by this realization: I was naked because everybody is when they are in this position. There was no point wearing clothes because this is all that I am, that is all that anybody is in this place. Surrounding myself with anything material would be pointless at such a conjunction.

I'm not entirely sure what I was in front of, but my feeling was at the time and still is that this was the sum total of all who have worked, worshipped and died before me, the whole assembled achievements of the company of heaven if you like, all those who had trodden the paths before me. The second thing I realized was that this unearthly gold structure was continuing to grow bigger and bigger, my tiny crouched figure diminishing before it. And then it occurred to me that in front of this I was absolutely nothing, really nothing whatsoever compared to everything that has been done before, all the saints and workers, all the deeds and the accomplishments of our ancestors. I've never had such a completely overwhelming sense of smallness, not just in terms of size but in terms of significance too, in terms of the content and qualities of my being: my achievements, experiences, desires and my own labours were as nothing. Possessions weren't just insignificant in this same way, they were entirely absent, they added nothing at all, irrelevant when it came to the sum total of spiritual achievements and events both in me and before me. This was not nakedness as any sort of purity but rather a result of searingly intense scrutiny of what actually matters, what counts.

The whole experience wasn't a particularly encouraging or comfortable feeling, but I think that what I learned from it is true. No matter how much of an effort I have made, physically and mentally, it really is as nothing compared to the sacrifices and achievements of the countless host who have gone before us. It was and is a quite jarring perspective: naked and nothing before something divine. And then I understood a third thing at the moment my vision of the gold cave faded: I may have nothing, but I am expected to give everything. It doesn't make sense on one level, but I understand that anything I do to the good is to form part of this accumulated edifice of past witnesses and labourers. That is what I must do, even though anything I achieve will be small to the point of vanishing.

So that was me put in my place.

On reflecting further about this vision, it has since occurred to me that nudity, like death, is one of the few irreducible conditions of humanity. It was a fixed point of incalculable pain and learning for me while I researched my thesis that a close friend was slipping away from a cancer that would not let him go. One afternoon between rounds of chemotherapy Bill had been walking in Richmond Park and came unexpectedly close to a deer. He stood for a moment as this fellow animal met his gaze. The last time we met, he spoke of the mountains of his native Scotland, the piercing clarity of a summit view, the bird's eye panorama and the ever-receding peaks fading to blue. I could see it in his eyes, and we both agreed, with and without faith to steer us, that we are inseparably part of this. When death is something I can discuss creatively with my many non-believing friends, family and acquaintances, it is what arises from my experiences of ecstatic connection to the landscape that I felt three times on St Herbert's Isle and most intensively on top of Carningli shortly after sunset, as the world below me went quietly to sleep. It is the simple and unarguable fact that we will become part of elemental creation once again, that it is us and we are it. I'm not surprised that mystical writers such as Lady Julian of Norwich are reluctant to believe that anyone, no matter how great a sinner, can be entirely disconnected from our Creator's love. It would ultimately be the same as saying that our body can be separated out from physical creation. This conclusion is not much use as an insight if your faith is motivated by the idea that lots of people will be going to hell, mostly people you disapprove of in some way. But that was my final revelation in witnessing a remote cave turn gold before me, that our feeble and few atoms are the indivisible material building blocks of all creation, both heaven and earth alike. And so death is nothing to fear, because from the Creator's perspective it does not exist.

Some of what I saw at nightfall in St Ninian's Cave might echo my own inclinations, which has made me question hard where it came from, particularly because nakedness before God is not exactly out of my comfort zone. But I can't really describe how extreme the feeling of insignificance that hit me, just as I thought I had got on top of this project, as I finished my work in the field and in the library. I was probably going to write introductions and conclusions that were rather more coloured by my own personal imagination and predilections than I have produced in this book: a love of rural solitude, a celebration of wild skinny-dipping, an affirmation that true religions trample over borders, a set of answers to environmental catastrophe, a ridiculously optimistic cry for ecumenical fellowship, and even a couple of good pub recommendations by the wayside.

But instead I knew I only had to write down what happened to me on my journey, so there you have it. This is what I did.

Doxology: Creator

Show me the place where the paint is made that colours the world
Where the light is created that makes shine the splendour of the dawn
Show me the well that feeds the rivers and the rain
The grass that makes the bread and fires the oven
Play me the chord that tunes the music of the spheres
The pulse that marks the rhythms of time and tide
Show me the mount from where all creatures can be seen
Naked limbs knit fast in the wonder of the womb
Show me the seed that touches heaven with its branches
The birds of every land that flock beneath its shade
Show me the hope that illuminates the darkness of the void
The lines and shapes of all forms

After Jesus Christ, after Carl Jung, after Julian Cope

Notes

Introduction

1 Patrick Francis Moran, 'St Patrick', *The Catholic Encyclopedia*, vol. 11 (New York: Robert Appleton Company, 1911) (adapted).

2 Adomnán, *Life of St Columba* iii.17, ed. Richard Sharpe (London: Penguin Classics, 1995), p. 219.

3 Alister McGrath, *The Reenchantment of Nature* (London: Doubleday, 2003), p. 34, is one of many examples. The word 'nature' is itself somewhat ana-chronous when applied to the early medieval period, since the word used for what we term the natural world was much more likely to be simply 'creation'. As will be seen, however, there was a sense that animals, the weather and the landscape were in a category distinct from humans, and were uniquely responsive to the presence of a holy man or woman.

4 The notion of Celtic Christianity as a thin veneer over Paganism is a common interpretation, most starkly put in P. Berger, *The Goddess Obscured* (London: Robert Hale Ltd, 1988). The view that there was a 'Celtic church' institution-ally opposed to Rome was common in the early twentieth century and before but has been discounted in recent decades.

5 One other specific criticism was levelled at the early British church, that they had failed to preach and convert the Anglo-Saxon invaders, but this sounds more a question of circumstances than a deliberate policy, and was only men-tioned once.

6 Ian Bradley, *Celtic Christianity: Making Myths and Chasing Dreams* (Edinburgh: Edinburgh University Press, 1999), pp. 3, 208; his most recent book, however, acknowledges there was an 'amalgam' of cultural and reli-gious influences, defying attempts to delineate early medieval society along strict tribal or ethnic lines: Ian Bradley, *Following the Celtic Way* (London: Darton, Longman & Todd, 2018), p. 8.

7 Recent DNA evidence reveals a far greater degree of ethnic mixing in areas once thought to be dominated by Anglo-Saxons, who contributed less than half the genetic signature even in south-east England: S. Leslie et al., 'The Fine-scale Genetic Structure of the British Population', *Nature* 519 (2015), pp. 309–14.

8 Adomnán, *Life of St Columba* iii.10, 22, mentions Genereus and another by name.

9 Bede, *History* iv.19.

10 In the anonymous *Vita sanctae Brigitae* 15.93, reproduced in the Bollandists' *Acta Sanctorum*, February, vol. 1 (1–6), p. 132.

11 Philip Carr-Gomm, *Sacred Places: 50 Places of Pilgrimage* (London: Quercus, 2011); Philip Carr-Gomm, *A Brief History of Nakedness* (London: Reaktion Books, 2012).

12 Andy Phillips, *Celtic Christianity Today* (Newlyn: Gwask Peran Sans (St Piran's Press), 2007), p. 11.

13 John Cassian, *Conferences* 1.7.1. For the translation, see *John Cassian: The Conferences*, trans. Boniface Ramsey (New York: Paulist Press, 1997), p. 45. Cassian was a devout follower of the pioneering Egyptian monk Evagrius Ponticus, whose predilection for nocturnal nude bathing disciplines is well documented, and discussed in detail in Chapter 6.

1 Sacred trees

1 C. J. Hefele (ed.), *A History of the Councils of the Church: From the Original Documents, to the Close of the Second Council of Nicaea* A.D. *787, Vol. 1* (Edinburgh: T & T Clark, 1896), p. 170.

2 Bede, *History* ii.2, in David Farmer (ed.), *Bede: A History of the English Church and People*, trans. Leo Sherley-Price, revised trans. R. E. Latham (London: Penguin, 1990), p. 104.

3 B. Eagles, 'Augustine's Oak', *Medieval Archaeology* 47 (2003), pp. 175–8.

4 Both meetings are recorded in the same chapter of Bede's *History* ii.2.

5 The Bosworth-Toller Anglo-Saxon Dictionary cites just this example of the word. T. Northcote Toller and Joseph Bosworth, *An Anglo-Saxon Dictionary: Based on the Manuscript Collections of the Late Joseph Bosworth: Supplement* (Oxford: Clarendon Press. 1921), p. 629.

6 D. Hooke, *Trees in Anglo-Saxon England* (Woodbridge: Boydell Press, 2010), pp. 169–72.

7 Bede, *History* iii.4, in Farmer, *Bede*, p. 148.

8 Tírechán, *Life of St Patrick*, chapter 51.

9 Hooke, *Trees in Anglo-Saxon England*, pp. 96–7.

10 Bede, *History* i.32, in Farmer, *Bede*, p. 94.

11 Bede, *Historia Ecclesiastica gentis Anglorum* i.30, ed. B. Colgrave and R. A. B. Mynors (Oxford: Clarendon Press, 1969), pp. 106–9. Although Bede gives the date of this letter as 17 June, historians working with the register of Gregory the Great's papacy date it to 18 July 601.

12 Ian Wood, 'The Mission of Augustine of Canterbury to the English', *Speculum* 69.1 (January 1994), pp. 1–17, at p. 12.

13 Bede, *History* ii.13, in Farmer, *Bede*, p. 130.

14 Hooke, *Trees in Anglo-Saxon England*, p. 32.

15 Hooke, *Trees in Anglo-Saxon England*, p. 34, with slight editing.

16 Constantius, *Life of St Germanus*, in T. F. X. Noble and T. Head (eds), *Soldiers of Christ: Saints and Saints' Lives from Late Antiquity and the Early Middle Ages* (London: Sheed & Ward, 1995), chapter 17, pp. 89–90.

17 I am indebted to members of a community that is actually called Forest Church for encouraging me to explore how far back the roots of nature

spirituality go; look up Ancient Arden Forest Church on the internet for details of this modern movement.

18 C. P. Charalampidis, *The Dendrites in Pre-Christian and Christian Historical-Literary Tradition and Iconography* (Rome: 'L'Erma' di Bretschneider, 1995), p. 68. Another example in the same geographical region is mentioned in John Moschus, *Pratum spirituale* 70, a hermit living in a plane tree in Thessalonica, in J. Wortley, *The Spiritual Meadow of John Moschus* (Kalamazoo, MI: Cistercian Publications, 1992), p. 53.

19 *Lives of the Desert Fathers*, in H. Rosweyd (ed.), *Vitae Patrum* (Antwerp: Balthazar Moret, 1628), VI.3.4 and VI.3.10.

2 Celtic nature theology

1 Bede, *Prose Life of St Cuthbert*, chapter 21, in Bertram Colgrave (ed.), *Two Lives of Saint Cuthbert: A Life by an Anonymous Monk of Lindisfarne and Bede's Prose Life* (Cambridge: Cambridge University Press, 1985), p. 225.

2 Genesis 3.17–19.

3 Colgrave (ed.), *Two Lives of Saint Cuthbert*, p. 225.

4 *Sancti Augustini opera: de genesi contra Manichaeos*, ed. Dorothea Weber (Wien: Verlag der Österreichischen Akademie der Wissenschaften, 1998), p. 85; the text was written in 389–390.

5 Augustine, *Confessions* 1.8, and particularly 1.11–12.

6 K. Pollmann, 'Human Sin and Natural Environments: Augustine's Two Positions on Genesis 3:18', *Augustinian Studies* 41 (2010), pp. 69–85; Hanneke Reuling, *After Eden: Church Fathers and Rabbis on Genesis 3:16–21* (Leiden and Boston, MA: Brill, 2006), pp. 162–3, discusses the extent to which scholars detect a shift in Augustine's writings on this matter.

7 Bede, *On Genesis*, ed. Calvin Kendall (Liverpool: Liverpool University Press), book 1, 1.29–30, p. 94.

8 Genesis 9.3.

9 Gildas, *De excidio* 4.3 (my own translation, which renders *exitiabiles* as 'deadly', something that other translators have avoided, perhaps because this literal meaning seems so counter-intuitive).

10 Some of the best writers of church history follow this line to a greater or lesser extent. See for example Diarmaid MacCulloch, *A History of Christianity* (London: Penguin, 2009), pp. 342–3; Nicholas J. Higham, *The Convert Kings: Power and Religious Affiliation in Early Anglo-Saxon England* (Manchester: Manchester University Press, 1997), p. 52; John Blair, *The Church in Anglo-Saxon Society* (Oxford: Oxford University Press, 2005), p. 49; Richard Fletcher, *The Conversion of Europe* (London: Fontana Press, 1998), p. 238; the historian Barbara Yorke, however, acknowledges the difficulty in substantiating claims about the instruction or otherwise of the lay folk, in Barbara Yorke, *The Conversion of Britain 600–800* (Harlow: Pearson Education Ltd, 2006), pp. 120 and 195.

11 Bede, *Historia Ecclesiastica gentis Anglorum* ii.5, ed. B. Colgrave and R. A. B. Mynors (Oxford: Clarendon Press, 1969), p. 153.

12 Bede, *History* iii.3, in Colgrave and Mynors (eds), *Historia Ecclesiastica*, p. 221.

13 Ronald Hutton, *Pagan Britain* (London: Yale University Press, 2014), p. 317.

14 Bertram Colgrave, *The Earliest Life of Gregory the Great* (Cambridge: Cambridge University Press, 1985), pp. 56–9.

15 *The Life of Gregory the Great*, chapter 15, in Colgrave, *The Earliest Life*. This is the earliest known hagiography of the pope, written at Whitby between 704 and 714, and most of the text focuses on events in England following his decision to send missionaries.

16 Bede, *Prose Life of St Cuthbert*, chapter 3, in Colgrave (ed.), *Two Lives of St Cuthbert*, p. 165.

17 Bede, *Metrical Life of St Cuthbert*, lines 113–14, my translation.

18 Augustine, *De Catechizandis Rudibus*.

19 Bede, *History* iii.22.

20 Bede, *History* iv.13, in Colgrave and Mynors (eds), *Historia Ecclesiastica*, p. 373.

21 Bede, *History* ii.13.

22 A productive study of this account is found in Julia Barrow, 'How Coifi Pierced Christ's Side: A Re-examination of Bede's Ecclesiastical History, II, chapter 13', *Journal of Ecclesiastical History* 62 (October 2011), pp. 693–706, at pp. 699–700. Professor Barrow suggests that Bede knew and heavily rewrote the earlier account with the croaking crow, but the differences are very stark and Bede usually acknowledges his sources.

23 Tírechán, *Collectanea de sancto Patricio*, chapter 26, in Ludwig Bieler (ed.), *The Patrician Texts in the Book of Armagh* (Dublin: Dublin Institute for Advanced Studies, 1979), pp. 142–3.

24 Isaac of Antioch, *Homilies* 77, in St Isaac of Antioch, *The Ascetical Homilies of Saint Isaac the Syrian / Translated by the Holy Transfiguration Monastery* (Boston, MA: The Holy Transfiguration Monastery, 1984).

3 The naked hermit of Mount Sinai

1 Michel de Montaigne, 'Apology for Raimond Sebonde', in George Savile and Charles Cotton (eds), *Montaigne's Essays in Three Books: With Notes and Quotations*, vol. 2 (London: B & B Barker, 1743), p. 172.

2 Mary Low, *Celtic Christianity and Nature: The Early Irish and Hebridean Traditions* (Edinburgh: Edinburgh University Press, 1996), pp. 105ff.

3 Sulpicius Severus, *Dialogues* i.17. Bernard M. Peebles, 'Sulpicius Severus: Writings', in *The Fathers of the Church*, vol. 7 (Washington, DC: The Catholic University of America Press, 1949), pp. 77–254, at p. 184.

4 This is at the start of 2 Corinthians 5, although Paul is talking metaphorically of a spiritual body.

5 Bede, *Life of St Cuthbert*, chapter 46. Bede even goes so far as to say in the preface to his *History* that one of the main purposes of the book is to encourage readers to imitate good people.

6 Bertram Colgrave (ed.), *The Earliest Life of Gregory the Great* (Cambridge: Cambridge University Press, 1985); contains the original Latin and a translation.

7 *The Earliest Life of Gregory the Great*, chapter 30.

8 See Chapter 1 on trees for more details.

9 Bede, *Historia Ecclesiastica gentis Anglorum* i.1, ed. B. Colgrave and R. A. B. Mynors (Oxford: Clarendon Press, 1969), p. 19.

10 Jonathan Wooding (ed.), *The Otherworld Voyage in Early Irish Literature* (Dublin: Four Courts, 2000).

11 E. A. Speiser, *The Anchor Bible: Genesis* (New York: Doubleday and Company, 1964), p. 86, n. 6.

12 Mark 12.28–31; Luke 10.25–28; Matthew 22.35–40; Deuteronomy 6.4–5.

13 Matthew 15.17.

14 Kallistos Ware, '"My Helper and My Enemy": The Body in Greek Christianity', in Sarah Coakley (ed.), *Religion and the Body* (Cambridge: Cambridge University Press, 1997). Ware claims that Symeon is exceptional among Greek theologians on this point, but there is a wealth of material suggesting otherwise. For one example, see Peter Brown, *The Body and Society: Men, Women, and Sexual Renunciation in Early Christianity* (New York: Columbia University Press, 2008), p. 96. For fasting, see Symeon's conclusion that it is intended to make the body 'healthier and more vigorous' (*On Fasting*, chapter 5, in C. J. deCatanzaro (ed.), *Symeon the New Theologian: The Discourses* (New York: Paulist Press, 1980), p. 170).

15 Ruth Barcan, *Nudity: A Cultural Anatomy* (Oxford: Berg, 2006), p. 21.

16 Isaiah 20; Micah 1.8; Job 1.21; 1 Samuel 19.24. The same Hebrew and Greek words are used to describe the state in which a baby emerges from the womb, equivalent to the English phrase 'birthday suit'.

4 A company of birds

1 Edward Thomas, *The Annotated Collected Poems*, ed. Edna Longley (Hexham: Bloodaxe Books, 2008).

2 Fyodor Dostoevsky, *The Brothers Karamazov*, trans. David McDuff (London: Penguin Books, 2003), book 6, chapter 3, pp. 413–14.

3 Brother Ugolino, *The Little Flowers of St Francis*, trans. Roger Hudleston (Grand Rapids, MI: CCEL, 1958), part 1, chapter 16.

4 Adomnán, *Life of St Columba* i.48, ed. Richard Sharpe (London: Penguin Classics, 1995). The bird might have been a crane rather than a heron, according to a note by translator Richard Sharpe.

5 W. Stokes, *Tripartite Life of Patrick: With Other Documents Relating to that Saint* (London: HMSO, 1887), pp. 114–15.

6 Susan Crane, *Animal Encounters: Contacts and Concepts in Medieval Britain* (Philadelphia, PA: University of Pennsylvania Press, 2012), p. 35, in a chapter generally full of useful insight into the hermit's relationship to animals.

7 Thomas O'Loughlin, *Celtic Theology* (London: Continuum, 2000), pp. 48–67, especially at pp. 54–5.

8 O'Loughlin, *Celtic Theology*, pp. 52–3.

9 Felix, *Life of St Guthlac*, chapter 39, in B. Colgrave (ed.), *Felix's Life of St Guthlac* (Cambridge: Cambridge University Press, 2007).

10 Jonas, *Life of St Columbanus* I.17, in *Ionae Vitae Sanctorum Columbani, Vedastis, Iohannis*, ed. Bruno Krusch (Hannover: Impensis Bibliopolii Hahniani, 1905).

11 D. H. Farmer (ed.), *The Age of Bede* (London: Penguin Classics, 1998), p. 242.

12 For an excellent overview of birds and many other natural vehicles for Celtic spirituality, see Mary Low, *Celtic Christianity and Nature: The Early Irish and Hebridean Traditions* (Edinburgh: Edinburgh University Press, 1996).

13 The latest translation of Bede's commentary on Genesis makes a very plausible argument that Bede himself did not approve of this highly unusual editorial change to the Bible, since he quotes the original verse correctly: Calvin Kendall (ed.), *On Genesis* (Liverpool: Liverpool University Press, 2008), p. 194, n. 293.

14 Anonymous, *Life of St Cuthbert* i.6; Bede, *Life of St Cuthbert*, chapter 13. Both citations are from Bertram Colgrave (ed.), *Two Lives of Saint Cuthbert: A Life by an Anonymous Monk of Lindisfarne and Bede's Prose Life* (Cambridge: Cambridge University Press, 1985).

15 Dostoevsky, *The Brothers Karamazov*, part 2, book 4, chapters 2 and 3.

16 Many of these tales are compiled in Dominic Alexander, *Saints and Animals in the Middle Ages* (Woodbridge: Boydell Press, 2008), although he tends to read these interactions allegorically rather than as the physical expressions of belief examined and recreated in this book.

17 Anonymous, *Life of St Cuthbert* ii.5.

5 A desert in the sea: hermit islands

1 Adomnán, *Life of St Columba* i.20, ed. Richard Sharpe (London: Penguin Classics, 1995).

2 This interpretation of Cain and Abel as representing a dichotomy between nomadism and city-dwelling has a long pedigree in Judaeo-Christian history (Josephus, *Jewish Antiquities* 1:53–4, and Ambrose, *Cain and Abel* 1.3.10), although other theories have been proposed for the source of their sinfulness/innocence.

3 Exodus 16.10.

4 Bede, *History* iii.3.

5 Bede, *History* iii.5, in David Farmer (ed.), *Bede: A History of the English Church and People*, trans. Leo Sherley-Price, revised trans. R. E. Latham (London: Penguin, 1990).

6 Bede, *On Genesis*, ed. Calvin Kendall (Liverpool: Liverpool University Press, 2008), p. 156.

7 James Dean, 'The World Grown Old and Genesis in Middle English Historical Writings', *Speculum* 57 (1982), pp. 548–68, at p. 560.

8 Bede, *Lives of the Abbots of Wearmouth and Jarrow*, in David Farmer (ed.), *The Age of Bede* (London: Penguin Classics, 1998), chapter 5.

9 T. Charles-Edwards, 'The Social Background to Irish Peregrinatio', in J. Wooding (ed.), *The Otherworld Voyage in Early Irish Literature* (Dublin: Four Courts, 2000), pp. 94–108, at p. 96.

10 Bede, *Historia Ecclesiastica gentis Anglorum* iii.27, ed. B. Colgrave and R. A. B. Mynors (Oxford: Clarendon Press, 1969), pp. 312–13.

11 Adomnán, *Life of St Columba* i.48.

12 John Ryan, *Irish Monasticism* (Dublin: Four Courts Press,1992), pp. 197–8.

13 Clare Stancliffe, 'Red, White and Blue Martyrdom', in Dorothy Whitelock, Rosamund McKitterick and David Dumville (eds), *Ireland in Early Mediaeval Europe* (Cambridge: Cambridge University Press, 1982).

14 D. A. Bray, 'Allegory in Navigatio Sancti Brendani', in Wooding (ed.), *The Otherworld Voyage in Early Irish Literature*, pp. 175–87, at p. 181 and n. 29, where she cites two further admonitions against pilgrimage from the ninth century.

15 Della Hooke, *Trees in Anglo-Saxon England* (Woodbridge: Boydell Press, 2010), p. 22 for Arles, p. 33 for Ælfric and Wulfstan.

16 B. Bitton-Ashkelony, *Encountering the Sacred: The Debate on Christian Pilgrimage in Late Antiquity* (Oakland, CA: University of California Press, 2005), pp. 61–2.

17 Anonymous, *Life of St Cuthbert* iii.1; Bede, *Life of St Cuthbert*, chapter 17.

18 Athanasius, *Life of St Antony*, chapters 11–13.

19 Jerome, *Life of St Paul the Hermit*, chapters 8 and 10.

20 Peter Brown, *The Cult of the Saints: Its Rise and Function in Latin Christianity* (Chicago, IL: University of Chicago Press, 1982), p. 108.

21 Adomnán, *Life of St Columba* ii.28.

22 *Adomnán's Life of St Columba* ii.27, ed. Alan Orr Anderson and Marjorie Ogilvie Anderson (Oxford: Clarendon Press, 1991).

23 Mark 5.1–20; Luke 8.26–39; Matthew 8.28–34; Sulpicius Severus, *Dialogues I*, chapters 20 and 22.

24 Constantius, *Life of St Germanus*, chapter 13, in T. F. X. Noble and T. Head (eds), *Soldiers of Christ: Saints and Saints' Lives from Late Antiquity and the Early Middle Ages* (London: Sheed & Ward, 1995).

25 Bede, *Metrical Life of St Cuthbert*, line 151, refers to St Aidan providing consecrated oil to aid a sea journey during a storm; Adomnán, *Life of St Columba* ii.34, refers to Germanus quelling the storm directly when he describes how Columba calmed a storm, once again on the waters of Loch Ness.

26 Bede, *History* iv.29; also in the anonymous *Life of St Cuthbert* iv.9, and Bede's *Life of St Cuthbert*, chapter 27.

27 Bede, *Life of St Cuthbert*, chapter 17, in Bertram Colgrave (ed.), *Two Lives of Saint Cuthbert: A Life by an Anonymous Monk of Lindisfarne and Bede's Prose Life* (Cambridge: Cambridge University Press, 1985).

28 Alastair McIntosh, *Poacher's Pilgrimage: An Island Journey* (Edinburgh: Birlinn, 2016).

29 Bede, *History* iv.29, in Farmer (ed.), *Bede*.

6 In for the chill: sacred bathing

1 Henry David Thoreau, *Walden* (New York: Cosimo Classics, 2009), p. 58.

2 *The Lausiac History, Ancient Christian Writers 34*, ed. Robert T. Meyer (New York: Paulist Press, 1965), p. 113; *Four Desert Fathers: Pambo, Evagrius, Macarius of Egypt, and Macarius of Alexandria, Coptic Texts Relating to the Lausiac History of Palladius Popular Patristics Series*, ed. Tim Vivian (Crestwood, NY: St Vladimir's Seminary Press, 2005), par. 22; *PG* XXXIV 1194B, chapter 86, for the original Greek; *PG* XXXIV 1192B for the censored Latin translation.

3 Louis Gougaud, *Devotional and Ascetic Practices in the Middle Ages* (London: Burns Oates, 1927), p. 159. Other studies include Colin Ireland, 'Penance and Prayer in Water: An Irish Practice in Northumbrian Hagiography', *Cambrian Medieval Celtic Studies* 34 (1997), pp. 51–66; Michael Herity, 'Early Irish Hermitages', in Gerald Bonner, David Rollason and Clare Stancliffe (eds), *Cuthbert, His Cult and Community to AD 1200* (Woodbridge: The Boydell Press, 1989), pp. 45–63, at p. 52.

4 Fergus Kelly, 'A Poem in Praise of Columb Cille', *Ériu* 24 (1973), pp. 1–34, at p. 9.

5 For example, Ronald K. Rittgers, *The Reformation of Suffering: Pastoral Theology and Lay Piety in Late Medieval and Early Modern Germany* (Oxford: Oxford University Press, 2012), p. 77; also *Encyclopedia of Monasticism*, ed. William M. Johnston (Abingdon: Routledge, 2015), p. 266.

6 Bede, *Life of St Cuthbert*, chapter 10, in Bertram Colgrave (ed.), *Two Lives of Saint Cuthbert: A Life by an Anonymous Monk of Lindisfarne and Bede's Prose Life* (Cambridge: Cambridge University Press, 1985).

7 One scholar comes close to considering the practical implications of this deep-water bathing, before pulling back and dismissing the scene as an allusion to the poetry of Roman writer Virgil: Michael Lapidge, 'Bede's Metrical Vita S. Cuthberti', in Bonner et al. (eds), *Cuthbert, His Cult and Community to AD 1200*, pp. 77–93, at p. 92.

8 Britton Brooks, 'The Reorientation of Creation in the Early Anglo-Saxon Vitae of Cuthbert and Guthlac' (unpublished PhD thesis, Oxford University, 2016), p. 89; the psalm is numbered 95 in modern Bibles, but 94 in the Latin Vulgate known to Bede.

9 J. T. Fowler (ed.), *The Life of St Cuthbert in English Verse* (Durham: Surtees Society Publications, 1889), p. 49.

10 British Library manuscript: *Yates Thompson MS 26*, f. 24r.

11 Bede, *History* i.1.

12 Nicholas Orme, *Early British Swimming 55 BC – AD 1719* (Exeter: University of Exeter, 1983), p. 38.

13 Olga Gusakova, 'A Saint and the Natural World', in P. Clarke and T. Claydon (eds), *God's Bounty? The Churches and the Natural World* (Suffolk: Boydell Press, 2010), pp. 42–52, at pp. 44–5; Dominic Alexander, *Saints and Animals in the Middle Ages* (Woodbridge: Boydell Press, 2008), p. 46.

14 Bede, *History* v.12.

15 Susan Crane, *Animal Encounters: Contacts and Concepts in Medieval Britain* (Philadelphia, PA: University of Pennsylvania Press, 2012), p. 25. Brooks, 'The Reorientation of Creation', pp. 67–73, 138, 151–2, detects a shift in Bede from monastic authority to pastoral ministry in his reworking of Cuthbert's *Life*, a trajectory of outreach that my own research follows further still. Other scholars claim that Cuthbert's bathing was designed as a lesson to the monks and nuns of Coldingham to curb their bodily appetites, since the monastery was eventually destroyed in a fire due to their immoral behaviour, but none of the accounts of this bathing scene make any reference to this context; Alexander, *Saints and Animals in the Middle Ages*, p. 46.

16 Anne Ross, *Pagan Celtic Britain* (London: Sphere Books Ltd, 1974), p. 48.

17 R. Sharpe (ed.), *Life of St. Columba* (London: Penguin Classics, 1995), n. 234, pp. 322–3. For details of finds at healing wells in Gaul, see Jessica Hughes, 'The Anxiety of Influence: Anatomical Votives in Roman Gaul, First Century BC–First Century AD', in *Votive Body Parts in Greek and Roman Religion*, Cambridge Classical Studies (Cambridge: Cambridge University Press, 2017), pp. 106–50.

18 Ronald Hutton, *Pagan Britain* (London: Yale University Press, 2014), p. 217. See also Miranda Green, *The Gods of the Celts* (Stroud: Sutton Publishing, 2004), pp. 143–4.

19 Adomnán, *Life of St Columba* ii.11.

20 L. Bieler (ed.), *The Patrician Texts in the Book of Armagh* (Dublin: Dublin Institute for Advanced Studies, 1979), p. 153.

21 Adomnán, *Life of St Columba* i.19, in Sharpe (ed.), *Life of St Columba*; the milk bucket is in ii.16.

22 J. Montgomery et al., 'Strategic and Sporadic Marine Consumption at the Onset of the Neolithic: Increasing Temporal Resolution in the Isotope Evidence', *Antiquity* 78.338 (2013), pp. 1060–72.

23 Just after returning from Orkney I read a remarkable book documenting a young woman's own healing on this island after a life of excess in London: Amy Liptrot, *The Outrun* (London: Canongate Books, 2016).

24 Ambrose, *De mysteriis* 6.30, *De sacramentis* 3.1.7. Five liturgical texts survive from the period with a foot washing: the *Stowe Missal*, the *Bobbio Missal*, the *Missale Gothicum*, the *Missale Gallicanum vetus*, and a liturgy at Saint-Maurice in Switzerland. See E. C. Whitaker and Maxwell E. Johnson (eds), *Documents of the Baptismal Liturgy* (London: SPCK, 2003), p. 283 (*Stowe Missal*), p. 273 (*Bobbio Missal*). See also Yitzhak Hen and Rob Meens, *The Bobbio Missal: Liturgy and Religious Culture in Merovingian Gaul* (Cambridge: Cambridge University Press, 2004), p. 72 for the *Missale Gothicum*; Gabriele Winkler, 'Confirmation or Chrismation? A Study in Comparative Liturgy', in Maxwell E. Johnson (ed.), *Living Water, Sealing Spirit: Readings on Christian Initiation* (Collegeville, MN: Liturgical Press, 1995), pp. 202–18, at p. 208 for the *Missale Gallicanum vetus*; and Everett Ferguson, *Baptism in the Early Church* (Grand Rapids, MI: Eerdmans, 2009), p. 846 for the Saint-Maurice baptistery.

25 Aphrahat of Syria, *Demonstrations* 12.10, translation in Bryan D. Spinks, *Early and Medieval Rituals and Theologies of Baptism* (Farnham: Ashgate, 2006), p. 52.

26 The causes and consequences of this disagreement have been eloquently compiled by an American scholar, Garry Wills, *Font of Life: Ambrose, Augustine, and the Mystery of Baptism* (Oxford: Oxford University Press, 2012).

27 Ambrose, *De sacramentis* 3.1.4–5, in T. Thompson and J. H. Srawley (eds), *St Ambrose: On the Mysteries, and the Treatise on the Sacraments by an Unknown Author* (New York: Macmillan, 1919).

28 John the Deacon, *Letter to Senarius*, §6, in Whitaker and Johnson (eds), *Documents of the Baptismal Liturgy*, p. 210. This letter, written around the year 500 by a senior deacon in Rome, even gives a theological justification for the requirement for nudity, and adds that it was treated with a degree of discretion in ecclesiastical documents. We will return to this later in the chapter.

29 My methods for studying such a 'family' of liturgical texts has been greatly helped by the recent work of Helen Gittos and others, particularly Helen Gittos and Sarah Hamilton (eds), *Understanding Medieval Liturgy* (Farnham: Ashgate, 2016).

30 Ambrose, *De sacramentis* 1.5.18, in Thompson and Srawley (eds), *St Ambrose*.

31 Ambrose, *De sacramentis* 2.7.20, in Thompson and Srawley (eds), *St Ambrose*; also in *De mysteriis* 2.7.

32 L. Duchesne, *Christian Worship: Its Origin and Evolution. A Study of the Latin Liturgy up to the Time of Charlemagne*, trans. M. L. McClure (London: SPCK, 1931), pp. 88–9; Paul Bradshaw, *The Search for the Origins of Christian Worship* (London: SPCK, 1992), pp. 161–84.

33 Thomas F. X. Noble and Thomas Head (eds), *Soldiers of Christ: Saints and Saints' Lives from Late Antiquity and the Early Middle Ages* (London: Sheed & Ward, 1995), p. 98, n. 26.

34 Paul Blowers, *Drama of the Divine Economy* (Oxford: Oxford University Press, 2012), pp. 251–7, 370.

35 Whitaker and Johnson (eds), *Documents of the Baptismal Liturgy*, p. 280.

36 John Chrysostom, *Baptismal Instructions*, §20–21, in Paul W. Harkins (ed.), *St John Chrysostom: Baptismal Instructions* (New York: Paulist Press, 1963), p. 138.

37 Cyril of Jerusalem, Lecture XX (second lecture on the mysteries), in P. Schaff and W. H. Fremantle (eds) and E. Gifford (trans.), *Nicene and Post-Nicene Fathers, Series 2, Volume 7* (Grand Rapids, MI: Eerdmans, 1893), p. 350.

38 Hippolytus, *Apostolic Tradition*, §21, in Whitaker and Johnson (eds), *Documents of the Baptismal Liturgy*, p. 7.

39 Laurie Guy, '"Naked" Baptism in the Early Church: The Rhetoric and the Reality', *Journal of Religious History* 27 (2003), pp. 133–42, at p. 140.

40 John Chrysostom, *Baptismal Instructions*, §28, in Whitaker and Johnson (eds), *Documents of the Baptismal Liturgy*, p. 43.

41 Bede, *History* ii.2, in *Historia Ecclesiastica gentis Anglorum*, ed. B. Colgrave

and R. A. B. Mynors (Oxford: Clarendon Press, 1969), p. 139 (adapted).

42 The latest of many scholars presenting this or a very similar viewpoint is Spinks, *Early and Medieval Rituals and Theologies of Baptism*, pp. 125–6.

43 A translation of Pope Gregory the Great's letter of 594 is in Whitaker and Johnson (eds), *Documents of the Baptismal Liturgy*, p. 206. The references to episcopal confirmation are in the *Life of St Samson of Dol* i.50, ii.7, Thomas Taylor (ed.), *The Life of St Samson of Dol* (London: SPCK, 1925).

44 Thompson and Srawley (eds), *St Ambrose*, p. 100, n. 2, describes the word *perfectio* as 'almost a technical term' for confirmation.

45 Whitaker and Johnson (eds), *Documents of the Baptismal Liturgy*, p. 3.

46 Ambrose, *De sacramentis* 2.2.6, in Thompson and Srawley (eds), *St Ambrose*; cf. *De mysteriis* 4.20.

47 Éamonn Ó Carragáin, *Ritual and the Rood: Liturgical Images and the Old English Poems of the Dream of the Rood Tradition* (London: The British Library and University of Toronto Press, 2005), p. 231.

48 *Gelasian Sacramentary*, section 35; in Whitaker and Johnson (eds), *Documents of the Baptismal Liturgy*, pp. 222–3.

49 Bede is still referring to the baptism ritual practised by Ionan priests as late as the 630s with the curious verb *recreati*, regenerated, even though he never uses the word again in that context, preferring instead the word *renatus*, reborn (Bede, *History* iii.1).

50 Eddius Stephanus, *The Life of St Wilfrid*, chapter 10, in Bertram Colgrave (ed.), *The Life of Bishop Wilfrid by Eddius Stephanus* (Cambridge: Cambridge University Press, 1985).

51 Gildas, *De excidio* 19.1, in Michael Winterbottom (ed.), *The Ruin of Britain, and Other Works* (Chichester: Phillimore & Co., 1978). The 'Scots' and their neighbours are also accused of a similar lack of inhibition in an exchange of letters between Augustine and a Pelagian, in Augustine: *Contra Julianum opus imperfectum* 4.44.2.

52 See <www.whitespring.org.uk> for the limited opening times.

53 Lisa Bitel, *Landscape with Two Saints: How Genovefa of Paris and Brigit of Kildare Built Christianity in Barbarian Europe* (Oxford: Oxford University Press, 2009), argues that there is no evidence for a Pagan deity called Brigit who was worshipped by the pre-Christian Irish, and perhaps not coincidentally also questions whether the category of 'Celtic' is applicable in either a Pagan or Christian context.

54 See, for example, the painting *The Holy Well* (1916) by William Orpen, showing pilgrims undressing to bathe in Ireland. Some critics have dismissed the scene as 'propaganda' but in reality it closely matches written records of traditional piety. See, for example, Dean Henry's disdainful description of the 'very indecent' spectacle of mixed-sex groups of pilgrims praying and then stripping naked to bathe at Holywell, Belcoo, in front of thousands of spectators in eighteenth-century Ireland, recorded in John Cunningham, *Fermanagh in Sight: The Fermanagh Highlands* (Belleek: Davog Press, 2008), p. 25.

55 Nicholas Orme, *Early British Swimming 55 BC – AD 1719* (Exeter: University of Exeter, 1983), p. 38; Thermae Bath Spa (2015), 'History of the Spa'. Available at: <www.thermaebathspa.com/news-info/about-the-spa/spa-history/>.

7 The serpent's lair: harrowing caves

1 Athanasius, *Life of St Antony*, chapters 7 and 8.
2 Gregory the Great, *Life of Benedict* in his *Dialogues* 2.1.
3 T. Taylor (ed.), *The Life of St Samson of Dol* (London: SPCK, 1925). The caves are mentioned in chapters 40–1, 50–1 and 58.
4 My fellow traveller Fr John Musther visited this cave before midge season and called it an 'attractive place', which it is during the day. For many more Celtic adventures and photographs, see his book *Sacred North* (Bridgend: Culture & Democracy Press, 2018), p. 52.
5 M. Carver, A. Sanmark and S. Semple (eds), *Signals of Belief in Early England: Anglo-Saxon Paganism Revisited* (Oxford: Oxbow Books, 2010), p. 29.
6 See <www.british-history.ac.uk/vch/derbs/vol2/pp69-75>.
7 K. C. Innemée, 'On the necessity of dress: Should a hermit wear clothes?' *Khil'a, Journal of Dress and Textiles in the Islamic World* 1 (2006), pp. 69–78.
8 Carver, Sanmark and Semple (eds), *Signals of Belief in Early England*, pp. 36–8.
9 Taylor (ed.), *The Life of St Samson of Dol*, chapter 48.
10 *Penitential of Theodore*, chapters 16 and 17. The earliest version of this *Penitential* is called the *Capitula Dacheriana*, and is online at: <http://individual.utoronto.ca/michaelelliot/manuscripts/texts/transcriptions/pthd.pdf>.
11 Felix, *Life of Saint Guthlac*, chapter 28.
12 For much more on this topic, see Peter Brown, *The Cult of the Saints: Its Rise and Function in Latin Christianity* (Chicago, IL: University of Chicago Press, 1982).
13 Adomnán, *Life of St Columba* iii.18.

8 Misty peaks

1 Marie Trevelyan, *Folk-lore and Folk-stories of Wales* (London: E. Stock, 1909), p. 45.
2 *The Welsh History Review* 14.1 (1988), p. 39.
3 S. Semple, 'In the Open Air', in M. Carver, A. Sanmark and S. Semple (eds), *Signals of Belief in Early England* (Oxford: Oxbow Books, 2010), pp. 21–48.
4 Bede, *History* iii.23, in David Farmer (ed.), *Bede: A History of the English Church and People*, trans. Leo Sherley-Price, revised trans. R. E. Latham (London: Penguin, 1990).
5 Examples include 1 Kings 13.32–33; 1 Kings 22.43–44; 2 Kings 12.3 and following chapters; and 2 Kings 18.4.
6 T. Taylor (ed.), *The Life of St Samson of Dol* (London: SPCK, 1925), chapter 48.
7 Adomnán, *Life of St Columba* iii.16, in R. Sharpe (ed.), *Life of St. Columba* (London: Penguin Classics, 1995).

8 Adomnán, *Life of St Columba* ii.44.

9 George Fox, *An Autobiography*, ed. Rufus Jones (Richmond, IN: Friends United Press, 1976), chapter 6.

10 Gildas, *De excidio* 4.3, in Michael Winterbottom (ed.), *The Ruin of Britain, and Other Works* (Chichester: Phillimore & Co., 1978) (amended).

11 W. Stokes, *Tripartite Life of Patrick: With Other Documents Relating to that Saint* (London: HMSO, 1887), p. 115 (slightly modernized).

12 Strabo, *Life of St Gall*, chapter 7, in M. Joynt (ed.), *The Life of St Gall* (Burnham-on-Sea: Llanerch Press, 1927), p. 72.

13 K. Meyer (ed.), *Hibernica minora, Being a Fragment of an Old-Irish Treatise on the Psalter* (Oxford: Clarendon Press, 1894), p. 44.

14 Felix, *Life of St Guthlac*, chapter 34, in B. Colgrave (ed.), *Felix's Life of Saint Guthlac* (Cambridge: Cambridge University Press, 2007), pp. 110–11.

15 W. J. Rees (ed.), *Lives of the Cambro British Saints* (Llandovery: Longman & Co., 1853), p. 295.

9 Lessons from the Celtic shore

1 In baptismal liturgy of the day, Ephesians 4 is quoted at this point: 'The old man is put off and the new man put on': *Gelasian Sacramentary*, in E. C. Whitaker and Maxwell E. Johnson (eds), *Documents of the Baptismal Liturgy* (London: SPCK, 2003), p. 223, the same passage that talks about 'complete' baptism of the whole body.

Bibliography

Primary sources

Adomnán, *The Life of St Columba*, in *Adomnán's Life of Columba*, ed. Alan Orr Anderson and Marjorie Oglivie Anderson (Oxford: Clarendon Press, 1991); another translation is *Life of St Columba*, ed. R. Sharpe (London: Penguin Classics, 1995).

Ambrose, *De mysteriis, de sacramentis*; *de sacramentis*, in *Saint Ambrose on the Sacraments*, ed. Henry Chadwick (London: A. R. Mowbray & Co., 1960); *De mysteriis* is in *Sources Chrétiennes, Les Editions du Cerf*, vol. 25; translations in T. Thompson and J. H. Srawley (eds), *St Ambrose: On the Mysteries, and the Treatise on the Sacraments by an Unknown Author* (New York: Macmillan, 1919).

Ambrosian Manual, in Marcus Magistretti (ed.), *Monumenta Veteris Liturgiae Ambrosianae Vol. 3* (Milan: Ulricum Hoepli, 1904).

Aphrahat, *Demonstrations*, in J. Parisot (ed.), *Aphraatis Sapientis Persae Demonstrationes*, Patrologia Syriaca 1 and 2 (Paris: 1894, 1907); partial translation in E. C. Whitaker and E. Maxwell Johnson (eds), *Documents of the Baptismal Liturgy* (London: SPCK, 2003).

Athanasius, *Life of St Antony*, translation in Carolinne White (ed.), *Early Christian Lives* (London: Penguin Books, 1998).

Augustine, *Confessionum Libri Tredecim* in *Patrologia Latina*, vol. 32.

Augustine, *Contra Julianum opus imperfectum*, in *Patrologia Latina*, vol. 45; translation in Roland J. Teske (ed.), *Answer to the Pelagians III*, in *The Works of Saint Augustine* I.25 (New York: New City Press, 1998).

Augustine, *De Catechizandis Rudibus*, in CCSL 46 (Turnhout: Brepols, 1969), pp. 121–78; translation in J. P. Christopher, *The First Catechetical Instruction: De Catechizandis Rudibus* (Westminster, MD: The Newman Bookshop, 1946).

Augustine, *De Genesi contra Manichaeos*, in Dorothea Weber (ed.), *Sancti Augustini opera: de genesi contra Manichaeos* (Wien: Verlag der Österreichischen Akademie der Wissenschaften, 1998).

Basil the Great, *On the Origin of Humanity* in *On the Human Condition / St Basil the Great*, trans. Nonna V. Harrison (Crestwood, NY: St Vladimir's Seminary Press, 2005).

Bede, *History* in *Historia Ecclesiastica gentis Anglorum*, ed. B. Colgrave and R. A. B. Mynors (Oxford: Clarendon Press, 1969); David Farmer (ed.), *Bede: A History of the English Church and People*, trans. Leo Sherley-Price, revised trans. R. E. Latham (London: Penguin, 1990).

Bede, *In Genesim, Bedae Venerabilis opera. Pars 2, Opera exegetica*, ed. C. W. Jones, CCSL 118A (Turnhout: 1967); translation in Calvin Kendall (ed.), *On Genesis* (Liverpool: Liverpool University Press, 2008).

Bede, *Lives of the Abbots of Wearmouth and Jarrow*, in David Farmer (ed.), *The Age of Bede* (London: Penguin Classics, 1998).

Bede, *Metrical Life of St Cuthbert*, original Latin in *Bedas metrische Vita Sancti Cuthberti*, ed. Werner Jaager (Leipzig: Mayer & Müller, 1935); this is the verse *Life of St Cuthbert* and to date has not been fully translated into English.

Benedict, *La règle de saint Benoît*, ed. Adalbert de Vogüé and Jean Neufville (Paris: Editions du Cerf, 1972).

Biblia Sacra iuxta Vulgatam versionem, ed. Robert Weber and Roger Gryson (Stuttgart: Deutsche Bibelgesellschaft, 2007).

Cassian, John, *Collationum XXIV Collectio in Tres Partes Divisa* in *Patrologia Latina*, vol. 49; translation in B. Ramsey, *John Cassian: The Conferences* (New York: Paulist Press, 1997).

Chrysostom, John, *Instructions to Catechumens*; translation in Paul W. Harkins (ed.), *St John Chrysostom, Baptismal Instructions* (New York: Paulist Press, 1963).

Cogitosus, *Vita sanctae Brigitae* in Karina Hochegger, 'Untersuchungen Zu Den Ältesten Vitae Sanctae Brigidae' (unpublished MPhil thesis, Universität Wien, Philologisch-Kulturwissenschaftliche Fakultät, 2009). Available online at: <http://othes.univie.ac.at/4797/>; translation in Liam de Paor (ed.), *St Patrick's World* (Dublin: Four Courts Press, 1993).

Colgrave, Bertram (ed.), *The Earliest Life of Gregory the Great* (Cambridge: Cambridge University Press, 1985); this volume contains the original Latin and a translation.

Colgrave, Bertram (ed.), *Two Lives of Saint Cuthbert: A Life by an Anonymous Monk of Lindisfarne and Bede's Prose Life* (Cambridge: Cambridge University Press, 1985); this volume contains the original Latin and a translation.

Constantius, *The Life of St Germanus*, in *Monumenta Germaniae Historica, Scriptores rerum Merovingicarum*, vol. 7 (Hannover: Impensis Bibliopolii Hahniani, 1920); translation in Thomas F. X. Noble and Thomas Head (eds), *Soldiers of Christ: Saints and Saints' Lives from Late Antiquity and the Early Middle Ages* (London: Sheed & Ward, 1995).

Cyril of Jerusalem, *Lectures*, in P. Schaff and W. H. Fremantle (eds) and E. Gifford (trans.), *Nicene and Post-Nicene Fathers*, second series, vol. 7 (Grand Rapids, MI: Eerdmans, 1893).

Eucherius, *In Praise of the Desert*, in *The Life of the Jura Fathers* (Cistercian Studies Series, no. 178), trans. Tim Vivian, Kim Vivian and Jeffrey Burton Russell (Kalamazoo, MI: Cistercian Publications, 1999).

Fairweather, Janet (ed.), *Liber Eliensis: A History of the Isle of Ely* (Woodbridge: Boydell Press, 2005).

Farmer, D. H. (ed.), *The Age of Bede* (London: Penguin Classics, 1998) (for a translation of the *Voyage of St Brendan*).

Felix, *Life of St Guthlac*, B. Colgrave (ed.), *Felix's Life of Saint Guthlac* (Cambridge: Cambridge University Press, 2007).

Fowler, J. T. (ed.), *The Life of St Cuthbert in English Verse* (Durham: Surtees Society Publications, 1889).

Gildas, *De excidio*; Latin original and translation are in M. Winterbottom (ed.), *The Ruin of Britain, and Other Works* (Chichester: Phillimore & Co., 1978).

Gonser, Paul (ed.), *Das Angelsächsische Prosa-Leben Des Hl. Guthlac* (Heidelberg: C. Winter, 1909), for the prose Anglo-Saxon *Life of St Guthlac*.

Gregory the Great, *Grégoire le Grand: Dialogues*, ed. Adalbert de Vogue (Paris: Éditions du Cerf, 1978–80); translation in *Life and Miracles of St. Benedict (Book II, Dialogues)*, trans. Odo J. Zimmermann and Benedict R. Avery (Westport, CT: Greenwood Press, 1980).

Isaac of Antioch, *The Ascetical Homilies of Saint Isaac the Syrian: Translated by the Holy Transfiguration Monastery* (Boston, MA: The Holy Transfiguration Monastery, 1984).

Jerome, *Life of St Paul the Hermit* in *Patrologia Latina*, vol. 23; translation in Carolinne White (ed.), *Early Christian Lives* (London: Penguin Books, 1998).

Jonas, *Ionae Vitae Sanctorum Columbani, Vedastis, Iohannis*, ed. Bruno Krusch (Hannover: Impensis Bibliopolii Hahniani, 1905); translation in *Jonas of Bobbio; Life of Columbanus; Life of John of Réomé; and Life of Vedast*, trans. Alexander O'Hara and Ian Wood (Liverpool: Liverpool University Press, 2017).

Kelly, Fergus, 'A Poem in Praise of Columb Cille', *Ériu* 24 (1973), pp 1–34.

Lives of the Desert Fathers, in H. Rosweyd (ed.), *Vitae Patrum* (Antwerp: Balthazar Moret, 1628); translation available online at <www.vitae-patrum.org.uk>.

O'Leary, James (ed.), *The Most Ancient Lives of Saint Patrick, Including the Life by Jocelin* (New York: P. J. Kenedy, 1880).

Palladius, *The Lausiac History*, in Cuthbert Butler (ed.), *The Lausiac History of Palladius, Introduction and Text* (Cambridge: Cambridge University Press, 1898); Robert T. Meyer (ed.), *The Lausiac History, Ancient Christian Writers*, vol. 34 (New York: Paulist Press, 1965); Tim Vivian (ed.), *Four Desert Fathers: Pambo, Evagrius, Macarius of Egypt, and Macarius of Alexandria, Coptic Texts Relating to the Lausiac History of Palladius, Popular Patristics Series* (Crestwood, NY: St Vladimir's Seminary Press, 2005).

Patrici, *Confessio*, in Ludwig Bieler (ed.), *Libri Epistolarum Sancti Patricii Episcopi, Clavis Patricii II* (Dublin: W. & G. Baird Ltd, Antrim, 1993).

Rees, W. J. (ed.), *Lives of the Cambro British Saints* (Llandovery: Longman & Co., 1853).

Severus, Sulpicius, *Vita Martini*, in CSEL 1 (*Opera*, ed. K. Halm (Vienna: Gerold, 1866)); *Dialogi*, in *Patrologia Latina*, vol. 20; translations in Bernard M. Peebles, 'Sulpicius Severus: Writings', in *The Fathers of the Church*, vol. 7 (Washington, DC: The Catholic University of America Press, 1949), pp. 77–254; Philip Schaff and Henry Wallace (eds), *Nicene and Post-Nicene Fathers*, second series, vol. 11 (Grand Rapids, MI: Eerdmans, 1894).

Stephanus, Eddius, *Vita sancti Wilfridi*, in Bertram Colgrave (ed.), *The Life of Bishop Wilfrid by Eddius Stephanus* (Cambridge: Cambridge University Press, 1985).

Stokes, Whitley (ed.), *Three Middle-Irish Homilies on the Lives of Saints Patrick, Brigit and Columba* (Calcutta: privately published, 1877).

Stokes, Whitley (ed.), *Tripartite Life of Patrick: With Other Documents Relating to that Saint* (London: HMSO, 1887).

Strabo, *Life of St Gall*, in M. Joynt (ed.), *The Life of St Gall* (Burnham-on-Sea: Llanerch Press, 1927).

Symeon the New Theologian, *Discourses*, in C. J. deCatanzaro (ed.), *Symeon the New Theologian: The Discourses* (New York: Paulist Press, 1980).

Taylor, Thomas (ed.), *The Life of St Samson of Dol* (London: SPCK, 1925).

Tírechán, *Life of St Patrick*, from *Collectanea de sancto Patricio*, in Analecta Bollandiana, vol. 2 (1883); translation in L. Bieler (ed.), *The Patrician Texts in the Book of Armagh* (Dublin: Dublin Institute for Advanced Studies, 1979).

Vita prima sanctae Brigitae, in Karina Hochegger, 'Untersuchungen Zu Den Ältesten Vitae Sanctae Brigidae' (unpublished MPhil thesis, Universität Wien, Philologisch-Kulturwissenschaftliche Fakultät, 2009). Available online at: <http://othes.univie.ac.at/4797/>; translation in Liam de Paor (ed.), *St Patrick's World* (Dublin: Four Courts Press, 1993).

Warner, George F. (ed.), *The Stowe Missal* (London: Henry Bradshaw Society, 1915).

Wilson, H. A. (ed.), *The Gelasian Sacramentary: Liber sacramentorum Romanae ecclesiae* (Oxford: Clarendon Press, 1894).

Secondary sources

Alexander, Dominic, *Saints and Animals in the Middle Ages* (Woodbridge: Boydell Press, 2008).

Barcan, Ruth, *Nudity: A Cultural Anatomy* (Oxford: Berg, 2006).

Barrow, Julia, 'How Coifi Pierced Christ's Side: A Re-examination of Bede's *Ecclesiastical History*, II, chapter 13', *Journal of Ecclesiastical History* 62 (October 2011), pp. 693–706.

Berger, Pamela, *The Goddess Obscured* (London: Robert Hale Ltd, 1988).

Bitel, Lisa, *Landscape with Two Saints: How Genovefa of Paris and Brigit of Kildare Built Christianity in Barbarian Europe* (Oxford: Oxford University Press, 2009).

Bitton-Ashkelony, B., *Encountering the Sacred: The Debate on Christian Pilgrimage in Late Antiquity* (Oakland, CA: University of California Press, 2005).

Blair, John, *The Church in Anglo-Saxon Society* (Oxford: Oxford University Press, 2005).

Blowers, Paul M., *Drama of the Divine Economy* (Oxford: Oxford University Press, 2012).

Bonner, Gerald, Rollason, David and Stancliffe, Clare (eds), *Cuthbert, His Cult and Community to AD 1200* (Woodbridge: Boydell Press, 1989).

Bonser, Wilfrid, 'Praying in Water', *Folklore* 48 (1937), pp. 385–8.

Bradley, Ian, *Celtic Christianity: Making Myths and Chasing Dreams* (Edinburgh: Edinburgh University Press, 1999).

Bradley, Ian, *Following the Celtic Way* (London: Darton, Longman & Todd, 2018).

Bradshaw, Paul, *The Search of the Origins of Christian Worship* (London: SPCK, 1992).

Brooks, Britton, 'The Reorientation of Creation in the Early Anglo-Saxon Vitae of Cuthbert and Guthlac' (unpublished PhD thesis, Oxford University, 2016).

Brown, Peter, *The Body and Society: Men, Women, and Sexual Renunciation in Early Christianity*, second edition (New York: Columbia University Press, 2008).

Brown, Peter, *The Cult of the Saints: Its Rise and Function in Latin Christianity* (Chicago, IL: University of Chicago Press, 1982).

Carr-Gomm, Philip, *A Brief History of Nakedness* (London: Reaktion Books, 2012).

Carr-Gomm, Philip, *Sacred Places: 50 Places of Pilgrimage* (London: Quercus, 2011).

Carver, Martin, Sanmark, Alex and Semple, Sarah (eds), *Signals of Belief in Early England: Anglo-Saxon Paganism Revisited* (Oxford: Oxbow Books, 2010).

Charalampidis, C. P., *The Dendrites in Pre-Christian and Christian Historical-Literary Tradition and Iconography* (Rome: 'L'Erma' di Bretschneider, 1995).

Coakley, Sarah (ed.), *Religion and the Body* (Cambridge: Cambridge University Press, 1997).

Corning, Caitlin, *The Celtic and Roman Traditions: Conflict and Consensus in the Early Medieval Church* (Basingstoke: Palgrave Macmillan, 2006).

Crane, Susan, *Animal Encounters: Contacts and Concepts in Medieval Britain* (Philadelphia, PA: University of Pennsylvania Press, 2012).

Dean, James, 'The World Grown Old and Genesis in Middle English Historical Writings', *Speculum* 57 (1982), pp. 548–68.

Dostoevsky, Fyodor, *The Brothers Karamazov*, trans. David McDuff (London: Penguin Books, 2003).

Duchesne, L., *Christian Worship: Its Origin and Evolution. A Study of the Latin Liturgy up to the Time of Charlemagne*, trans. M. L. McClure (London: SPCK, 1931).

Eagles, B., 'Augustine's Oak', *Medieval Archaeology* 47 (2003), pp. 175–8.

Ferguson, Everett, *Baptism in the Early Church* (Grand Rapids, MI: Eerdmans, 2009).

Fletcher, Richard, *The Conversion of Europe* (London: Fontana Press, 1998).

Gittos, Helen and Hamilton, Sarah (eds), *Understanding Medieval Liturgy* (Farnham: Ashgate, 2016).

Gougaud, Louis, *Devotional and Ascetic Practices in the Middle Ages* (London: Burns Oates, 1927).

Green, Miranda, *The Gods of the Celts* (Stroud: Sutton Publishing, 2004).

Gusakova, Olga, 'A Saint and the Natural World', in P. Clarke and T. Claydon (eds), *God's Bounty? The Churches and the Natural World* (Suffolk: Boydell Press, 2010), pp. 42–52.

Guy, Laurie, '"Naked" Baptism in the Early Church: The Rhetoric and the Reality', *Journal of Religious History* 27 (2003), pp. 133–42.

Hefele, C. J. (ed.), *A History of the Councils of the Church: From the Original Documents, to the Close of the Second Council of Nicaea AD 787*, vol. 1 (Edinburgh: T & T Clark, 1896).

Hen, Yitzhak and Meens, Rob, *The Bobbio Missal: Liturgy and Religious Culture in Merovingian Gaul* (Cambridge: Cambridge University Press, 2004).

Herren, Michael and Brown, Shirley Ann, *Christ in Celtic Christianity: Britain and Ireland from the Fifth to the Tenth Century* (Woodbridge: Boydell Press, 2002).

Higham, Nicholas J., *The Convert Kings: Power and Religious Affiliation in Early Anglo-Saxon England* (Manchester: Manchester University Press, 1997).

Hooke, Della, *Trees in Anglo-Saxon England* (Woodbridge: Boydell Press 2010).

Hughes, Jessica, 'The Anxiety of Influence: Anatomical Votives in Roman Gaul, First Century BC–First Century AD', in *Votive Body Parts in Greek and Roman Religion*, Cambridge Classical Studies (Cambridge: Cambridge University Press, 2017), pp. 106–50.

Hutton, Ronald, *Pagan Britain* (London: Yale University Press, 2014).

Innemée, K. C., 'On the Necessity of Dress: Should a Hermit Wear Clothes?', *Khil'a, Journal of Dress and Textiles in the Islamic World* 1 (2006), pp. 69–78.

Ireland, Colin, 'Penance and Prayer in Water: An Irish Practice in Northumbrian Hagiography', *Cambrian Medieval Celtic Studies* 34 (1997), pp. 51–66.

Johnston, William M. (ed.), *Encyclopedia of Monasticism* (Abingdon: Routledge, 2015).

Leslie, S. et al., 'The Fine-Scale Genetic Structure of the British Population', *Nature* 519 (2015), pp. 309–14.

Liptrot, Amy, *The Outrun* (London: Canongate Books, 2016).

Low, Mary, *Celtic Christianity and Nature: The Early Irish and Hebridean Traditions* (Edinburgh: Edinburgh University Press, 1996).

MacCulloch, Diarmaid, *A History of Christianity* (London: Penguin Books, 2009).

McGrath, Alister, *The Reenchantment of Nature: The Denial of Religion and the Ecological Crisis* (London: Doubleday, 2003).

McIntosh, Alastair, *Poacher's Pilgrimage: An Island Journey* (Edinburgh: Birlinn, 2016).

Mayhew-Smith, Nick, *Britain's Holiest Places* (London: Lifestyle Press, 2011).

Meyer, K. (ed.), *Hibernica minora, Being a Fragment of an Old-Irish Treatise on the Psalter* (Oxford: Clarendon Press, 1894).

Montgomery, J., Beaumont, J., Jay, A., Keefe, K., Gledhill, A., Cook, G., Dockrill, S. J. and Melton, N. D., 'Strategic and Sporadic Marine Consumption at the Onset of the Neolithic: Increasing Temporal Resolution in the Isotope Evidence', *Antiquity* 78 (2013), pp. 1060–72.

Musther, John, *Sacred North* (Bridgend: Culture & Democracy Press, 2018).

Noble, Thomas F. X. and Head, Thomas (eds), *Soldiers of Christ: Saints and Saints' Lives from Late Antiquity and the Early Middle Ages* (London: Sheed & Ward, 1995).

Ó Carragáin, Éamonn, *Ritual and the Rood: Liturgical Images and the Old English*

Poems of the Dream of the Rood Tradition (London: The British Library and University of Toronto Press, 2005).

O'Loughlin, Thomas, *Celtic Theology* (London: Continuum, 2000).

Orme, Nicholas, *Early British Swimming 55 BC – AD 1719* (Exeter: University of Exeter, 1983).

Phillips, Andy, *Celtic Christianity Today* (Newlyn: Gwask Peran Sans (St Piran's Press), 2007).

Pollmann, Karla, 'Human Sin and Natural Environments: Augustine's Two Positions on Genesis 3:18', *Augustinian Studies* 41 (2010), pp. 69–85.

Reuling, Hanneke, *After Eden: Church Fathers and Rabbis on Genesis 3:16–21* (Leiden and Boston, MA: Brill, 2006).

Rittgers, Ronald K., *The Reformation of Suffering: Pastoral Theology and Lay Piety in Late Medieval and Early Modern Germany* (Oxford: Oxford University Press, 2012).

Ross, Anne, *Pagan Celtic Britain* (London: Sphere Books, 1974).

Ryan, John, *Irish Monasticism* (Dublin: Four Courts Press, 1992).

Schalansky, Judith, *Atlas of Remote Islands* (London: Penguin Books, 2010).

Speiser, E. A., *The Anchor Bible: Genesis* (New York: Doubleday and Company, 1964).

Spinks, Bryan D., *Early and Medieval Rituals and Theologies of Baptism* (Farnham: Ashgate, 2006).

Stancliffe, Clare, 'Red, White and Blue Martyrdom', in Dorothy Whitelock, Rosamond McKitterick and David Dumville (eds), *Ireland in Early Mediaeval Europe* (Cambridge: Cambridge University Press, 1982), pp. 21–46.

Thoreau, Henry David, *Walden* (New York: Cosimo Classics, 2009).

Toller, T. Northcote and Bosworth, Joseph, *An Anglo-Saxon Dictionary: Based on the Manuscript Collections of the Late Joseph Bosworth: Supplement* (Oxford: Clarendon Press, 1921).

Trevelyan, Marie, *Folk-lore and Folk-stories of Wales* (London: E. Stock, 1909).

The Welsh History Review 14:1 (1988).

Whitaker, E. C. and Johnson, Maxwell E. (eds), *Documents of the Baptismal Liturgy* (London: SPCK, 2003).

Wills, Garry, *Font of Life: Ambrose, Augustine, and the Mystery of Baptism* (Oxford: Oxford University Press, 2012).

Winkler, Gabriele, 'Confirmation or Chrismation? A Study in Comparative Liturgy', in Maxwell E. Johnson (ed.), *Living Water, Sealing Spirit: Readings on Christian Initiation* (Collegeville, MN: Liturgical Press, 1995), pp. 202–18.

Wood, Ian, 'The Mission of Augustine of Canterbury to the English', *Speculum* 69:1 (January 1994), pp. 1–17.

Wooding, J. (ed.), *The Otherworld Voyage in Early Irish Literature* (Dublin: Four Courts, 2000).

Wortley, J., *The Spiritual Meadow of John Moschus* (Kalamazoo, MI: Cistercian Publications, 1992).

Yorke, Barbara, *The Conversion of Britain 600–800* (Harlow: Pearson Education Ltd, 2006).

Copyright acknowledgements

Plate 8(a), a twelfth-century manuscript from Durham Cathedral, is reproduced by permission of the British Library. Image © British Library Board, BL Yates Thompson MS 26, f. 24r.

Plate 8(b), an icon of St Ethelflaeda, is reproduced by permission of the author's wife, Anna Mayhew-Smith, <www.annasicons.co.uk>.

Index